Charles A. J. (Charles Alden John) Farrar

Wild Woods Life

Or, A Trip to Parmachenee

Charles A. J. (Charles Alden John) Farrar

Wild Woods Life
Or, A Trip to Parmachenee

ISBN/EAN: 9783337140854

Printed in Europe, USA, Canada, Australia, Japan

Cover: Foto ©ninafisch / pixelio.de

More available books at **www.hansebooks.com**

LAKE AND FOREST SERIES.

WILD WOODS LIFE;

OR,

A TRIP TO PARMACHENEE,

CONTAINING

THE ADVENTURES OF THE PARTY OF BOSTON BOYS WHO FIGURE IN "EASTWARD HO!" AND WHO IN THIS VOLUME PENETRATE FARTHER INTO THE WILDERNESS, AND MEET WITH A GREAT VARIETY OF THRILLING ADVENTURES AND AMUSING EXPERIENCES.

A REALISTIC STORY OF LIFE IN THE WOODS.

(FULLY ILLUSTRATED.)

BY

CAPT. CHARLES A. J. FARRAR,

AUTHOR OF "EASTWARD HO!" "MOOSEHEAD LAKE AND THE NORTH MAINE WILDERNESS, ILLUSTRATED," "THE ANDROSCOGGIN LAKES, ILLUSTRATED," "CAMP-LIFE IN THE WILDERNESS," ETC., ETC.

———oo⁂oo———

BOSTON:
LEE & SHEPARD, PUBLISHERS,
NEW YORK:
CHARLES T. DILLINGHAM.
1884.

To

MY DEAR BROTHER,

ANDREW E. FARRAR,

WITH WHOM I HAVE PASSED MANY HAPPY DAYS IN
THE WOODS OF MAINE, AND TO WHOM
SOME OF THE INCIDENTS
IN THIS STORY

MAY RECALL PLEASANT REMINISCENCES,

This Volume

IS AFFECTIONATELY DEDICATED.

PREFACE.

THE cordial reception tendered to the first volume of this series, "Eastward Ho!" by the press and the public, encouraged the author to go forward in the work he had undertaken, of writing six volumes on Life in the Woods, as experienced by him on many camping-out excursions, extending over a period of twenty years.

It was his intention to have these volumes follow each other closely, at least one each year, until the series was completed; but the cares of an extensive and rapidly growing business, combined with a large amount of other literary work, have widened the gap, until four years have elapsed since the launching of the first volume on the crowded sea of literature.

In reply to many inquiring letters from interested readers of "Eastward Ho!" he would state that the succeeding volumes of the series will make their appearance, at the farthest, within twelve months of each other, and possibly sooner.

He would also take this occasion to tender his heartfelt thanks for the many commendatory letters received from kind friends from all parts of the country, the most of whom being personally strangers to him makes their congratulations doubly valuable.

The scene of the two next volumes is laid in the vast wilderness of Northern Maine, in a country much more isolated and wilder than any visited in the two books already published.

Hoping that those who have followed our party through the first two volumes will look forward with pleasure to a renewal of their acquaintance in the third, we lay aside the pen for the present, wishing the kindest regards to our numerous circle of readers.

C. A. J. FARRAR.

ROCKVIEW, JAMAICA PLAIN, MASS., April, 1884.

CONTENTS.

                                                                                   Page

CHAPTER I.—Northward Bound—Almost an Accident—A Stage Ride—Runaway Horses—A Fault-finding Passenger—Colebrook—Panther Excitement—Brook Fishing—The Panther's Lair—The Countryman's Astonishment—Arrival at Dixville Notch—A Good Supper.   13

CHAPTER II.—Sight-seeing—A frightened Granger—A Panther Hunt—Sudden Appearance of the Animal—A frightened Crowd—The Chase—In at the Death—Return to the Hotel—A Funny Deer—A Good Joke—Off for Colebrook—Collision on the Road—Settling Damages.   37

CHAPTER III.—Good-by to Colebrook—Through a Bridge—The Wheelman—Connecticut Lake—The Ride to Second Lake—Shooting Partridges—A Glance at a Moose—Arrival at Second Lake—Tom Chester's Camp—The Deer Story—Trout Fishing—Crossing the Carry—Arrival at Parmachenee.   65

CHAPTER IV.—The first Meal in Camp—Cooking under Difficulties—Under the Blankets—An Alarm in the Night—What was It?—The Attack of the Minges—Good Fishing—Prospecting for a Camp Site—The Hunting Party—What they found—A Bear in a Trap—His Capture—Bringing him to Camp—Arrival of more Stores—A Square Meal—Around the Camp-fire—Bruin and the Singing—Christening the Bear—A good Night's Rest.   102

CHAPTER V.—Early Fishing—Moving Camp—Getting to Rights—An Inquisitive Guide—Feeding the Bear—A Trial at Jack Shooting—Baking Beans—Berrying—A Caribou—An unsuccessful Chase—A Visit to Flint's Camp—Potatoes and Chains—Teaching the Bear—A Sunday Dinner—Wild Lightning—Looking for a Beaver Dam—The Eagle's Nest—The Big Pine—Back to Camp.   128

CHAPTER VI.—Fishing and Berrying—The Eagle's Nest—Chopping the Pine—An Interference—Fight with the Eagles—The Boys getting the Worst of It—St. Clair to the Rescue—Return to Camp—A Visit to Chester's—Evening Recitations—A Trip to Moose Brook—Discovery of a Deer in the Lake—Its Chase and Capture—Changing Cooks—St. Clair's Speech.   154

CHAPTER VII.—A Rainy Sunday—Moving up River—A Tramp through the Woods with Nap and Lightfoot—A Good Supper—Around the Camp-fire—A Mysterious Alarm—A Bad Shot—Plenty of Venison—Claude and Phil visit Chester's Camp—Visitors—Tough Yarns—Ascent of Camel's Rump—Discovery of a Cave—The Skeleton—Frightened by a Bat—Table-talk—Return of Claude and Phil.   179

CHAPTER VIII.—Claude's Story—An Unpleasant Adventure—Oversleeping—A Foggy Morning—"Quack! Quack! Quack!" the First Ducks—Phil's Story—An Excursion to Little Boy's Falls—A Hot Day—Maynard and the Bear—Building a Shanty—Roast Duck for Supper.   207

CHAPTER IX.—An Early Turn-out—A Visit to Rump Pond—Phenomenal Fishing—Two at a Time—A Whale—A Sudden Dive—Quick Retribution—The Two Bathers—Capture of the Large Fish—Return to Camp—A Visit to the Cave—The Storm—Buried Alive—Short Rations—A Hard Bed.   242

CHAPTER X.—The Kitchen Finished—A Terrible Storm—Thunder and Lightning—Killing Time—The Two Strangers—Pork and Hardtack—Building a Fire Under Difficulties—A Rainy Night—Where are the Boys?—Determination of Maynard to Seek them in the Morning.   265

CHAPTER XI.—Troubled Sleepers—The Nightmare—The Rescuing Party—Removing the Boulder—The Prison Doors Opened—Back to Camp—A Jolly Supper—A Quiet Night—Departure of the Woodsmen.   278

CHAPTER XII.—Claude and Phil Visit Flint's—The Saucy Loons—Returning to Camp—A Large Flock of Ducks—Successful Shooting—St. Clair, Le Roy, and Wingate Start for Arnold's Bog—A Quiet Sunday—Writing to Old Chums

	Page
— A Circus in Camp — Maynard Takes a Bath — The First Snow — Worrying About the Absent Ones — Camp-fire Flickerings — A Wakeful Night — An Unsuccessful Moose Chase — Return of the Wanderers.	294
CHAPTER XIII. — Around the Camp-Fire — St. Clair's Story — A Night at Black Pond — Deer by Moonlight — Arnold's Bog — The Camp at the Forks — Moose-Hunting at Night — A Sleepy Hunter — The Battle between the Moose — Locked Horns — Large Game — A Visit from Indians — Building a Raft — Lake Megantic — A Night at a Hotel — Return up the Lake — A Hard Tramp — Lost — Climbing a Mountain — The Forks Again. — Back to Camp.	315
CHAPTER XIV. — Moving Down-river — Rafting the Menagerie — Camping at the Foot of the Lake — The Pursued and Pursuers — Fighting the Hounds — Lightfoot's Death — Removal to Forks of the Magalloway — A Fifty-Dollar Bear — Down-river again — Upper Metalluc Pond — Camping Overnight — Early Risers — Good Duck Shooting.	331
CHAPTER XV. — Early Birds — Fine Duck-Shooting — Moving — The Camp at Lincoln Pond — A Prolonged Storm — Housed-up — Fair Weather — Early Fishing — Splendid Luck — Three and Four Pounders — A Windy Day — A Poor Hunt — Bears as Thieves — A Logger's Story of an Inquisitive Bear.	357
CHAPTER XVI. — A Deer-Hunt — A Ludicrous Fright — A Sociable Bear — Trailing a Caribou — Peculiar Pedestrianism — Successful Shots — The Caribou Killed — Aid from Camp — Boat-racing on Lincoln Pond — Formation of the Lake and Forest Club — Peppering a Loon — Last Night in Camp.	366
CHAPTER XVII. — A Noisy Waking. — Good-by, Lincoln Pond — Down to Flint's — The Brown Farm — A Surprise Party — Old Friends — A Charming Re-union — The Ride on the Steamboat — The Lakeside — A Good Hotel — Trading in a Country Store — A Beautiful Drive — Climbing Speckled Mountain — The View from the Summit — Moose Cave — The Jail — Screw Auger Falls — Arrival at Bethel — Homeward Bound.	388

LIST OF ILLUSTRATIONS.

	Page
The Panther's Leap	Frontispiece
Old Man of the Mountain, Dixville Notch, N.H.	49
On a Buckboard	75
Parmachenee Lake, looking North	103
Capturing a Bear	127
Moose-Shooting on the Magalloway River	141
A Hard-Fought Battle	155
An Obstacle	169
Parmachenee Lake, looking West	191
Steamer Diamond	221
Kennebago Lake, from Snowman's point	255
Duck-Shooting at South Arm	281
A Moose Fight	321
Lake Umbagog, from Steamboat Landing	353
Androscoggin River, between Bethel and Newry Corner	385

WILD WOODS LIFE;

OR,

A TRIP TO PARMACHENEE.

CHAPTER I.

Northward Bound. — Almost an Accident. — A Stage Ride. — Runaway Horses. — A Fault-finding Passenger. — Colebrook. — Panther Excitement. — Brook Fishing. — The Panther's Lair. — The Countryman's Astonishment. — Arrival at Dixville Notch. — A Good Supper.

As the northward-bound train over the Boston, Concord, & Montreal Railroad stopped at Wells River on the afternoon of Tuesday, Aug. 8, 1876, six young Americans rushed from the drawing-room car out upon the platform, and began casting eager and searching glances upon the crowd around them.

"There he is, boys," cried Claude Emerson, the oldest of the party, pointing off to his right, and, elevating his voice a little, sang out, "This way, Phil; here we are, old fellow!"

The young gentleman thus addressed heard the call, and, catching sight of the party, made a rush for them, and, as he reached the boys, held out both hands, each one of which was grasped by three of his friends.

"How are you, fellows?" queried the young gentleman who had thus been unceremoniously pounced upon, and who was none other than Mr. Philip De Ruyter, of Brooklyn, N.Y., who had come on to join his Boston friends for a trip to the woods and lakes of Maine.

"First-rate, Phil."

"Never better."

"Bang up."

"Gay and festive."

"Young and saucy."

"Well and hearty," answered his friends in one breath.

"How did you leave your folks, Phil, and are they coming up this way this summer?" interrogated Andrew St. Clair, who had visited his friend at his home, and who had an especial regard for his friend's sister.

"Oh, father and mother were well. They are going to Mount Desert in August, and to the mountains in September, and I think quite possible they may visit the lakes. Violet was down to Long Branch, stopping a few weeks with some friends who have a cottage there. She will return home though in time to visit the mountains with father and mother. The folks sent their regards to all of you."

"Remember us to them," replied Claude, "in the first letter you write."

While the train is speeding on its way, a little information about the characters in our story to those who have not read the first volume of this series may not come amiss. The six young gentlemen first introduced were Claude Emerson, Andrew St. Clair,

Charles Wingate, Frank Maynard, Thomas Le Roy, and John Adams, Jr., of Boston, who two years before had made a trip to the Maine woods, and who had enjoyed themselves so much on that occasion that they had determined to try it again. During their first excursion they had met Philip De Ruyter, on the steamer on Umbagog Lake, who with his relatives and friends were going up the Magalloway. The parties all became well acquainted, and St. Clair had fallen in love with De Ruyter's sister, and the young lady had smiled upon him, and he had continued to be very attentive to her, and hoped some time to marry her. De Ruyter had visited his Boston friends once since their first meeting in the Maine wilderness, and St. Clair and Emerson had visited him in Brooklyn, where he lived.

There had been nine in Claude's party on the first excursion, and of the missing three, William Foster was in California, his folks having moved there; David Smith had died the past winter of typhoid fever, and George Robbins had gone down to Florida to live with an uncle who had started a large orange grove, and who was intending to make the cultivation of the fruit his whole business.

"Did you bring your boats along, Claude?" inquired De Ruyter.

"Yes, sir. They are in the baggage-car."

"We had them freshly painted," added St. Clair, "and they look as good as new."

"Don't you think it a little risky to try this trip without guides, Claude? Isn't there danger of one getting lost? And then the cooking, and the other work. I am afraid it will be too much for us."

"Not a bit of it," answered the leader of the party. "We talked the guide business over thoroughly, and came to a unanimous conclusion that we would try it one year without them. Of course we do not intend to kill ourselves with hard work. For instance, we can hire some men to carry our boats, and the heaviest of our stores from Second Lake to Parmachenee. We can have them hauled as far as Second Lake by team. As for the cooking, we are all accomplished cooks. Have been taking lessons at home for six months, and the other work connected with camping, such as cutting wood, carrying water, etc., will not be very hard divided among seven of us."

"It will toughen our muscles, and give us good appetites," put in Maynard with a laugh.

"Yes, Phil, it will do you good to cut a cord or two of wood in the morning before breakfast," chimed in Le Roy.

"Me? I couldn't cut a cord of wood in a week," and De Ruyter glanced at his hands, which were white and soft, in a manner that brought forth a shout of laughter from his friends.

"I'll bet on you," said Claude, "when the time comes."

A few moments after this a sharp whistle was heard from the engine, and the air-brakes were applied with such suddenness as nearly to throw every one out of their seats, and the train with a jar and a shock came suddenly to a halt.

"I wonder what that means," said Adams.

"I don't know," replied Claude; "let's get out and see. I hope they are not trying to pass another train on the same track. That generally makes bad business."

"You are right there," remarked Phil, as the boys left their seats.

They stepped out beside the cars, and found several more of the passengers hurrying toward the engine. As they neared the locomotive they discovered the cause of the trouble. The place where the train had been brought to its sudden stand-still was at the beginning of a sharp curve, and between two high banks, and from the one on the right a large boulder had been dislodged, probably by the jar of a passing train, and had rolled down the side of the cutting and landed in the middle of the track. Owing to the curve the train had come very near it before the engineer saw it, and hence the suddenness and force with which the air-brakes had been applied. It had been a narrow escape from what would assuredly have been a bad accident, and the passengers had reason to be thankful.

When the boys reached the engine, the train hands, from brakemen to conductor, were trying to roll the huge stone off the track; but they could not budge it an inch. As one of the brakemen remarked, "They hadn't beef enough."

"We shall have to procure a long lever, and get some of the passengers to help us before we can start that fellow," said the engineer to the conductor. "That rock will weigh two or three tons."

The conductor ordered two of the brakemen to get axes from the baggage-car, and go to a piece of woods a few rods away, and cut a yellow-birch or maple stick about six inches through and twenty or thirty feet long. The brakemen went for the lever, while the passengers — about all that were on the train had " come to the front "— were busily engaged in giving the engineer and conductor advice as to the best method of removing the boulder. The fireman having procured a crow-bar from one of the cars, a hole was made in the ground on one side the boulder, so as the lever could be pushed well under it, and the engineer brought a large flat rock as a bait for his pry. By this time the brakemen had returned with a stick about twenty-five feet long, — a tough piece of yellow-birch. They champered one end of the pry a little, then pushed the stick as far under the boulder as it would go, and placed the flat stone that was to serve as a bait close up to it, then the engineer invited all the "strong men" to give them a lift. Several of the passengers responded to his invitation by pulling off their coats, and taking hold of the pry.

"All ready!" cried the engineer. "Now give it to her! All together, with a will. There she rises!" and the heavy stone was turned up about a foot. "Now trig it!" yelled the engineer as one end of the lever was brought to the ground. "Jack" — to his fireman — "put a rock under that boulder, quick!" This was done, and the lever readjusted, and then as many as could took hold again, and the boulder was carried up so high that it balanced.

"Now comes the tug of war!" cried the engineer. "Ten or twelve of you who are standing there looking on, throw the rock over, if you can, while we hold the cant of it." A crowd responded to this appeal, and pushing, slowly, the boulder finally went over and lodged in the ditch, out of the way of the trains. Then a shout of triumph went up from all hands, the tools were placed in the car, the passengers took their seats, and, with a prolonged whistle from the engine, the train started off after an hour's delay.

"It's lucky that rock did not come down in the night," remarked St. Clair, as the boys made their way through the train to the parlor-car.

"That is so," answered Claude, "it would probably have wrecked a train if it had. And if our engineer had not been tending to his business, I think we should have had something more than a little shaking up."

"Do you suppose they will make up the time?" queried Wingate. "If they don't we may miss our connections with the Grand Trunk train."

"If we do," replied Claude, "we can hire a team at Groveton, and drive up to North Stratford. It is only thirteen miles. However, I don't propose to worry about it."

At Lancaster the train had made up half an hour of the lost time, and they reached Groveton Junction only twenty minutes behind, and found the Grand Trunk train awaiting them. Everything had to be changed here, and Claude and his friends were anxious about their boats, not knowing whether they could get them on the Grand Trunk train.

After the baggage had been changed, Claude spoke to the Grand Trunk baggage-master, and he said the boats would have to go in the express-car if they went at all, as there was no room in his car for them. And an inspection of it by Wingate showed that he spoke the truth. Then the boys tackled the express agent, and he agreed to take them in his car for fifty cents each.

Claude willingly paid this, and the boats were loaded. Then the train was off, and after half an hour's ride they reached North Stratford, a little after seven o'clock.

As soon as they left the cars the boys went over to the Willard House and had supper, and made an engagement with the landlord, who had a livery stable, to haul their boats and the most of their baggage to Colebrook, the next day. By this time the stage was ready, and they climbed up on the outside, and as the seats would only hold five, besides the driver, Le Roy and Adams made themselves as comfortable as they could on the roof.

It was quarter past eight when the driver cracked his whip, and yelled "G'lang" to his horses, and with the boys outside, three passengers, all men, inside, and a rack piled high with baggage and express-matter, the coach turned the corner of the hotel, and the horses, fresh from the stable, took the hill at a gallop.

"Hope you won't capsize us, driver," remarked Claude, who was seated beside the Knight of the Ribbons, as the stage reached the top of the hill, and bowled along at a rattling pace.

"I guess there aint much danger of that," replied the driver with a laugh ; "I never tipped a team over in my life."

"There has to be a first time for everything," said Phil, who occupied the seat with the driver and Claude.

"So I suppose," said the reinsman, as he touched up his horses ; "but I shan't capsize this coach to-night all the same."

"It seems to me you have chosen a cheerful subject for conversation, Claude," sang out Le Roy from his perch on the roof. "If the old ark should go over, where do you suppose Adams and I would go to?"

"'Go to grass,' I guess, if there was any by the road side," put in Maynard, merrily.

By the time they had reached the Columbia post-office it had began to cloud up, the sky having the appearance of rain. As the coach rattled along, the darkness momentarily increased, until finally, after having nearly run down a single team, the driver of which anathematized the Knight of the Ribbons, in curses both loud and deep, the stage-driver pulled up his horses, asking Claude to hold the reins while he went down and lit his lamps. He had lighted one and was passing around behind the stage to get at the other when a bird or a bat flew in front of the leaders, and frightened them, and with a wild jump they started on a gallop, the pole horses following their lead. The driver had neglected to put on the brake when he left his seat, and the coach started easier than it would otherwise have done.

Here was a situation that Claude had not counted on, and he hung to the reins with all his strength.

Meanwhile the king, who had so suddenly lost his throne, was running after the stage as fast as a heavy overcoat would permit him, for the evening had grown chilly, and he had donned his outside garment during their stop at Columbia, and was shouting at the top of his voice for Claude to "stop!" and "hold on!" and "pull up those horses, can't you?" without having much effect on the team, and as the distance between them increased his voice grew fainter and fainter, and finally the boys lost it altogether.

"Saw their mouths with the bits, and then you can

pull them up," suggested Phil to Claude, who sat all nerved up, his feet braced against the foot-board, two turns of the reins wound around his hands, and pulling as if his life depended on it.

"Pull your grandfather up!" shouted Claude. "I believe the rascals have the bits between their teeth, I can't make any impression on them."

"If you don't stop them soon we shall all go to Kingdom come," remarked Wingate. "If we happen to meet a team, now, you will see the splinters fly." "Come down beside me, St. Clair," called Claude, "and put on the brake. Jam it down for dear life, and I'll give them a pull at the same time. I can't see much, but I believe we are coming to an up grade, and perhaps we can stop them on the top of the hill. Be careful and not get thrown off when you change seats."

The men inside the coach, who had been talking loudly among themselves, and who were undoubtedly alarmed at the rapid rate they were travelling, and the way they were bounced around, now made themselves heard. "What is the matter outside?" shouted one, with his head out of the left door; "what are you driving so fast for?"

"Because we can't help it," answered Phil, who was on that side, and he chuckled in spite of the situation.

"Yes you can, too," returned the man, angrily, as one of the wheels went over a rock and he was tossed up against the roof of the coach, banging his hat (he wore a beaver) down over his eyes. "If you don't drive slower, I'll come up and take the reins myself."

"I wish to heavens you would," shouted Claude,

who had caught the latter part of the remark; "I am not crying for the job."

By this time St. Clair had put the brake down, and with both feet jammed hard on it, pressed it against the wheels with a force that made them squeak, while Claude tugged harder than ever on the reins. The hill was quite steep, and the united pressure of Claude's pull and the brake, was a little more than the horses could stand. Besides, they had recovered somewhat from their fright, and as they climbed the hill they went slower and slower, until they settled down to a walk, and then Claude told St. Clair to let off the brake.

When they reached the top of the hill Claude brought the horses to a stop, and St. Clair volunteered to get down and hold the leaders until the Knight of the Ribbons should make his appearance, which Claude was very glad to have him do, not knowing but what the horses might take it into their heads to run again.

The man who had spoken before now poked his head out of the window.

"Where's the driver?"

"Oh, back on the road a couple of miles, I guess," returned Phil, nonchalantly.

"Why didn't you stop the stage before?" in a very angry tone of voice.

"Because I could not," replied Claude. "I don't know anything about horses; never drove one half-a-dozen times in my life."

"What business have you up there with the driver?"

"You are becoming impertinent, now," returned Claude, coolly.

"Impertinent! me? You had better talk. You're

a saucy young scamp, and you came near breaking all our necks."

"Small loss if he had broken yours," sang out Wingate.

"What did you say, young man?" shouted the irascible passenger.

"I said it may rain to-morrow, if it is not pleasant," returned Wingate, with a chuckle.

"Oh, shut up, old sore-head! Give us a rest," said Phil, as he climbed down and lit the lamp on that side, taking a look at the open-mouthed passenger as he did so, whom he found to be an old man about sixty years of age.

Just then the driver, puffing and panting, came along and wanted to know if everything was all right.

The boys told him they believed it was, and he climbed up to his throne, just as the old fellow from the inside broke out with, "You're a smart man, driver, you are. You ought to be sent to the penitentiary for this."

"Go to Jerusalem!" returned the driver, who did not seem to have much veneration for his passenger, and as he took the reins, and whipped up the horses once more, he told the boys that the old man lived two or three miles beyond Colebrook, and was the worst growler in the whole country.

"I have seen pleasanter men," said Claude, laughing at the graphic description the driver gave of him.

"Pleasant!" grunted the Knight of the Ribbons as he laid the whip to his horses, "he's about as pleasant as a mad dog, and I'd just as leave travel with one."

"Your lamps don't light up very well," remarked Phil, who on his side was vainly endeavoring to pierce the darkness. "I don't know how you can see anything, or what prevents you from running into teams if you meet them."

"Good luck and guessing," returned the driver, "and it is seldom we have such dark nights as this; besides, I know every inch of the road."

The words had scarcely left the driver's mouth when bang went the left hind wheel against a large stone, the coach being a little out of the road.

"Knew where that rock was, didn't you?" asked Phil, laughing; "anyhow you struck it fair."

"Get into the road there; what are you doing?" and the driver tugged at his reins, and gave the horses the whip, completely ignoring Phil's remark.

"How far are we from Colebrook, now?" inquired Claude.

"About four miles and a half. We'll come to a bridge in a few minutes. It's four miles to the village from that bridge."

"Is it a Bridge of Sighs?" sang out Adams from above.

"Punch him, Le Roy," cried St. Clair. "If we give him any encouragement, he'll overwhelm us with his cheap jokes before we reach Colebrook," and the boys laughed, as Le Roy threatened to throw him off the stage if he tried to perpetrate another pun.

At eleven o'clock, without farther adventure, the stage rolled up to the Parsons House, and the boys alighted, glad of the chance to stretch their limbs after their tiresome ride. They were all well tired out, and it did not take them long to find the landlord, secure rooms, and retire to rest.

After breakfast the next morning, they fell into conversation with the landlord, and learned from him the best places to buy their stores, and how they should get to Connecticut Lake. They inquired about the fishing in the vicinity of Colebrook, and whether there was any shooting in the country around them.

The landlord told them a long yarn about a huge wild-cat, or panther, that had been committing devastation upon sheep between Colebrook, and Dixville Notch, and informed them that several parties had been out hunting after the animal, but although the hunters had tracked it some ways, none of them had seen it.

Claude laughed, and told Mr. Bailey that they were going to Dixville Notch before they went up to the lakes, and that they would shoot the wild-cat if they obtained a sight of it.

"Ha! ha! ha!" laughed Mr. Bailey. "If you run across the wild-cat, or panther, or whatever it is, you had better give it a wide berth. I don't want anything to do with such critters as that."

Leaving the landlord, the boys walked out, visited a number of stores, and obtained prices on articles that they should be likely to buy when they started northward.

About ten o'clock their boats and baggage arrived, and, after they had seen to the disposition of their things, they took out their fishing-tackle, and guns, and ammunition, and made ready for their excursion to the Notch.

As soon as they had finished dinner they hired from Mr. Bailey a two-horse wagon containing three seats, and, with their sporting-traps, started off. It was ten miles to the Notch; and they told the driver he could take them about six miles, and they would walk the rest of the way and fish some of the brooks.

It seemed that the wild-cat the landlord had told them of had made quite a stir in the town, as that was all the driver talked about on the way, and he told them he should hate to be out after dark anywhere near the Notch.

The boys looked from one to another somewhat annoyed, and winked back and forth, as the driver went on telling how many sheep the animal had destroyed, and how it had tackled a cow, which it would have killed but for the timely arrival of a farmer and his son to whom the animal belonged, and who frightened off the ferocious beast, only to find, after it had left, that the cow was so badly wounded that it could not live, and they had been obliged to kill it.

"I should think," remarked Claude, as the driver stopped a moment for breath, "that you would form a party and hunt the animal down and slay it. There must be plenty of young men in a village like Colebrook who own guns or rifles, and know how to use them."

"Bless your soul!" answered the driver, "they have tried it two or three times; but the critter is too sharp for them. The last party followed it to the thick woods, somewhere this side of the Notch, and tracked it into a kind of pokerish place, and they let it go. The fact was, I guess, they didn't dare to come to close quarters with it in the forest, where the animal would have every advantage; and I snum, I don't blame them."

"You think, then," said St. Clair, "that it is somewhere about the Notch, at present?"

"Can't say; may be there, and may not. One night it will kill a lamb way up to the north part of the town, and the next be raising the Old Harry down here."

"Well, if we run across it when we are all armed, we will let daylight into it," added Wingate, who was a capital shot with a rifle.

"If you see it," warned the driver, "you had better make tracks, or it may let daylight into you."

"We'll risk it," returned Maynard, and the subject was changed to fishing, the driver telling them where they would be likely to have the best luck.

About three o'clock he stopped his horses beside the road, a little less than four miles from the Dix House, and the boys taking their guns, rifles, ammunition, and fishing-tackle, struck for a trout brook, near them, that headed somewhere in the Notch. As the driver turned his team around, Claude called back to him to come for them at the Dix House on Friday afternoon.

In fifteen minutes they had reached the brook, and Claude, St. Clair, Wingate, and De Ruyter put their rods together, selected their favorite flies, and scattered along the stream in quest of some promising pools, Maynard, Le Roy, and Adams agreeing to carry all the fire-arms, besides their own rods, so as to relieve the fishermen.

Phil caught the first fish, a troutlet about three inches long, and with some disgust returned it to its native element. Ten minutes afterward, however, he was more fortunate, striking a half-pounder in the same pool, which he secured, and threw into the basket slung from his shoulder. St. Clair was the next lucky man, and his first catch was a trifle larger than Phil's, and he claimed that it would weigh three-quarters of a pound. Claude, in making his first cast, caught his fly in a tree on the opposite side of the stream, which he was obliged to wade, before he could clear it, and Wingate hooked into an old snag under water, and spent half an hour in clearing his hook rather than run the risk of breaking his tackle.

Thus the sport went on, with all the pleasures and vexations that brook-fishing is subject to; and the boys found, in spite of a gentle breeze that occasionally fanned their hot faces, that it was warm work.

The amusing incident of the afternoon was while the whole party were climbing over a snarled and twisted mass of windfalls, when Maynard stumbled and fell head-first down into a hole, from which he found it utterly impossible to extricate himself. After standing on his hands and head for two or three minutes, which time he spent in futile attempts to free himself, he called lustily to his friends, who were all ahead of him, to come and help him out. Claude and St. Clair went back, and found him in the hole, his heels two or three feet below the top of the windfalls. When they saw him they burst out laughing in spite of their fears that he might be injured. He presented such a comical sight they could not help it.

"Are you hurt any, Frank?" inquired Claude, as he reached the hole and peered down into it.

"No, but I can't get out. I hav'n't room to turn around. Grab me by the feet and lift me up, and don't be all day about it."

"What are you doing down there, Maynard, have you started for China?" asked St. Clair, as he climbed over to the opposite side of the hole.

"None of your fooling, St. Clair. I am not in a mind for joking at present. Just get me out of here, will you?"

"All right, my boy; we'll snake you out before you can say Jack Robinson! Look out for yourself, now. I'll take hold of his foot this side, Claude, and you get hold of the one on your side, and I guess we can fetch him. Now then."

The boys seized both of Maynard's feet as St. Clair had suggested, and, lifting with all their strength, for he was a dead weight on them, managed to pull him to the top of the trees, where it was discovered that with the exceptions of a lump on his forehead and a small scratch on his nose, he was none the worse for his singular tumble.

"Well, Frank," declared Claude, as he gazed down into the place, which was between seven and eight feet deep, "if you are not a lucky fellow I never saw one. Nothing but a kind Providence kept you from breaking your neck. I wouldn't fall into that hole as you did, and take the chances, for a thousand dollars."

"It was nothing to fall in," replied Maynard, laughing, "the trouble was to fall out. Where is my rod? I dropped it somewhere when I took that dive."

The boys looked about and soon found the rod, uninjured, and then made their way to their friends, where Maynard's nose and forehead were immediately a subject of comment.

"What is the matter, Maynard?" inquired Phil;

"have you run across that panther, and been fighting him single-handed?"

"Tumbled over a windfall," suggested Adams, with a laugh.

"Or run across a hornet's-nest," added Wingate,

"How smart you fellows are!" replied the victim of the accident. "You'll live forever if you don't die some time."

"The truth is," said St. Clair, "he's thinking of joining a circus, and has been practising on tumbling."

"Tumbled well, did he?" queried Le Roy.

"He tumbled into a well would be a better way to put it," answered Claude laughing; "only it was a dry well."

"That was well done," remarked Adams.

"I'll do you," declared Maynard, joining in the laugh against himself, "if you don't shut up. It's time we were moving on" (looking at his watch) ; "it is most six o'clock."

"How many fish have been taken?" inquired Phil.

The four fishermen counted up, and found they had thirty-five. Claude announced the count, and said he thought that would be enough for their supper, and he agreed with Maynard that it was time they were heading for the hotel.

They had to go through a thick piece of woods to reach the road, and among the trees was considerable underbrush. As they were slowly making their way through this they came to a spot where the bushes and young trees had been beaten down some, and here they found fragments of wool and a torn sheepskin, besides several bones, showing conclusively that some wild animal had dined here on a lamb. This was a discovery; and amid startled exclamations, the boys looked with alarm around them. In the immediate vicinity they saw several trees with the bark scratched off where some animal had been trying his claws, and from the looks of the marks they judged it must be a large one.

"It strikes me," said Claude, excitedly, "that we are pretty near where that panther took his last meal, and as he may be hungry again by this time, we had better load up;" and, drawing a couple of shells from his pocket loaded with buck-shot, he slipped them into his gun, while the other boys followed his example.

"I don't believe he would attack so many of us," remarked St. Clair.

"Perhaps not. But if he is lurking about here it is just as well to be prepared for him."

"Hang the panther!" Wingate said. "He probably is not within ten miles of here now, and I am getting confoundedly hungry. Let's push along."

"All right," returned Claude, as he started on; "only keep your eyes open."

The boys reached the road without further cause for alarm, and struck out for the Dix House. Phil had been over the road two years before, and told his friends that as near as he could remember they were about two miles from the hotel.

They soon reached a small house, the occupants of which stared at them from the door with wide-opened eyes, and a man, near the barn, asked them if they were not afraid to be out in the woods, telling them that there was a wild-cat around there, and that it carried off one of his lambs the night before.

"He didn't carry it far," said Claude, laughing; "we ran across the place where he eat it, just back here in the woods half a mile."

"Is that so?" remarked the man. "Consarn his pictur', I mean to set a trap for him to-night, and I shall house all my sheep."

"That will be useless trouble," replied St. Clair. "Lightning don't strike twice in the same place."

"Perhaps yer right about lightnin', but that ere durned critter, in my opinion, is likely to come prowling around here ag'in, and if he does I calkerlate he'll get inter trouble, durn him!"

"How far is it to the Dix House?" inquired Maynard.

"'Bout a mile an' a half. Goin' ter stop there to-night?"

"Yes, sir."

"Met with some accident, ha'n't ye? I see yer got a lump over your eye and a scratch on yer nose."

"He nose it," chuckled Adams.

"And I nose that he nose that you nose it," added Phil, with a grin at the bewildered look on the countryman's face; and the boys resumed their walk.

They kept a sharp lookout for wild-cats and panthers during the rest of the distance, but nothing appeared to disturb them, and they reached the hotel about seven o'clock, and informed the landlord that the sooner he could get supper for them the better it would suit them.

"Can you cook these trout for our supper?" asked Claude as the boys emptied their baskets.

"I guess we can."

"How long will it take?"

"About half an hour. If you'll step into the office the clerk will show you rooms, while I carry your fish to the kitchen, and see about your supper."

"All right, Mr. Parsons," said Phil. "Come on, boys; I know the ropes here. We stopped here three days when our folks went through two years ago, but the old gentleman has evidently forgotten me."

"Shows you are not worth remembering," laughed Adams.

The boys stepped into the hotel, and, taking the shells from their guns and rifles, stood them in a corner, and then registered their names; after which the clerk showed them to their rooms, and they carried up their things and had a good wash, which made them feel better, for the latter part of the road had been dusty, and they had felt sticky and dirty.

After performing their toilets they descended to the piazza and enjoyed the beauty and quiet of the scene around them, watching and commenting on the other guests of the house, of whom there were several in sight. In about fifteen minutes the clerk informed them that their supper was ready, and led the way to the dining-room, and gave them a table by themselves. Although the regular supper hour was six o'clock, a few tardy ones were still eating.

"Now, boys," said Claude, smiling, as they sat down, "show your bringing up, and don't frighten the girl to death when she comes to take your orders."

"Bless her dear soul!" replied St. Clair, as a rosy-cheeked girl, in a neat dress, wearing a dainty white apron, approached the table, "I wouldn't harm a hair of her head."

"Keep still," added Phil, "she'll hear you."

The girl took their orders, which must have been unusually numerous, as an amused smile played across her face for a moment, lighting it up prettily, and then she disappeared in the kitchen. In a few moments she returned, accompanied by another girl, the second one bearing in one hand a large platter upon which lay the trout in browny crispness, surrounded by thin slices of pork, in the other a dish of fried potatoes. These were placed in the centre of the table, and the girl went out, while the first one added bread, berries, cold beef and chicken, to the fish and potatoes, and then, through a slide in the wall, called for tea and coffee. These were soon furnished; two plates of doughnuts and a basket of cake were also placed on the table, and the girl withdrew a short distance.

The supper was highly satisfactory, judging by the way the boys cleared the dishes; and they kept the young lady who waited upon them so busy that Wingate tried in vain to carry on a conversation. The fact that she was a little shy, and not disposed to meet his advances half-way, did not help him any, nor did the remarks of his friends, who, seeing how the land lay, bothered him with exasperating speeches, and gave him occasional kicks and punches under the table. The meal over, the boys returned to the piazza and scraped acquaintance with some of the other guests.

An old fellow, half hunter, half guide, who was employed in various capacities around the house, hearing the boys speak of the panther, asked them a few questions about what they had seen, and then branching off on another course, began to tell of hunts of his own, and entertained them until ten o'clock with stories of his own prowess in the forest, which, if not true, — and the boys sagely thought that many of them were not, — at least had the merit of being interesting. Finally, at the conclusion of a wonderful bear hunt, the old fellow said he must go to bed, and the boys followed his example.

CHAPTER II.

Sight-seeing. — A frightened Granger. — A Panther Hunt. — Sudden Appearance of the Animal. — A frightened Crowd. — The Chase. — In at the Death. — Return to the Hotel. — A funny Deer. — A good Joke. — Off for Colebrook. — Collision on the Road. — Settling Damages.

THURSDAY morning, after breakfast, the boys started out to see the sights in the vicinity, under the guidance of De Ruyter, who was sufficiently acquainted with the neighborhood to know where all the objects of interest were. With a wholesome dread of the panther, they all carried their guns and rifles, determined if they ran across the beast to give him a warm reception.

They visited the top of Table Rock first, and, after stopping half an hour, took a look at the Snow Cave, a few yards away, then descended to the road; upon looking at his watch Claude found it had been two hours since they had left the house.

They sat down on some rocks beside the path, and, after resting a few minutes, visited Columnar Rock and Pulpit Rock, and took a look at the Profile Cliff, or Old Man of the Mountain, as some call it. From here they continued down the highway toward the eastern end of the Notch, on their way to the Flume. Just before reaching the path that led to the Flume, situated on a stream a few rods from the road, they met a countryman, in a dilapidated wagon, driving a horse that looked more like a scarecrow than anything else. When they first saw the team the driver was belaboring the poor old horse in great shape, laying a large alder stick over his body with such resounding whacks that the boys could hear them some way off.

"Just see that old brute pound his horse," cried Claude, indignantly. "I should like to lay the stick over him."

"They need the society with the long name down here," remarked Phil, "to look after such fellows as he."

"The horse is nothing but skin and bones, now," added St. Clair.

"The old buffer is probably drunk," suggested Adams.

"Took his bitters early, then," put in Wingate.

As they neared the team the old man stopped belaboring his nag and pulled up by the side of the road.

"What was you pounding your horse for?" asked Le Roy, as the boys stopped at the wagon.

"'Cause I was in a hurry," answered the old man, with some excitement. "Just back here a little ways I heerd the awfullest noise I ever heerd in my life, on the left side of the road. And a minute arterwards I seed suthin' go across the road like a streak o' lightnin'. Dunno whether it was a wild-cat, or what in the deuce it was, but I was afraid it might take a notion to go for me, and I just stirred the old mare up a leetle."

"How large an animal was it?" asked Maynard.

"As near as I could tell from what leetle I'd seen of it, its body was about four feet long and its legs about a foot."

"Nonsense," replied Claude, laughing. "You was so frightened it probably looked twice as large to you as it really was."

"Mebbe, mebbe," returned the countryman; "but it was a durned sight bigger animal than I want ter tackle."

"Probably it's the panther that has been making such havoc above here, killing cows and carrying off sheep," said St. Clair.

"Sho! yer don't say. Are you fellows arter him?"

"Not exactly," answered Claude. "But if he comes in our way we'll give him a dose of leaden pills that will trouble his digestion."

"Pity yer couldn't kill him," remarked the countryman, as he clucked to his mare, and gave her another taste of the stick; "the farmers around here would gin ye a leather medal if yer did."

"No doubt of it," yelled St. Clair after him as he drove away; "they are too mean to give you anything that would cost a cent."

"What are we to do now?" queried Adams, — "go back to the house or keep on and run our chances of being eaten by the panther?"

"For one," answered Claude, "I say go on. We have four rifles and three shot-guns, and if we are not able to cope with any animal smaller than a grizzly bear, we must be mighty poor shots."

"That's the talk, Claude; I'm with you," said St. Clair. "Go ahead, Phil, and show us the Flume, panther or no panther."

"Before we go any farther," suggested Wingate, "I think it would be only prudent for us to load our pieces.

If we should run across the animal he might attack us before we were ready for him."

"A good idea," acknowledged Claude; "but do, fellows, take care, and not shoot each other. Carry your pieces at half-cock, and take care and not stumble when we go into the woods."

"No danger of that," said Phil. "There is a good path from the road to the Flume."

The boys now continued their walk, and soon reached the path, into which they turned. The woods grew close on each side of them, and it was but natural that they should keep a sharp lookout on either hand, and halt for a moment if they heard any unusual noise. They reached the Flume, however, without having seen anything to shoot at larger than a squirrel, and sat down to rest. From where they sat they could see the fall at the head of the Flume, and, after enjoying the beauty of the cataract for a few moments, left their seat on the mossy ledge, and, going to the edge of the ravine, stooped down on their hands and knees and looked down into the chasm. The ledge on which they now were shelved in and back from the bed of the stream, and Adams, who was the farthest to the right, discovered, at the base of the shelving ledge, just beyond the flow of the water, the panther, stretched at full length, apparently enjoying the coolness of the place. With a startled cry, he sprang to his feet, and shouted, "The panther! the panther!"

"Where? where?" asked his friends, anxiously, as they jumped up and grasped their weapons.

But either through fright or excitement, Adams was

speechless, and could only point in a nervous way to the bottom of the Flume.

The next moment, however, the boys heard a noise below them, and, with a blood-curdling yell, the panther sprang to the top of the opposite bank. The boys all saw him, but only Claude and Wingate had the presence of mind to fire, and apparently they both hit him; for the huge cat shook himself, turned and bit savagely at one of his hind legs, and then, with another fearful yell, gathered himself together, and, with a frightful bound, cleared the chasm, and was among them.

As he jumped, St. Clair and Phil fired at him, and this undoubtedly saved some of their lives, as they both wounded him, and the panther, who had evidently intended to attack them, turned, on reaching the spot where they were, and started down stream through the woods on three legs, with the blood pouring from his wounds.

"Hurrah!" cried Claude, "we've sickened him, and now let's finish him;" and, taking the empty shell from his gun, he put in a loaded one, and started on the trail, which was plain and easy to follow.

His friends hurried after him, and for half an hour or more they traced the wounded beast by means of his blood, which was plainly perceptible along his track, until they reached a point where he had entered the stream.

"He has probably crossed the brook," said Claude, as he stooped down to get a drink, for it was hot in the woods, and the perspiration was streaming down his face.

"Perhaps he has a den about here," suggested St. Clair.

"It's one o'clock, fellows," remarked Adams, looking at his watch. "I move we let him slide, and go back to the hotel. I am getting hungry."

The others loudly protested against this proposition, Maynard declaring that now he had got his hair down smooth again, he wanted a shot at him, and adding, to the edification of his friends, that when the panther gave that first yell, his hair stood on end, and he forgot all about his rifle.

"Come on, boys," cried Phil, as he waded into the brook, the water being about six inches deep; "we shall find his track somewhere on the other side."

The rest of the party followed, and, after hunting for five minutes, they discovered the trail a little below where they had crossed, and saw that it ran away from the stream. They followed it for three-quarters of an hour, and then found it led to a huge old growth of a yellow-birch tree, over two feet in diameter. On the rough bark they could see the marks of the animal's claws where he had climbed the tree, and also occasional blood-spots.

"He's our game now," cried St. Clair, exultingly; "he is up in this tree somewhere. Who can see him?"

This question was not so easily answered, for the tree had a wide-spreading top, with very thick foliage, and although the boys walked around it, and craned their necks in every direction, they could not catch a glimpse of the game.

"Confound him!" said Claude, "if he won't show himself, let's pepper him. He's up there somewhere. Stand back from the tree a little, fellows, and I'll see what a charge of buck-shot will do. The rest of you be ready to fire, if you see him."

Stepping back from the birch, as Claude had directed, the boys stood with their pieces elevated, while Claude, aiming amid the branches at the top of the birch, pulled the triggers of both barrels.

The reports were followed by a shower of leaves and small twigs, and also a growl from the panther, as he left the place he had been resting in, and, running out on a large horizontal limb, leaped into a large spruce growing near. The boys saw him when he jumped, and all but Claude gave him a volley. This brought him to the ground, a distance of about seven yards, but he was on his feet a moment after he had struck, and charged on the boys, who scattered in all directions; but it was noticed that the brute still travelled on three legs.

The wounded animal now headed for the stream again, and before he was out of sight Claude discharged both barrels at him, and reloaded his gun as he kept on in pursuit.

"He's a tough customer, that chap," declared St. Clair; "but he'll probably stop at the brook a moment, and we must try and finish him there. If we don't we shall lose him."

"Yes," assented Phil, "if he gets into the mountain, on the other side of the Notch road, our chances in him are not worth ten cents, for there are so many large holes there he would be sure to hide in some of them."

"Walk a little faster, then, boys," urged Claude, "and let's catch him at the stream. Your pieces are all loaded now, I believe."

Quickening their steps, they hurried forward, and

reached the brook just in time, as the panther was about leaving the stream on the opposite side.

"There he is," cried Wingate, who saw him first; "let him have it;" and, throwing his rifle quickly to his shoulder, he took a hurried aim, and fired, his friends following his example, and the ugly beast dropped dead in his tracks.

Crossing the brook the boys examined him, and found he was about three feet long, thick through the body, and guessed he would weigh from a hundred to a hundred and fifty pounds. On looking him over, his skin was found to be completely riddled with shot and bullets, showing that some of the boys had fired with better effect than they had supposed. The animal's claws were about two inches long, and would have made bad work on either of the party if one of them had been in close quarters with him.

"Now he is dead what shall we do with him?" inquired Adams.

"That is a pretty question," answered Le Roy. "Carry him to the hotel, of course."

"But it's confounded hot," said Adams.

"What of it?" remarked Claude. "A little perspiration, more or less, will not kill any of us, I guess; and, if we take turns in carrying him, it won't tire us much."

"How shall we carry him?" asked Wingate; "one fellow take hold of each of his paws?"

"I guess not," returned Claude, laughing; "you could carry him but a short distance that way without being tired."

"Tie him to this pole," said St. Clair, who had found

a maple stick lying on the ground near them, about ten feet long and two inches in diameter.

"The very thing," acknowledged Claude; "that was just what I was about to propose," and, diving into his pockets, he produced some stout string, nearly as large as cod-line, and, tying the fore paws of the animal together, and then the hind ones, ran the pole between them until the panther was in the middle of it. "Now, who takes the other end? I am good for this one;" and Claude grasped the end of the pole beyond the animal's head.

"I'm with you," remarked St. Clair, and the two boys hoisted the pole to their shoulders, their companions carrying their guns for them.

The weight of the panther caused the pole to bend considerably, but the boys went along quite comfortably. When they reached the road Phil and Maynard took a turn at carrying the game, and thus, with frequent changes, and all taking their share of the burden, they reached the hotel about three o'clock, somewhat hot and tired, and as hungry as wolves.

As they approached the house they fired several shots in the air, and this brought all the people about out on the piazza, and the boys, marching up to the hotel, deposited the panther in front of the door, where all could see it.

"What have you shot, boys?" asked Mr. Parsons.

"Can't say, certainly," answered Claude, "but I judge we have killed the panther that has been working such havoc among the sheep in this vicinity."

"You don't mean it?" returned the old man, as he stooped and examined the animal, while the others drew near and looked it over.

"Oh, what horrid claws!" cried one of the ladies present, as Mr. Parsons untied its feet, and spread out its toes and nails. "I don't see how you dared to shoot it."

"There were so many of us there was not much danger," replied Wingate.

"The State ought to pay you a bounty for that," observed Mr. Parsons, "and you deserve it. There have been two or three crowds from Colebrook out after that panther, and never got a shot at it."

"I'll give up my share of the bounty in prospective for a dinner at present," said Adams, who began to think of his stomach again.

"I declare," remarked the landlord, "I forgot you have had no dinner. I'll have the girls get you some at once;" and the old gentleman started for the kitchen as if he meant business, while the young hunters went up to their rooms to wash and brush up.

When they came down Claude found the hostler and offered him half a dollar to skin the panther, as the boys wished to carry home this proof of their first hunt. That good-natured individual readily promised to do it, and, going to the piazza, shouldered the brute, carried it out to the stable, and hung it up in the middle of the harness-room, so that he could more readily perform the job. While the young fellows were talking with him, the bell rang for their dinner, and they started for the table without loss of time.

The maid with the cherry cheeks waited upon them, and after she had filled their orders Wingate attracted her attention, and began to tell her about their panther-hunt, and, with unblushing effrontery, claimed the honor of having fired the shot that killed the beast.

At this his friends all laughed, and they told her that Wingate had run away the minute he saw the brute; that his hair had stood on end; that he was so frightened he intended to go home as soon as he reached the hotel, and various other things that caused the young lady to look askance at her admirer, while he, with a mouthful of hot plum-pudding, vainly protested that he was telling the truth, and that his companions were libelling him.

With Wingate's assertions and his friends' denials, the fair waitress was evidently in doubt as to the truth of the story, and between them they had a jolly time, until the young lady, finding they had no intention of leaving the table as long as she was present, excused herself and retired to the kitchen. The boys waited some time for her return, but as she did not put in an appearance, finally took the hint, and went out on the piazza, where they rested and lounged until supper time.

After supper they took a walk for about a mile out on the road toward Colebrook, and on their retrun found some of the guests in the parlor singing, and the landlady invited them to join with the others; which they did, and passed a very pleasant evening.

When the party broke up it was about half-past nine, and Claude missing Wingate asked the other boys if they knew where he was. None of them could tell, and Claude told them to follow him, and, going silently out on the piazza, they found him buzzing the cherry-cheeked lass, who fled like a deer on their approach.

"You're a nice young man now, aint you?" exclaimed Claude, shaking his finger at him in mock severity, while his friends laughed in chorus.

"Oh, confound you!" cried Wingate to his tormentors, "can't a fellow have a quiet chat with a young lady without being broken in on by a party of boobies?"

"Boobies, indeed!" remarked Adams. "What will your ma say? We shall have to appoint a committee of one to look after you, and protect you from the seductive wiles of the girl who serves up the hash."

The boys all laughed, and Wingate, declaring they were all like the fox who cried "Sour grapes," betook himself upstairs, and the others soon followed. As they were all very tired, they went to bed at once, and were soon sound asleep.

They did not get up very early the next morning, and it was nine o'clock before they were through breakfast. As they expected the team to come to take them back to Colebrook after dinner, they could not go off for a very long tramp. After considerable argument as to how they should spend the time until dinner, Claude, St. Clair, and Phil concluded to take a walk over to Nathan's Pond; Wingate and Maynard announced their intention of climbing Table Rock again, and of following the edge of the mountain along to the Profile, and inspecting it from above; Le Roy and Adams said they had had tramping enough the day before, and concluded to stop at the house and amuse themselves reading or chatting with some of the other guests; and then the party separated, those who left the hotel agreeing to return as near noon as possible.

After leaving the house Wingate and Maynard changed their plan, and, instead of climbing to Table Rock, continued along the road until they reached the

Old Man of the Mountain, Dixville Notch, N.H.

place where the best view of the Profile was to be obtained, and, after studying the " Old Man " from that spot, started to climb the mountain from nearly underneath the Profile. They found it harder work than they had anticipated; but, by zigzagging, more or less, and helping each other as they worked their way upwards, they finally reached the top of the mountain without accident, but not without several narrow escapes from a bad fall, and when they stood, at last, on the jutting rock forming the " Old Man's " head, they made up their minds that they would not care to take the climb a second time.

The result of their labor also was unsatisfactory, for at the top of the cliff it was hard discerning the slightest likeness to the huge and impressive face as seen from the road. After resting a few moments they started along the mountain towards Table Rock, as they could make the descent easier by the path. They kept back from the edge of the mountain some way intending to take another look at the Snow Cave. They had left the Profile but a short distance behind them, when they caught sight of a fox just beyond them, and each picking up a stone gave chase. The animal had heard them, and, after taking one look at them, started on a trot that enabled him to keep ahead of them easily. But the boys, thinking they might possibly get near enough to Reynard to bring him down with a rock, kept up the pursuit, stumbling and jumping occasionally, for the ground they were passing over was very rough and rocky, and was often crossed by gullies.

It was a hot day, and the scorching rays of the sun fell squarely upon them, and the perspiration was soon pouring down their bodies in streams. For fifteen minutes they did their best, and then, as fatigue and heat began to tell upon them, their pace began to slacken, and the fox, taking a last look at them, gave utterance to a short bark, that sounded in the ears of the excited boys like a taunt, and disappeared in the woods.

As the fox vanished, Maynard, who was several rods ahead, threw the stone that he had clung to all the time at him, and the next moment, to Wingate's surprise and alarm, disappeared from view as suddenly as if the earth had opened and swallowed him.

"My gracious!" exclaimed Wingate, as he reduced his run to a walk, and kept on carefully toward the spot where he had last seen his companion, "what has happened to Frank? Oh, I hope he is not hurt!" and raising his voice, he shouted his friend's name.

At first he heard no answer. But proceeding a few steps farther, and continuing his call, after a while he heard a faint response that seemingly came from the bowels of the earth, and a few steps more brought him to a huge rent in the mountain, some twenty feet deep, and at the bottom of this he saw Maynard.

"Are you hurt, Frank?" inquired Wingate anxiously, as he peered over the top of the hole.

"I guess not; but I got a confounded shaking-up when I lit in here; I did not know for a few moments whether I was alive or dead."

"This must be the Snow Cave you are in?"

"Not much. This hole is deeper and larger than the Snow Cave, and what puzzles me is how I am going to get out. You see the walls are as smooth as glass, and there is no climbing them."

"If we only had a rope now, or an axe, I would soon have you out. I see there is snow down there."

"It was snow once. It is ice now, and it is as cold and damp as a refrigerator here. I am afraid I shall take cold if I don't get out soon. I was wet through with perspiration when I came down here, and I am cooling off too fast."

"Take a little exercise, old fellow; anything to keep in motion, and tie your handkerchief around your throat, and I will see if I can find a pole or dead tree, or anything, that I can put down in there for you to climb up on."

"Be as quick as you can, Charlie. I feel like a rat in a trap down here. Blast that fox! I hope he will get shot before he is a week older."

Wingate needed no urging, and, leaving the chasm, he went to the woods that grew near them, and, after fifteen minutes' search, succeeded in finding a dead fir that had partly fallen, it being lodged in a scrub-spruce. He managed, with hard work, to get this clear; but it was so heavy he could scarcely drag it, and it took him nearly half an hour to get it to the place where his friend was imprisoned, and several minutes more to get it down into the hole.

As soon as it touched bottom, Maynard climbed up on it, and, although the tree did not reach to within two feet of the top, it answered his purpose, for when he reached the end of it, Wingate leaned over, and, grasping one of his hands, helped him a little, and he was soon on the outside of the hole. Taking a few steps, he gave himself a kind of shake, and, swinging his arms, assured himself that he was all right.

"Now," said Wingate, as they went along, "I would advise you, in future, to look ahead a little and see where you are going to. This is the second scrape of this kind you have been in in three days, and, in fact"— a smile playing over his features — "you are the holiest fellow in our crowd."

Maynard laughed at the joke, and declared his intention in future to look before he leaped.

Without farther accident they reached Table Rock, and, descending by the path to the road, reached the hotel a few moments before twelve, and found the other boys had not arrived. The team had come from Colebrook, and the driver greeted them as they stepped on the piazza. Wingate asked him what time he was going back, and he told them he would return any time they were ready.

"I think three or four o'clock will be early enough to start," suggested Le Roy; "it is only a two-hours' drive, and it will be cooler toward evening than it is now."

"I agree with you," said Maynard; "but here comes Claude; we'll see what he says."

The three boys who had been to the pond now joined their friends, and Maynard told them that they were discussing the time to leave. The new-comers agreed with Maynard, and they told the driver to be ready with the team at four o'clock. The boys then went to their rooms to wash, and came down again just as the dinner-bell rang.

As they took their seats at the table Wingate remarked that he thought that Claude, St. Clair, and

A Funny Deer.   55

Phil appeared unusually smiling, and he asked Claude what luck they had had on their trip to the pond.

At this question St. Clair and Phil burst into a shout of laughter, and were finally joined by Claude.

Their four friends looked at them curiously, and Adams told them they need not keep all the fun to themselves, but to let the others know what they were laughing at.

"Shall I, Claude?" chuckled Phil, with an interrogatory glance at his companion.

"Yes; I don't mind,— go ahead;" and Claude was seized with another spasm of laughter.

"After we left the hotel, this morning," began Phil, "we went over to the pond. We saw nothing on the way worth shooting but a rabbit and a few squirrels, and we would not waste cartridges on them. We stopped about half an hour at the pond, and saw some deer tracks, but no deer. Not wishing to be late to dinner, we started back about eleven o'clock, and were within about half a mile of the house, we judged, when Claude, who was ahead, saw an animal cross the path some way beyond. He claims he did not have a fair sight at it, for which we will give him due credit," and Phil and St. Clair laughed again, while their companions listened and wondered.

"The deer tracks we had seen at the pond had probably stirred up Claude's hunting instinct; but however that might be, he yelled, 'A deer! a deer!' and started on the run, St. Clair and I following. Just as we caught up to him he fired both barrels, and, stepping aside, cried, 'He's in there; give it to him!' and pointed to the left, where we just caught a glimpse of the branches of some trees moving, as if an animal was making its way through them. Of course St. Clair and I fired as he directed, and then we all rushed in to be at the death, and found we had shot a young calf,"— here a universal roar broke from the other boys,— " and," continued Phil, struggling with his laughter, " it was as dead as Julius Cæsar, ana probably belongs to Daddy Parsons."

For some moments after Phil's story nothing could be heard but the uproarious laughter of the boys, and the other occupants of the dining-room gazed at them in astonishment.

Finally, Wingate, with the tears running down his face from laughter, asked Claude why he had not brought the head along with him, and sent it to Boston to be set up; and Adams suggested he had better get the skin and have it tanned.

When they had sobered down a little, Le Roy suggested that they would have the calf to pay for.

"That is nothing," replied Claude; "it won't cost more than five or six dollars."

Wingate here beckoned to the cherry-cheeked lass who waited upon them, and who had been watching them with a great deal of wonder depicted on her face, and when she reached his chair, he nodded toward Claude, and informed her in a whisper that could be heard all over the dining-room, that Mr. Emerson had shot a deer that forenoon. This started the boys laughing again; but they quieted down after a few moments, and finished their dinners.

When they went out-doors, a gentleman who had

sat at a table near them asked Adams what they had found so funny at dinner, and Adams told him, and the gentlemen enjoyed the story hugely.

When they paid their bill, Claude told Mr. Parsons about the calf, and that gentleman only charged them a fair price for it; but he laughed a great deal at hearing the story.

At four o'clock they left the house, and the four horses, having been well rested and fed, started on a sharp trot for Colebrook. The driver had heard the deer story, and although the boys had the panther-skin with them, and he had acknowledged that they had done a big thing in shooting the panther, still he seemed to take more pleasure in alluding to the deer-hunt than he did to the panther-chase, which I suppose was only natural.

About half way to Colebrook they came up with a countryman driving a skinny-looking horse in an old wagon that looked as if it might collapse at any moment.

The old trap threw up a cloud of dust, that came back in the boys' faces and made it very disagreeable for them.

"Can't you pass that wagon?" said Claude to the driver. "We don't want to swallow that fellow's dust all the way to Colebrook."

"I'll leave him behind in a moment," and the driver reined his horses to the right of the road.

But just as he did this the old man looked back, and, seeing that it was Dick's intention to pass him, called back, "Ye can't go by me, Dick Williams, till ye gin yer hosses a little more oats," whipped up his old plug and rattled ahead.

"It's old Smith," said Dick, who had recognized him, "and he's the ugliest old cuss yer ever saw. He's goin' clear to Colebrook, and he won't let us pass him if he can help it."

"Whip up, and try it," said St. Clair.

Dick did as ordered, and, touching up his horses, began to gain on the team ahead. But the old man was not asleep, and, seeing that they were gaining on him, he plied his stick with renewed vigor, and the horse broke into a gallop, and again widened the gap.

The boys now began to get excited, and Phil told Dick that if he'd pass the old buffer he would give him five dollars.

That was a big offer in the driver's eyes, and, touching up his leaders, and laying the whip over the pole horses again, they started on a gallop, and began to gain rapidly on the old man.

"The old beggar 'll stick ter the middle o' the road, darn him!" said Dick, as they neared the wagon, "and it'll be hard gettin' by him."

"Run him down, then," said Claude. "I'll pay the bills. If he's going to act like a hog, we'll take some of the bristles off of him. The first show you have of getting by him pass him if you take off his wheels. We'll see whether he is entitled to the whole of the road or not."

"That's the talk," assented Phil. "We'll beat him or wreck him."

The race was now an exciting one. The old man stood up in his wagon, and lathered the old horse as if his life depended on it, and Dick cracked his whip and yelled at his leaders to encourage them. The few teams they passed drew off to the side of the road, to keep out of the way, and watched the race with interest.

Dick's leaders put their noses over the rear of the old man's wagon just as the two teams reached the top of a short hill that descended at an easy grade, and the boys shouted with triumph.

"Turn out, now," cried St. Clair, "and go by him."

Dick followed instructions.

Sheering his horses a little to the right, and laying the whip over them, they shot by the old man's team, taking off both his wheels, and nearly capsizing themselves; for, as the old fellow had stuck to the middle of the road, Dick had been compelled to turn out more than he intended, and the wheels on the right side of the coach had gone into the ditch. For a moment the wagon was balanced on two wheels, but the boys jumped up to the left side, and Dick made a sharp turn to the left, and the carriage gradually returned to an upright position.

Dick stopped his horses as soon as he could, and the boys looked back. The old man was just scrambling to his feet, and was shaking his fist at them, while the horse, that been thrown down, had rolled over on one of the shafts, and, after breaking it, had cleared himself from the wreck, and was just getting up, and after gaining his feet, walked about in a manner that showed he was all right. The wagon was scattered about the road, and appeared to be pretty well used up.

"Drive on," said Claude, who had made up his mind

that neither the old man nor his horse had been hurt except in their feelings; "that will learn him to be a little more accommodating another time. It won't cost much to repair the damage, and that we are willing to do."

"He'll probably have us arrested," suggested Wingate.

"No fear o' that," said the driver, "if yer willing to pay him anything near what it'll cost him to fix up his old wagon; he won't trouble ye otherways; he knows darned well he'd no business to block up the road. Yer see we've got him there."

"I'm willing to pay whatever is right, and no more," returned Claude. "I don't propose to have him swindle us because he acted like a hog and had his wagon stove. It served him right, and I hope it will be a good lesson to him."

Without further adventure the boys reached the hotel, and Phil handed Dick a five-dollar bill, which made the driver feel very happy, and he told them he should like to drive for them wherever they went.

The boys then went to their rooms, washed up, and walked in to supper.

After satisfying their hunger they went out on the piazza and sat there talking about the "collision," as they called the smash-up, and told the landlord, who was present, all about it. He laughed heartily at Claude's humorous account of the affair, and just as he had finished narrating the story the old man came along. He had mended the broken shaft by means of a stick and a piece of marline, and had a pole lashed under the two axles on the side the wheels were off. He was walking, and leading the horse, and he stopped just in front of the piazza.

"What's the matter, Smith?" said the landlord; "you look as if you had met with an accident."

"No accident about it," returned the old man, snappishly; "that good-for-nothing Dick Gammon run inter me, and tried ter kill me, and you've got ter pay for it. Jest look at my team."

"It does look as if it needed repairing," acknowledged the landlord, with a smile, while the boys laughed and winked at each other.

"Repairin'! I should say it did. It'll cost a hundred dollars to make it as good as it was before."

At this the boys roared, and the landlord laughed also.

"A hundred fiddlesticks," replied Claude, contemptuously. "That is more than your whole team, horse and all, are worth."

"And himself besides," added Wingate, in a low tone.

"Let's see what the damage is," said the landlord, as he walked down and examined the wagon, and continued: "Dick brings a charge against you also. He says you kept in the middle of the road, and would not let him pass you. That isn't fair driving, Mr. Smith."

"He lies, then!" cried the old man, excitedly. "I got way out o' the road two or three times to let him go by, and he run inter me purposely."

At this deliberate falsification of the facts the boys shouted again with laughter, and the old man asked the landlord " what them chessy cats up there were grinnin' at."

"I am afraid you have forgotten the facts in regard to the accident," returned the landlord; "but, anyway, fifteen dollars will make your wagon better than it was before."

"Fifteen dollars, indeed! Twenty-five won't pay the bill. What do yer take me fur?"

"A beat," said Phil, a little under tone.

"A mad granger," added Claude, with a laugh.

"You can't talk any twenty-five dollars to me," said the landlord, as he returned to the piazza; "I've had too many teams repaired myself."

"Then I'll take the law on ye!" threatened the old man.

"Go ahead, if you want to," replied the landlord; "but you know, Smith, that law is expensive business."

"Well, I'll tell you what I'll do, Bailey," returned the old man, after he had pondered over the subject a few moments. "Me and you never had any trouble, and I'll split the difference, and call it twenty dollars."

The landlord was about to refuse this offer, but Claude nodded to him to accept it, and, taking two ten-dollar bills from his pocket, handed them to the landlord, who passed them over to the granger, who took them with a chuckle of satisfaction, studied them attentively for a few moments, and then buried them in the depths of a greasy, dirty black leather pocket-book. Then, giving a general nod to the landlord and the boys, he led his team off toward a carriage-shop a short distance from the hotel.

"That is more money than the old rascal will earn in the next month," observed the landlord, as he went in to supper.

"How the old sinner did lie!" remarked Maynard, as the boys arose and went on a stroll about the village.

The most of Saturday was spent in purchasing the necessary stores for their trip, and in getting them together and having them packed. As one team would not carry them and their boats, they had Mr. Bailey send the boats up in the morning on an extra team, and charged the driver to see that they were carefully handled, when he left them, and put in a safe place.

They completed all their preparations about three o'clock, and then went off fishing, and returned about seven with good appetites but a poor string of fish, they having caught but half-a-dozen small trout.

They spent the Sabbath quietly, going to church in the forenoon, and to Sunday school in the afternoon. In the evening they took a walk down to the river, and whiled away an hour or two on the bank, where they sat and talked over their future plans.

When they returned to the hotel they went up to the parlor and sang awhile, and, being joined by some of the other guests who were fond of music, the evening slipped rapidly away.

As they all had liked Dick for a driver, Claude spoke to Mr. Bailey about his going with them; and the landlord agreed to let him drive them up to the lake, and told Claude that he would have the team at the door by half-past seven, so they could start at eight.

Phil suggested that the driver had better go to the stores in the morning with the team and pick up the things they had bought the day before; and the landlord said he would have him do it before he called for the boys.

As everything was now arranged for their departure on the morrow, Claude suggested they had better retire, so as to be up early in the morning, and, calling to Phil, who roomed with him, they went to bed; and their friends, not caring to sit up any longer, also sought their rooms.

CHAPTER III.

Good-by to Colebrook. — Through a Bridge. — The Wheelman. — Connecticut Lake. — The Ride to Second Lake. — Shooting Partridges. — A Glance at a Moose. — Arrival at Second Lake. — Tom Chester's Camp. — The Deer Story. — Trout Fishing. — Crossing the Carry. — Arrival at Parmachenee.

AFTER breakfast Monday morning they settled their bill, bade Mr. Bailey good-by, and took their seats in the team, where Dick sat holding the reins all ready for a start. Quite a little crowd had gathered to see them off, and the landlord, and also the loafers, wished them good-luck, as Dick cracked his whip and started his horses into a trot.

It was a lovely morning, and the boys talked and joked with the driver as the team bowled along, and enjoyed themselves hugely. The road lay along the east side of the river, and the scenery was very pretty.

"How far shall we get to-night, Claude?" inquired Le Roy, breaking in on the silence.

"To the hotel at Connecticut Lake. It is twenty-five miles there, and that is far enough to travel in one day."

"And yer won't find any such road as this above there," put in the driver. "It's rough going between the First and Second Lakes. I've logged up there, and know something about it. You'll have to take a buckboard to get to Second Lake, and I don't know how ye'll get yer boats there; have to hire some men to lug 'em, I guess."

"We had them hauled from Andover to the South Arm of the Richardson Lakes two years ago, over a very rough road, and they were not hurt a bit. I guess we can manage it some way."

"Well, perhaps yer can. But you'll have ter watch 'em sharp or they'll get chafed. They're mighty purty boats, too. Where were they made?"

"They were built in South Boston," answered Wingate.

"Were they? Wall, I wouldn't mind owning one like 'em myself."

"Here comes a two-horse team," said Wingate, "and I don't see how we shall pass it; the road is very narrow here."

"That's the stage from Stewartstown. He'll wait there until we get up with him; the road's wider there. He's hauled up now. Come! gee up, a lang there!" and Dick snapped the end of the whip about the leaders' ears in a way that accelerated their movements.

"It's going to be a hot day," remarked Claude, as the sun struck in on them.

"Yes, sir, it is," replied the driver. "Those horses have begun to sweat now, and I aint worked them at all. What do yer say, boys," and Dick glanced around with a smile, "had I better take his wheels off?"

"I guess not," returned Claude, laughing; "he seems disposed to give us half the road."

As the teams passed each other the stage-driver and his two passengers, who were young women, gazed at the boys as if they had just come out of a curiosity-shop.

"Mornin', Bill," said Dick. "How are ye?"

"Fust-rate," returned the stage-driver.

"Where ye bound?"

"Connc't'cut Lake."

"Comin' back to-night?"

"Dunno. Guess so."

"Why do all your country folks stare at people so?" inquired St. Clair, as they left the stage behind.

"Guess they want ter know ye ag'in when they see ye," answered the driver, with a laugh.

"It's nothing but insatiable curiosity," observed Claude. "And if it was only the staring you might put up with it; but they are so confounded impertinent! They want to know everything about you: who you are; where you come from; where you are going; what you are going for. And they ask you the sauciest questions imaginable without the slightest idea of their impertinence."

"Yes," added Phil, with a laugh, "and the moment one of them finds out anything he runs to somebody else with it, and that person in turn tells it to the first person he meets, and in a few hours it is all over town."

"Well," said Dick, who thought the boys expected him to say something, "yer see there aint much going on down here in the country, and we think more of little things than yer do in the city, and what 'ud interest us you'd look on as small pertatoes and few in a hill."

"Well answered," returned Maynard, "and, if you always come as near to the truth as you have now, you'll not be hung for lying;" and the boys and driver laughed in concert.

About ten o'clock they reached the village of West

Stewartstown, and the driver pulled up near the hotel and watered his horses, while the boys took advantage of the short stop to visit a store in the neighborhood, where they succeeded in buying some very small and very sour apples. As soon as they had taken their places in the wagon again, Dick started his team, and they crossed the river by a bridge into Canaan.

"Now yer in Canaan, Vermont," said the driver, as they rode through the village.

"So this is the 'happy land of Canaan,' that they sing about, is it?" asked Claude, as he offered the driver some apples.

"I don't know about that; but some of the men who live here are pretty happy, and they get happy altogether too often to suit my idees."

"In other words, they get drunk," suggested Adams.

"You've spelled it," said Dick.

"Where shall we get our dinner?" inquired St. Clair.

"About five miles farther on there's a house where yer can get some; or yer can wait until we get to ther lake."

"How long will that be?" asked Le Roy.

"About three o'clock," returned Dick.

"Three o'clock!" yelled Adams. "I protest! Let's get something to eat before that time, if we have to stop at a farm-house."

"We might get a bowl of bread-and-milk at the house the driver speaks of," suggested Claude, "and that will stay our stomachs until we reach the house at the lake."

Lunch at a Farm-house.

"If that is the way you are going to do it," said Adams, "I'll call for a six-quart pan of milk and a loaf of bread for myself," at which his friends all laughed.

The river was now on their right, and furnished them many pretty views as they followed its banks northward. For a few moments it appeared a long dead reach like some pond, and then would be broken into noisy rapids, and occasional falls. Crooked, like all New England streams, it turned and twisted apparently to every point of the compass. In the five miles to the house where they were to get lunch they only met one team, and nothing unusual occurred.

The driver pulled up at the farm-house, and the boys stepped down from the coach. Claude knocked on the door, and interviewed the farmer's wife, who, after listening to his request, agreed to furnish them with some bread and milk, which she promised to have on the table in ten minutes. While she busied herself getting their lunch, the boys walked about out of doors and "stretched their legs a little," as the driver put it. From the field back of the house came the smell of new-mown hay, and the party could see the farmer and his men hard at work, some mowing, and others spreading. It was a busy season of the year, along their route, for, wherever there was any hay to cut, a crew were at it with a will. The driver said it had been very poor hay weather through July, and, now that the right kind of weather had come, those who had hay to harvest were making the most of it.

The old lady now appeared at the door and beckoned them to come in, and, followed by the driver, whom

Claude had invited to take a bite with them, they took seats about the old-fashioned round table and were soon discussing the relative merits of bread and milk, while with table-spoons they gave force to their arguments.

In eating and talking a half-hour glided swiftly away, and, at the end of that time, the boys arose from the table, and Claude settled the bill, a very moderate one. The driver had not taken his horses from the team, and a few moments saw them in their seats on the coach again, and once more progressing northward.

The day was perfect; hot and pleasant, with just enough of a west wind blowing to temper the sun's rays, and keep them from feeling laggy. Within three miles of the lake hotel the road crossed a small stream by means of a wooden bridge. As they approached it the driver told them it was getting old, and was considered by some to be unsafe. While speaking of it the team rolled heavily on it, and the horses had just stepped off of the farther side when the whole structure collapsed, and down into the bed of the stream went the wagon, minus the forward wheels, which the horses had taken with them. The driver, clinging to the reins, had been dragged out of the team by his horses, which, although somewhat frightened at the crash, he had succeeded in stopping, and, tying them to a tree, he went back to see how his passengers fared.

They had been pretty well mixed up for a few minutes, but were now crawling off from each other, and alighting in the brook, the water being only two or three inches deep, with stones plentifully sprinkled about, many of them being several inches above the water, and offering dry footing, of which the boys availed themselves. They clambered up the banks of the stream, which were about six feet high where the accident occurred, and found that, beyond a few scratches and bruises and a sudden fright, they had sustained no injury.

"Are you hurt any, boys?" asked the driver anxiously, as he looked from one to the other.

"Oh no! we are all right," replied Claude, "but how about the wagon? I see the rack is broken, and the boxes and other things that were on it, are in the brook."

"Yes, and they ought to be taken out at once," broke in St. Clair, "some of the things will be spoiled if they get wet."

"I'll take care of 'em," and Dick scrambled down to the stream, and, picking up the articles that had been on the rack, passed them up to the boys, who deposited them beside the road.

After doing this, the driver examined the wagon carefully, and found that the axle, wheels, and springs were all right, and the damage was very slight.

"If I only had a man or two with me now," he remarked, as he finished his survey, "I could get this wagon out of the brook."

"Here are seven good men and true," replied Claude, smiling; "we will give you all the assistance you desire."

"Good boy!" said Maynard, patting Claude on the shoulder, "you have expressed the spirit of the party exactly."

"Wall, I didn't know as yer'd want to take hold," answered the driver, "but if yer do, we'll snake the wagon out'n that brook quicker'n chain lightning ever went through a gooseberry bush."

"Now you are talking," put in Wingate; "tell us what to do first."

"Wait a minute, till I unhitch the horses from the forward wheels," and Dick scrambled up to the road and went to work.

After he had cleared the horses he took hold of the pole, and drew the forward wheels along the road a short distance, until he reached a place where the land sloped gently away from the road, and turning off he went into the field, and drew the wheels to the brook, striking it a short distance from the road where the banks were very low. He run the wheels into the bed of the brook, and backed them up near the wagon, and then called to the boys to come and help him.

"What will you have?" asked Claude, as they reached the brook.

"See if there's beef enough in yer to lift up the front end of the wagon so I can shove the forward wheels under."

The boys hauled off their shoes and stockings, rolled up their pants, and, all taking hold with a will, lifted the wagon and held it until the wheels were pushed under and the bolt dropped into the axle.

"Good enough!" exclaimed Dick, with a satisfied air. "Now if yer'll clear away that rubbish," alluding to the remains of the bridge, "and throw it t'other side of the wagon, I'll go and get the hosses and hitch on."

"All right," replied Adams. "Hurry up for we are getting hungry."

The boys had soon removed the *débris* around the

wagon, and in less than ten minutes Dick had his horses in their places, and was in his seat. Starting his team carefully, he drove down the bed of the stream a few rods, and then, turning to the left, gained dry ground, and, shortly after, the road. When he reached the spot where the things had been deposited after the accident he was obliged to turn completely around. But the road was quite wide in that place, and he made the turn without any trouble.

It took some fifteen minutes to load, and then they were once more under way.

"Do we cross any more bridges?" queried Le Roy, as Dick laid the whip over his leaders to make up for lost time.

"No, only over ditches, or something of that kind. There's no more bridges of any size."

"Then I hope you'll succeed in getting us there without breaking our necks," said Phil. "It's almost a miracle that we went through that bridge without getting injured."

"Wall now, if there aint a durned fool!" exclaimed the driver, gazing earnestly ahead, without paying the slightest attention to Phil's remark.

"Where? Oh, I see!" and Claude, who had asked the question, laughed.

"What's the critter on anyway?" inquired Dick, with open-mouthed wonder.

"Why, a velocipede," said St. Clair. "Didn't you ever see one?"

"No, sir! What are they fur?"

"To ride," answered Maynard. "Don't you see how that fellow comes along?"

"Yes; and, consarn him, he'll be frightening my hosses. I should like to know how he got way up in here with that thing. I didn't see him go up."

"He's dismounting," cried Phil. "He is going to take a rest until we go by."

In a few moments the wagon had reached the wheelman, who lifted his cap and bowed, as the horses were pulled up.

The boys saluted him, and Claude asked him where he had come from.

"Boston was my starting-point. Rode from there to Rangeley, then took the steamer across the lakes to the Magalloway river. Then went up to Parmachenee in a boat, crossed to Connecticut Lake, and reached there Saturday evening, stopping at the hotel until after dinner to-day. Am going as far as Colebrook to-night, and down to North Stratford in the morning, then to the White Mountains by the way of Lancaster."

"On that durned thing?" broke in the driver, contemptuously.

"Yes, sir," replied the wheelman. "I can make as many miles a day with my steed as you can with yours."

"In a horn yer can," laughed Dick.

"We are from Boston," said Claude. "Do you live there?"

"No. I live in Hartford."

"I suppose we ought to know each other," and Claude, after mentioning his own name, introduced the other members of his party.

"My name is John Hawthorne, but my friends call me Jack. You are bound on a camping-out racket, I take it?"

ON A BUCKBOARD.

"Yes," replied Claude; "we are going to Connecticut Lake, and from there across to Parmachenee, and spend a few weeks in that vicinity."

"It's a pretty country over there," returned Hawthorne. "I wish I could be with you. But I must move, for I wish to reach Colebrook before dark. Good-by, and good luck to you!"

"The same to you," answered Claude.

"We tumbled through a bridge, a few miles back," cried Maynard, as the wheelman started off; "look out you don't fall into it."

"Thank you; I'll keep my weather-eye open," shouted back Hawthorne, as he rapidly widened the distance between them.

"Go, ahead, Dick!" now sang out Adams, urgently; "that dinner will be supper by the time we reach it."

The driver "gerlanged" to his horses, and once more they were bowling along the road. The boys laughed and joked about their delays, and wondered what would turn up next.

To the great satisfaction of Adams, however, nothing further hindered their onward progress, and at half-past four they reached the hotel, and were out of the wagon as soon as it had stopped.

The landlord met them at the door, and "the hungry man" went for him on the dinner-question before he had time to open his mouth.

"Don't be in such a hurry," said Claude; "let's see if we can get rooms."

And the leader of the expedition turned to the Boniface and asked him if he had rooms for them all. Receiving a satisfactory answer on that point, Claude then spoke to him about the dinner.

"Dinner! Oh, yes! Can give you dinner, if you want it, in half an hour. But supper will be ready in about an hour. Don't you think you had better take both meals in one?"

Claude looked around at his friends to see what they thought of the proposition, and Phil said he could wait an hour easy enough if the others could. The rest of the boys concluded they could stand it if Phil and Claude could; so nothing more was said about dinner, and they sat down and talked over their future plans until supper-time.

The driver told the landlord about the broken bridge, and he ordered one of his men to harness up a team, take a lantern, and ride down to the bridge, and put it up there, so that no one would ride into the brook during the night. He also told him to notify a Mr. Jones, who had charge of the road, that the bridge was down, so it could be repaired the next day.

After supper Claude made a bargain with the landlord to take the party, with their boats and baggage, to Second Lake. Feeling tired after their ride, the boys went to bed early, to obtain a good night's rest.

They were up betimes Tuesday morning, and, after a good breakfast, put on their hunting-suits, and prepared for the start. The boats were carefully loaded into a hayrack, and secured in such a manner that they could not chafe, and their supplies and other traps were loaded upon two buckboards. The distance from the hotel to Second Lake was about eight miles; but, as the horses would have to walk all the way, they did not expect to reach Chester's Camp until noon.

At half-past seven they bade the landlord good-morning, and started on the "war-path," as Adams expressed it. Claude and St. Clair loaded their guns as they left the hotel, in the hope of getting a shot at a few partridges.

The first two miles the boys rode on the buckboards, but, becoming tired of riding so slowly, they left the teams, and went ahead, after learning from the drivers that they could not by any possibility lose the road.

"How long will it take to cross the carry to Parmachenee Lake?" asked Wingate of Claude as they trudged along.

"I suppose we can go over in half a day easy enough," replied Claude; "but it will take one whole day, perhaps longer, to get the boats and stores across."

"Are you sure we can hire men at Chester's to take our things over for us?" inquired Adams.

"Well, no, not absolutely sure. But the landlord at the Connecticut Lake House told me there were generally three or four guides at Chester's Camp, and I guess we shall be able to get some one to do the 'toting,' as these fellows call it up here. Besides, if it come to the worst, we could get the things over ourselves."

"It would take us a week," added Phil, with a wry face at the bare idea.

"I guess we should be weak by the time we finished the job," put in Le Roy, laughing.

"I don't propose to borrow any trouble about it," said Claude.

They were now passing through a piece of woods, and, calling to St. Clair to accompany him, Claude asked the rest of the party to keep back, and perhaps his companion and himself might get a shot at some partridges.

The two gunners went on in advance of the others, and in about fifteen minutes came upon three partridges sunning themselves in the middle of the road. The birds did not seem at all startled at the noise the boys made, and, instead of flying, walked a few steps, and then stopped and looked at them.

"Let them have it!" cried Claude, and the two boys fired simultaneously, killing the three birds at the first fire; but, as they were only about thirty feet away from them, it would have been strange if they had missed.

"So much towards dinner," said St. Clair, as they picked up the birds, which were young and fat.

Then they each put a fresh cartridge in their guns, and waited for their friends to come up.

"First game," announced Claude, as the other members of the party came hurriedly toward them, having heard the reports of the guns.

"Three partridges, boys," sang out Maynard, as he caught sight of the birds.

"Yes," replied Claude, "and if some of you will carry them, Andrew and I will push ahead again, and see if we can't find some more to go with them."

Adams took the birds, and the two gunners went on again.

"Great Scott! I wish I had my rifle," exclaimed Wingate, as a large bald-headed eagle flew over their heads, as they stood in a group waiting for Claude and St. Clair to get out of sight.

"If either of us had a rifle that fellow would not have come so near us. They know a thing or two, those eagles do."

"Perhaps not; but I mean to get a shot at one before we go home."

"I should like to knock one of those baldies over," chimed in Phil; "they look very handsome when they are well set up."

"They differ a good deal from men, then," said Adams.

"Differ from men? What do you mean?"

"Why a man generally does not look very well when he is 'set up,'" returned Adams, with a sly grin.

"Oh, rest your mouth!" cried Maynard; "it's too early in the day for that kind of talk."

"He can't help it any more than a mule can kicking," added Le Roy; "but let's be moving along, the boys are far enough ahead by this time."

"When we reach the lake I suppose we had better put in our boats, load our things into them, and go by water to Chester's Camp. What do you say, Claude?"

"Certainly, Andrew, that will be the easiest way to do it."

"Do you suppose there are any brook-trout in Second Lake, Claude? The landlord down to the other hotel told me there were very few in Connecticut Lake, but that there were plenty of lake-trout."

"I guess they are all brook-trout in Second Lake; but I don't know sure. However, we shall find out when we get there."

"This is a pretty hard road we are travelling on," said St. Clair.

"Yes, it is nothing but a lumber road; is not used much in summer, I guess."

Just then a large animal came out of the woods on their right, and, leisurely crossing the road, disappeared in the forest to the west. Both of the boys saw it, and gave an excited shout of "A moose! A moose!" and, with more zeal than discretion, started in pursuit. But they might as well have chased a whirlwind, for the moose, startled by the outcry they had made, tore through the woods at a pace that effectually discouraged pursuit, and the only glimpse the boys obtained of him was the one they had caught from the road.

A half-hour's rapid pursuit had, however, well tired them, for the day was very hot, and they stopped and sat down on an old windfall, to rest a few moments before going back to the road.

While sitting on the fallen tree they heard a noise behind them, and, looking around, they saw a flock of partridges, and counted seven. The birds were on the ground, moving slowly about, apparently in quest of food, and were within easy gunshot.

Claude whispered to his companion to fire, and himself blazed away. They shot four birds out of the seven, the other three flying. The boys watched them, and noticed where they alighted, and, stealing carefully up towards them, knocked them over with their remaining barrels.

Picking up their game, they retraced their way slowly to the road, and came out just as the teams drove along. They learned from the teamsters that their friends were ahead, and they started on in advance of the teams. It was half-past ten when they joined their friends at the foot of the lake, and Phil told them the rest of the party had been there half an hour, and were beginning to worry about them.

"Did you notice anything in the road, Phil," asked Claude, "when you came along after we left you this time?"

"Nothing particular. Did you see anything worth looking at?"

"I guess we did."

"What was it?"

"A moose," put in St. Clair.

"Oh, nonsense!"

"It's a fact," asseverated Claude, "and we followed him for half an hour into the woods on the left of the road, and shot these partridges in there."

"Was it a large one?" inquired Adams.

"A regular old reefer," returned Claude, — "half as large as an elephant."

"Why didn't you shoot him?" queried Maynard.

"Because we never got sight of him again after he crossed the road, and, at the rate he travelled, I guess he is in Canada by this time."

"That was too bad," said Le Roy. "I wish you had shot him."

"So do I," added St. Clair. "But you know, if wishes were horses, beggars might ride."

"Did you see anything of the teams?" asked Adams.

"Yes," replied Claude. "We met them when we came out of the woods."

"Are they very far behind?"

"Not a great way. I think they'll be here soon; but while we are waiting for them let's pluck these partridges."

The boys now busied themselves in removing the feathers from the birds, and, after they had picked them clean, dressed them, and had them all ready for Tom Chester's cook, when they should reach his camp.

At eleven o'clock the teams arrived. The boats were unloaded and placed in the water, and the stores, tents, and other baggage packed away in them. With a "Good-by!" to the drivers, the boys jumped into their boats and pulled for the camp, which stood on the west shore of the lake, about two miles beyond. Claude, Maynard, and Phil were in the "Fairy," St. Clair and Adams in the "Go Ahead," and Wingate and Le Roy in the "Water Witch." Pulling abreast of each other, the oarsmen kept their boats in that position until they reached the camp. They were in no hurry, and pulled a long easy stroke. As the light craft rippled through the placid waters of the lake they presented a beautiful sight.

As they came within sight of Chester's Camp they were discovered by the occupants, who stepped out to watch them, headed by old Tom himself. As the boats floated in to the shore, the by-standers passed many complimentary remarks upon them.

The boys stepped carefully out of the boats, after passing the time of day with those on shore, and Claude, as spokesman for the party, asked Chester if he could accommodate them until the next day.

"Sartenly, sartenly," answered the old man, and he

busied himself in helping unload the boats. After this was done, the boys each took a valise, containing their special belongings, up to camp, leaving the rest of their things on the shore.

Claude turned the partridges over to Tom, and told him they would like them for dinner. The landlord said they should have them, and that he would have dinner ready for them by one o'clock.

The boys found the present occupants of the camp to be two New York gentlemen and their guides, and three other guides, who were waiting for a party whom they were daily expecting. One of these last was called Ned Norton, and Claude fell into conversation with him, while awaiting their dinner, and, after some talk, made a bargain with him and his two companions to get their boats and baggage across the carry, and, as the tents would be the first thing they would need, Norton agreed to take them over that afternoon and set them up for the party.

"But you can't get back to-night?" said Claude.

"No, but we can be here by seven to-morrow morning."

The party were favorably impressed with Camp Chester, and, indeed, it was very pleasantly located. It stood a short distance back from the water, facing the lake and the boundless forest beyond, stretching away mile upon mile to the eastward. Of the three Connecticut lakes, Second Lake is by far the handsomest, and has a decided advantage over the large lake below, from the fact that on all sides it is surrounded by a heavy growth of hard and soft woods, which, as yet, have escaped the ruthless hands of the Connecticut

River Lumber Company. Large game of all kinds are to be found in the vicinity, and one of the New York gentlemen told Claude that they had shot two deer while they had been there, in a little over a week.

Just then the welcome sound of "Dinner" came from the Camp, and the boys left off talking to repair to the table.

After the meal was over the party adjourned outdoors, and the boys put their fishing-rods together with the intention of trying their luck with the trout later in the afternoon. Norton and his two companions started about two o'clock for Parmachenee Lake, carrying the tents and a few other articles, and agreed to be back the next morning.

When he had put his rod together Claude found the landlord, and interviewed him about the fishing-grounds. Tom told him the most likely place to visit, and then suggested that four o'clock was early enough to start.

"Do you get much game about here, Mr. Chester?" asked Claude.

"Yes, considerable. Deer and moose, and, sometimes, caribou are plenty enough about here, and there's lots of otter and beaver."

"I never saw a beaver," returned Claude, "but I have a moose. One of our party, Maynard, shot one over to the Richardson Lakes, when we were there two years ago."

"Wall, if you was goin' ter be around here any length of time I'd take you to a beaver dam; but, perhaps, you'll run across one over Parmachenee way."

"Hope I shall; I would like to see one."

As it still lacked an hour of the time when they had decided to start after the trout, Claude brought out his sketch-book, and made a picture of the lake from the camp, while his friends amused themselves in various ways.

St. Clair told the New York gentlemen about the moose that he and Claude had seen in the morning, and they concluded to start off, accompanied by their guides, the first thing after supper, and see if they could not run across him.

One of the gentlemen informed St. Clair that the guides had a way of enticing the moose toward them by using a sort of trumpet of birch-bark, making a noise similar to that made by the moose, and known among woodsmen as the " moose-call."

" Have you done much shooting?" asked St. Clair, who was interested in anything appertaining to hunting.

"Considerable. But all I have ever done never gave me as much pleasure as the first deer-hunt I had on snow."

" Tell us about it," urged St. Clair ; and his companions, scenting a story, gathered about to listen.

Lighting a cigar, the gentleman threw himself on the ground at full length, and surrounded by the boys, each in the position that best suited his convenience, held forth as follows : —

" Some twenty years ago business brought me, in winter, to Portland, Me., and, being an enthusiast in sporting matters, I brought my gunning equipment with me. After successfully completing my business, I went up to Bethel, and from there to the Magalloway

Settlement, where I engaged a guide, who had a good dog, and we started out on a week's hunt.

"One morning, after a fearfully cold night, when the snow lay on the ground to the depth of four or five feet in sheltered places, but less over tracts exposed to the wind, Nay Bennett and I crawled out of our pit below the crust, under the lea of Emery mountain, where we had passed the night very comfortably, in spite of the intense cold, with our feet at a good log fire, and, slipping on our snow-shoes, commenced our journey toward Parmachenee Lake, in search of moose."

"There's where we are going," said Adams.

"So Mr. Emerson told me. I wish I was going with you, but we leave for home Monday morning."

"Don't interrupt the story, Adams," said Maynard.

The gentleman smiled at Maynard's remark, and proceeded.

"We had not made more than a couple of miles over the crisp, sparkling crust, which was hard enough to bear us, and were about entering a track of black-growth timber, near the summit of a moderate hill, when we observed numerous deer-tracks, and fresh-bitten shrubs, which indicated that we were in a deer-yard."

"What is a deer-yard?" inquired Maynard.

"Now who is interrupting?" queried Adams, with a sarcastic grin.

Maynard blushed at being caught "on the hip," and the gentleman proceeded with his story, and answered Maynard's inquiry at the same time.

"It is the habit of these animals, as well as of moose, in northern latitudes, when the snow is deep and crusty in the month of March, to stop and yard until the snow melts away, or becomes soft enough for them to travel about without cutting their legs. This is done by selecting a spot where there is an abundance of undergrowth and shrubbery, which, in the warm days of that month, throw out their smelling buds in anticipation of more favorable weather. Upon these sweet and tender buds the deer will browse contentedly until the snow is nearly gone. By running over the snow, as the crust begins to form, and by depressing it, a firmer crust is formed than in the surrounding forest, which enables them to run about more readily in quest of food. Sometimes the area of a yard is more than two or three hundred acres, but generally less, depending upon the number of deer yarding together. In this instance we found the yard to be a large one, and, although we were in search of moose, we concluded, in the absence of venison or other fresh meat from our larder, to take in some if possible. We therefore prosecuted our search up and down and across the yard until nearly two hours had passed, and we were seemingly no nearer our game than at the commencement of our search, although the signs were most encouraging.

"As we had been travelling briskly, we concluded to take a short halt, and let our dog, Zip, make the search alone for a while. Zip was a veteran in this line of exertion, and immediately put himself out vigorously at the order from Nay. Hardly had he disappeared in advance before his quick running yelp announced the finding of game. We speedily followed, and found that we had halted in close proximity to a number of deer, which Zip had started from their beds in the snow. We saw plainly the hollows or resting-places from which they had been so suddenly started, and down the hillside we saw the road or ploughed furrow by which they had escaped. It was wide and deep, and indicated the passage of a dozen or more. We could plainly hear the yelping of Zip not far ahead, who apparently was not making any rapid progress.

"I hastily gave Nay my pack and gun, and rushed down the hill in pursuit as rapidly as my snow-shoes would allow me, leaving Nay to follow as fast as he could with his increased burden.

"An important object after starting deer in this manner is to hurry them up as much as possible at first, which increases their alarm and occasions more floundering and fatigue than would result from a slow following. Deer, when closely pursued at first, will soon lose courage and strength if the travelling is difficult; but, if allowed to get over the first flurry, will settle down into a more cool and steady exertion. I soon came up with Zip, who was doing all he could, but who found the crust too soft to fully sustain him. I left him behind, which annoyed him very much, as evinced by his redoubled exertions and yelping. A mile more of rapid travelling brought me in sight of the deer, — a splendid drove of thirteen, — led by a large buck, which I mentally resolved should be mine."

"I wish I had been there," cried Le Roy, who was getting excited over the story.

"At my near approach their exertions were increased, but only to still more hopelessly flounder in the snow; and, upon my reaching them, they separated from each other, as usual in such cases, each taking care of himself. Singling out the big buck, I brought him to bay, the others soon being lost to my sight. The old fellow would turn and face me upon my near approach; but, finding himself unmolested, would exert himself to escape, until again crowded. My object was to detain him until Nay or Zip should come up. Finally Zip arrived, and immediately commenced a furious onslaught, after the manner of dogs of his class, which, being trained to hunt moose, do not close in, but keep up a perpetual springing and barking, which serves to annoy and hold the game at bay until the hunter arrives with his gun. A dog of good metal and hold-fast qualities would most likely lose his life in endeavoring to seize and hold a full-grown moose, owing to the effective manner this animal has of striking out with his forefeet; and the dogs employed by moose-hunters in that part of the country are of an ordinary character, and are effective in their way. Zip was one of this sort; and, although the animal we had at bay was much inferior to a bull moose, I could not get him to lay hold, while the buck was gradually working his way to a hill-side not far distant, where the snow was partially blown away, which I feared he might reach, and, perhaps, escape, before Nay came up with the gun."

"Hang such a dog as that!" broke in Phil, with emphasis.

Without taking any notice of the interruption, the gentleman went on : —

"I therefore kept very close, and urged Zip on continually. The buck would start on as speedily as possible until Zip's running nips would bring him around, when he would charge in a gallant manner; but Zip's ability to keep out of harm's way was only too evident. In vain I urged him to hold, but hold he would not, though most noisy and persistent in his peculiar warfare. The buck finally became very furious at this continual goading, and employed nearly all his time in charging and striking at Zip, giving out in his fear and rage an angry, hissing sound. In the excitement I had approached within ten or twelve feet of him, when suddenly, disregarding the dog, who, as usual, made good his escape, came upon me so quickly that, in my efforts to retreat, I locked my snow-shoes, and came down upon my back."

"Holy mackerel! you was in a fix then," exclaimed St. Clair.

"I think I was," remarked the gentleman, with a smile.

"I saw his leap, and his body coming down upon me with his forefeet close together in striking condition. I had barely time to twist my body a little on one side, when down in the snow close beside my waist came his cleaving feet. I had in my right hand a buck-horn handle-knife with a thirteen-inch double-edged blade, running to a point. I had drawn this out on my near approach to the buck, and, as I felt his breath on my face, I suddenly threw both arms around his neck, to detain him from coming down upon me again with his sharp feet; but his strength was so great that he instantly rose in the air with me hanging to his neck, while Zip, who had grown more courageous, seized him firmly by the rear. The buck was now in a decidedly bad fix" —

"Had him where the wool was short," interrupted Adams.

"This fact he seemed well aware of, and I was very much astonished at the rapidity with which he leaped up and down, despite the heavy burdens he carried in the front and rear. I came to the immediate conclusion that his strength would outlast mine, unless abated by some extreme action. So, finally, compressing my left arm, which was hooked over his neck, and rapidly seizing his throat with my left hand, I liberated my right arm and brought my knife blade down to the hilt in his neck; it seemed like cutting butter, the knife slipped into his flesh so readily. Down came buck, dog, and myself in a confused sort of way, myself underneath; but the buck had ceased to struggle, and I pushed aside his head to keep off the hot red blood which spurted from his wound and nostrils, and rose to my feet, well tired from my exertions. The buck was dead, and I had been lucky enough not to receive a scratch. Nay soon arrived, and we dressed and hung up the buck in a tree, above the reach of animals. Cutting from him enough meat to supply our immediate wants, we pursued our way towards Parmachenee Lake. When we returned, two weeks later, we found his frozen carcass hanging as we had left it. Nay rigged up a rough sled, and hauled him out to the settlement, where we found his weight to be one hundred and eighty-nine pounds."

"He was a rouser!" said Phil.

Claude thanked the gentleman for his story, and, telling his friends it was time they were off if they were going to have any time for fishing, led the way to the boats. Launching their light craft, they pulled to the location that Chester had told them of, and, separating a little, began whipping the lake. As only two could conveniently fish from a boat, Phil, who was with Claude and Maynard, amused himself by watching his companions, at the same time holding himself in readiness to net any fish that either of his friends might get near enough.

The day had been so warm that the trout were slow to rise, and, after a couple of hours' fishing, the party pulled back to camp, having only captured thirteen small trout, the largest of which would not run over three-quarters of a pound.

Claude took the trout up to camp, and asked Tom to cook them for their supper. This he promised to do, and told him as they had caught so few trout, they should have some moose meat to keep them company.

Claude informed his companions that Chester had promised to give them some moose meat for supper; at which they were all delighted, more especially Phil, who had never eaten any.

As they did not intend to do any more fishing until they reached Parmachenee, the boys filled up the time while waiting for tea by packing up their rods.

A little before seven the New York gentlemen, who had eaten their supper before the boys, started off with their guides, to try and get a shot at the moose that Claude had told them about. They took their rifles, blankets, and a few other necessary articles, intending to be out all night. The boys felt interested in the success of the expedition, and wished them good luck, and Claude asked one of the gentlemen to send them word whether they killed the moose; if the boys had left when they came back to camp; and Mr. Loud promised to do so.

After supper the boys gathered with Tom outside the camp, near the door-way, and listened to the old trapper spin his yarns, amid a cloud of tobacco-smoke, that, like a huge incense, rose above him. Story after story of hardship and adventure in the woods fell from his lips, that were eagerly devoured by his attentive listeners. Many of them were laid in Eastern Maine, where Tom had spent several years, trapping in the unbroken wilderness about Katahdin, and Tom told the boys that some time they should visit the Penobscot region, which they mentally vowed they would do, after listening to the stirring adventures which the trapper had experienced in that portion of the wilds of Maine. Time passed so quickly that it was eleven o'clock before they knew it; and then, telling them that he must go to bed, their host showed them to their bunks, and turned in himself.

The boys had hardly gone to bed when an owl, in a tree back of the camp, began his "Te whit, te whit, te woo!" and this was answered by the dismal cry of a loon, somewhere in the lake, who thought, perhaps, that the owl was calling him.

Maynard proposed that they should turn out and try and shoot the owl and the loon; but Claude declared that it was late, and that they needed all the sleep they could get, as the next day's travel would be hard; and, therefore, his friend gave up the idea, and, by midnight, silence reigned throughout the camp, only broken by an occasional snore from some one of the tired sleepers.

It seemed to Claude that he had slept scarcely an hour

when Tom gave him a gentle shake, and informed him that it was six o'clock, and that breakfast would be ready in half an hour. Yawning and stretching, Claude turned out, and called to his friends: —

"Come, boys! all hands on deck! It is the middle of the day, and breakfast is all over!"

"What's that you say?" inquired Adams, who had only caught his last words, as he started up in alarm. "Did you say breakfast was all over?"

"Certainly," answered Claude, turning around to conceal a smile.

"Then it's a cold day for you, John," declared Maynard, poking Adams in the ribs.

"I guess we shall find something," added St. Clair, as he began dressing. "Claude is only trying to frighten us, to take our appetites away;" and, amid much laughter, and a running-fire of joke and repartee, the boys finished dressing.

As soon as they had completed their toilet they hurried out-doors to see what the weather looked like, and found they would have another warm, pleasant day; and while they were discussing what they should carry, Tom called them to breakfast.

Just as they arose from the table, Ned Norton and his two companions came in, and Ned told them that he should be ready to start again as soon as they had eaten breakfast.

"How far have you come this morning, Mr. Norton?" asked Claude.

"Six miles. We started at four o'clock."

"And shall you start right back without resting any?" inquired St. Clair.

"Certainly. A six-mile walk is nothing," and the guide laughed as if St. Clair had asked him something funny.

"What had we better have go next, boys?" queried Claude, as he looked around at his friends.

"The boats," said Wingate.

"The blankets," cried Phil.

"Some grub," chimed in Adams.

"How much can you carry?" asked Claude.

"Oh, we are good for seventy-five pounds apiece!" answered Norton, smiling at their looks of astonishment when he mentioned the weight they could carry.

It seemed a hard matter to determine what they needed the most; but, after a general expression of opinion among the boys, aided by suggestions from Tom and the guide, it was decided that the members of the party should each carry their fire-arms and fishing-tackle, and, in addition, Claude should take their iron kettle, St. Clair the coffee-pot and teapot, Wingate the two frying-pans, Maynard the wooden water-pail, in which was packed twelve dozen of eggs; Le Roy the iron pot, Adams a ten-quart tin pail filled with butter, and Phil, what dishes he could make a convenient-sized bundle of. All of these things could be hung to their guns or rifles, and could thus be carried much easier.

Norton was to take one of the boats, the oars and paddle being lashed firmly inside, one of his friends some blankets and flour, and the other a few pounds of pork, some potatoes, a ham, and a few cans of condensed milk.

Chester agreed to take care of the two boats and the other things left behind, until Norton and his friends could "tote" them across, and went over with the boys to the other side of the lake. The "Fairy" was taken out of the water, and left for Norton and Chester, after bidding the boys "good-by," and wishing them "good luck," returned with the other two boats to camp.

"Now then, fellows, let's be off," said Claude, as he passed the barrels of his gun under the bale of the kettle, and swung the gun on his shoulder, taking his rod-case in his left hand. "It won't pay to hurry on this tramp; we'll take it easy."

The others loaded in the same manner, and were soon stringing along in single file, like a party of Indians on the war-path. As the sun climbed high in the skies, the heat in the thick forest was intense, and the sweat rolled down the faces of the boys, who stopped occasionally to change their loads and rest. About eleven o'clock Norton and the two guides passed them, and Ned told them they had acomplished half the distance.

After hearing that, Claude proposed that they should rest and eat a lunch that they had brought from Chester's with them; to which his companions gladly assented. At noon they started again, and at four o'clock met Norton and the guides on their return, who told them they were only a mile from the lake, which was welcome news to the tired trampers.

Norton asked what they should bring over the next day, and Claude told him the two boats, a few blankets, and some more provisions. Telling Claude that he would find their tents all set up, and that they might look for them the next day at noon, they left them, and a moment later were out of sight.

"What walkers those fellows are! they travel like

horses," said St. Clair, who had admired the free-and-easy strides with which the guides had left them.

"Yes, and they carry like horses, too. The idea of a man lugging seventy-five pounds across here on his back!" and Phil shrugged his shoulders as if the thought was not pleasant.

"We shall not reach the lake to-night if we stand here all day talking," sang out Le Roy; "remember we have our own supper to get to-night."

"Yes," chimed in Adams, "and I'm as hungry as a bear."

"You're always hungry," declared Wingate, giving him a poke; "you must have swallowed a tape-worm when you was a child."

"I can swallow you in about two minutes," retorted Adams, "if you keep on talking that kind of nonsense."

"Look here," cried Claude, "if the rest of you wish to stay here and be eaten up by flies and mosquitoes, you can, but I am going along;" and, picking up his things, he started, followed by his friends, who, one by one, fell into line.

It was a quarter of five when the boys reached the tents, which they found had been pitched on a level piece of land, clear of underbrush, and but a couple of rods from the water. Quite a large piece of the upper end of the lake was in sight from the camping-ground. Laying their things in the store-tent, they sat down a few moments for rest and consultation.

"Now, fellows," said Claude, as he looked from one to the other, "we may as well organize our force before we begin work. As you all know, there are a certain round of routine camp duties that must be performed, if we are going to live agreeably and comfortably; and I think I know you all well enough to say that I don't believe any of you will shirk your proper amount of the labor. As we are all supposed to be cooks, I propose that each one shall take his turn at a week's cooking, and that whoever is cook during the week shall be boss of the camp, and shall have authority to call on any of us for what help he needs."

"But I don't know anything about cooking," protested Phil. "I have not been taking lessons at home all summer, as the rest of you have."

"That's nothing," returned Claude, "you can learn here. We can make you cook for the last week of our stay, and you ought to learn the business by that time."

"I'll break him in," said Maynard, grinning.

"As we are in the middle of a week now," continued Claude, "I'll be cook for the balance of this week and through next, and a week from Sunday somebody else can take my place."

"Confound these mosquitoes!" exclaimed Phil; "they are getting thick."

"That is so," replied Maynard, as he killed two on his forehead at one crack. "Let's get out of here and build a smudge. Where's the axe?"

"That's the question," said Claude, as they all rose to their feet. "I'll bet five dollars they are all at the other lake."

A few moments' search convinced them that this was the fact.

"Here's a nice go," growled Adams.

"A sheer piece of stupidity," echoed St. Clair.

"Well, we were all fools, that is a fact," assented

Claude, "not to have had an axe brought over. The very article we needed the most."

"I should have supposed the guides would have thought of that," added Le Roy.

"There's no use in crying for spilled milk," remarked Claude, cheerfully; "so let's all skirmish around and find what dry wood we can, and break up enough to get supper with."

CHAPTER IV.

The First Meal in Camp. — Cooking under Difficulties. — Under the Blankets. — An Alarm in the night. — What was It? — The Attack of the Minges. — Good Fishing. — Prospecting for a Camp Site. — The Hunting Party. — What they found. — A Bear in a Trap. — His Capture. — Bringing him to Camp. — Arrival of more Stores. — A Square Meal. — Around the Camp-fire. — Bruin and the Singing. — Christening the Bear. — A Good Night's Rest.

THE boys had no intention of stopping where their tents were now pitched any longer than was necessary for Norton and his friends to get over the balance of their things. As they had left Boston with the intention of being away until the first of October, they had brought a large supply of provisions and ammunition with them, besides plenty of thick clothing, and a pair of woollen blankets, and one rubber blanket for each member of the party. A sheet-iron stove, mosquito netting, a table that folded up into a shape four feet square and six inches thick, seven folding camp-stools, three hammocks, and some other articles that were not carried by camping parties in general, were among their outfit. The store tent was Λ-shaped, six by ten feet, and the tent in which they were to live and sleep was a wall tent, twelve feet square, with perpendicular walls five feet high, giving a very roomy space inside. Both of these tents the boys had ordered made expressly for this trip; and, while the duck from which they were manufactured was light, it had been soaked in oil until it was thoroughly water-proof.

Parmachenee Lake, looking North.

They had a good stock of canned meats, vegetables, fruits, etc., besides common groceries; for they were all good livers at home, and did not intend to be dependent upon fish and game for their living. As Claude expressed it, "they were not going into the woods to starve." They had brought only a limited supply of such stores as flour, potatoes, and pork, intending to replenish these articles from some of the camps in the vicinity of the lake.

"Now, boys, start a fire, will you?" said Claude, as they all threw down their wood a short distance from the tent, "and I will see what I can find for supper."

Upon looking over what things had been brought across the carry, Claude found that no baking-powder had come with the flour, so the idea of making bread of any kind that would be palatable was out of the question. Le Roy, luckily, had filled the iron pot with hard-tack before starting, and thus the bread could be dispensed with. The stove had not come over, and the absence of the axes was a chronic thorn in Claude's side.

It was with some difficulty that he rigged a crane over the fire, on which to suspend the kettle, in which he boiled the potatoes; but he managed it after awhile. Cutting several slices of ham, he put them in the frying-pan, and, after the ham was cooked, some eggs; and, when the potatoes had boiled, announced that supper was ready, St. Clair, in the meantime, having set the table. Phil had brought all the tin plates, dippers, knives and forks over, so that they could eat what they had to eat in a decent way. None of the tea or coffee had come, but a pail of water from the lake supplied this deficiency.

The walk had given the boys a healthy appetite, and they went for the ham and eggs and hard-tack as if they did not know where the next meal was coming from.

"I propose we have some trout for breakfast in the morning," said Adams, with a glance at Claude.

"All right, my boy. If the trout are caught I will cook them. I think it would be a good idea, myself."

"How are we going to sleep to-night?" asked Phil, who had been investigating before supper. "Only three pairs of blankets have come over."

"We shall have to do the best we can," replied Claude. "I see there is plenty of spruce about here, and after supper we shall have to break off some small boughs and spread them along one side of the tent, lay two of the blankets on them, and put the others over us. It is going to be a pleasant night, and not very cold."

While Claude and St. Clair washed up the dishes and cleared away the things, the rest of the party gathered boughs for their bed.

No fire was built out-of-doors that evening, as the boys found it rather difficult to get fuel without an axe.

Before dark they put their rods together for fishing in the morning, and also loaded their guns and rifles.

Claude appointed St. Clair as his assistant in the morning, and Phil and Le Roy wood-gatherers, while Adams, Wingate, and Maynard agreed to try their luck with the trout.

Not having either fire or lights, the party went to bed early, and by half-past nine were all asleep.

Along in the night Claude was awakened by a noise out-of-doors, sounding as if some animal was around the camp. He sprang up quickly, and groping his way to the table picked up his gun, and hastened to go out. His movements awakened St. Clair and Phil, who had been sleeping either side of him, and they called out to learn what the trouble was.

"Hist!" replied Claude. "I hear some animal out-doors, and am going to see what it is."

His two friends were on their feet in a moment at this report, and their action awoke the other members of the party, and they all went out together. It was very dark, and they could scarcely distinguish one tree from another.

Keeping quiet for a few moments they heard a rustling and tracking in the store tent, and Claude crept carefully up to it and looked in. As he lifted up the flap to see what was there, he heard a noise between a snort and a growl, and the next moment a large animal rushed by him into the middle of the party, completely upsetting Maynard and Adams, and took to the woods.

Springing by and beyond his friends Claude fired both barrels of his gun, which were loaded with buckshot, in the direction of the noise, and sang out, "Take that, with my compliments."

"What was that, — an elephant?" inquired Maynard, as he picked himself up.

"I thought a travelling tornado had struck me," said Adams, who had fallen upon a rock, and barked his shins. "What was it, anyway?"

"I think it was a bear," remarked Wingate; "but it was so confounded dark you couldn't see anything."

"That is my opinion, also," chimed in Claude;

"but it is too dark to determine the matter to-night; let's turn in again."

"So I say," added Phil; "this night-air is chilly; I begin to feel cold already."

"I wonder what time it is?" queried St. Clair.

Claude scratched a match and looked at his watch. "Half-past twelve. Let's get to bed again."

As nothing could be done in the darkness to discover what kind of an animal their nocturnal visitor had been, they crawled under their blankets and were soon sound asleep, nothing more occurring to waken them during the night.

About four o'clock in the morning the minges swarmed into the tent, and in a few moments everybody was wide awake, slapping, rubbing, and growling. Sleep any longer was out of the question, and the whole party turned out.

Taking their rods, Adams, Wingate, and Maynard launched the boat and went off fishing, while the others, after examining the ground, to see what it was that had disturbed them in the night, began gathering wood for the breakfast fire. It did not require a great deal of search to convince them that their visitor had been a bear, as in one or two places the tracks of its feet were clear and well defined, and Claude suggested that as soon as they had time they should try and find Mr. Bruin, and see if they could not pay him for the scare he had given them.

The fire was soon lighted, and the smoke cleared the minges away from their immediate vicinity. Some potatoes were peeled and sliced, the pork tried out, and as soon as the fishermen hove in sight the potatoes were fried and the hard-tack placed on the table.

The boys had been highly favored, and had brought back about sixty trout. On their arrival all of the party took hold and helped dress the fish, and they were soon spluttering in the frying-pan.

The breakfast was the same as the supper the night before, with the exception that the trout and fried potatoes took the place of the ham and eggs. It was about six o'clock when they sat down to breakfast, and the two hours they had been up had given them a relish for anything in the shape of eatables.

"What shall we do this forenoon, fellows?" asked St. Clair, as he paused in his eating a moment.

"Follow up that bear track and shoot the bear," answered Maynard.

"Go a-fishing," said Adams, whose excellent luck in the morning had given him strong hopes for the future.

"What time do you expect Norton and his men, Claude?" inquired Phil.

"He said he would be here at noon, and we must be on hand when he comes. If he leaves the axes behind this time I shall give him a Dutch blessing.

"I hope he'll bring coffee, tea, and sugar," remarked Le Roy, who had missed the three mentioned articles very much.

"We don't want to stay here any longer than necessary," said Claude, "and we had better look out a permanent camp site, or, at least, a spot where we can stay two or three weeks, and move our things to it to-day. After we clear up the breakfast things I will take

Wingate and Phil, and we will row up to the inlet, and select a suitable place for a camping-ground. The rest of you can pick up a little more wood, enough to get dinner with, and then amuse yourselves as you please until noon. I will try and return by eleven o'clock, and have dinner at twelve."

No one objected to this arrangement, and when the camp-work had been done, Claude, Wingate, and Phil started in the boat for the inlet. They landed to the west of it, and, after prospecting a little, found a good, level place, plenty large enough for both tents, that had been at some time cleared, but which was now partially overgrown with bushes. Not having any axe, they set to work with their hands, and, as the soil was light, soon had the entire crop of weeds and bushes torn up by the roots and thrown into a pile to burn.

Just beyond the spot they had cleared to set their tents on, a bright, sparkling brook came tumbling down from a hill behind them and emptied its waters into the lake. For all camp purposes this was as good as a spring, for the water was as clear as crystal, and almost as cold as ice, while it was filtered over a bed of cobblestones and sand. Their clearing, also, was only about four rods from the shore, and commanded a view of the picturesque islands that dot the surface of the upper end of this beautiful lake. A little to the south of their camping-ground a slight undulation of the lake-shore made a small cove ending in a tiny sand beach, — a safe harbor for their boats.

The three boys found plenty of good firewood close to their camp site, and several large pine and spruce trees from which to hang their hammocks.

"I think this is the boss place for a camp," remarked Phil, as having done all the work they could, and all the prospecting they cared for at present, they made their way to the "Fairy," and embarked for the return to the carry.

"Suits me to a T," added Wingate.

"I think it is as pretty as any place we camped in on our last trip," said Claude, as he dipped the oars in the water and shot the light boat from the shore, while Phil, in the stern, with a dexterous stroke of the paddle, turned her in the right course.

The members of the party whom Claude and his companions had left behind had quite a spirited discussion as to how they should spend the forenoon, after the boat had left them.

Although neither of them cared to go off alone, they each made different propositions as to what they should do. Adams, still enthusiastic over his morning's success, spoke earnestly in favor of fishing, but his ardor dampened a little when Le Roy told him they could do nothing where they were then without a boat. Maynard, who was especially fond of field-sports, said there was more fun in beating the woods for partridges than anything else; while St. Clair and Le Roy, with an ambition to distinguish themselves, coaxed their friends to go with them on the track of the bear, and see if they could not shoot it. By dint of strong argument they brought the others over to their way of thinking, and taking their guns and rifles loaded, with a few extra cartridges, they picked up the trail of the bear and followed it as fast as they could trace it.

Old Bruin's track led them south, according to Maynard's compass, along the side of a large hill that swept back from the lake. At times it was very distinct, and at others completely obliterated, causing them several minutes of careful search before they found it.

After an hour's travel, however, the trail suddenly became broader and plainer, and looked altogether different from what it had at first, leaving the boys at a loss to account for the sudden change in its appearance. But having no difficulty now in following it at a rapid pace, a half-hour's walking enabled them to solve the mystery, as, swinging around a huge boulder that appeared in their way, they came suddenly upon Bruin, and found that one of his hind feet had been caught in a trap, and that he had been dragging that, as well as the clog, with him the entire distance from where the trail had first broadened. To increase his misfortune the trap had caught against a maple about six inches through, and, by accident, probably, the bear had made a turn around the tree with the chain attached to the trap, and was now a prisoner in two ways. As he caught sight of the boys he made a movement to run, but the chain and trap held him fast, and he fell over, growling and showing his teeth as he did so.

Le Roy raised his rifle, and a second later Bruin would have had a bullet in him, but Maynard, catching his arm, cried, "Don't shoot! I believe we can capture him alive."

This remark, while creating a sensation among his friends, was received with sarcastic credulity.

"Capture your grandmother!" cried St. Clair, laughing. "Why don't you go up and shake hands with him?"

"Or," suggested Adams, "you might put a bit in his mouth and ride him back to camp."

"Foster could if he was here," said Le Roy, with a chuckle, alluding to an incident in their former trip.

"Well, don't be in a hurry to shoot him," urged Maynard, "he is having a pretty hard time of it as it is."

"Kill him, and put him out of his misery, I say," and St. Clair cocked both barrels of his gun.

"He isn't hurt any," protested Maynard; "a black bear is as tough as a boiled owl. If we can get him to camp, we'll have no end of fun with him."

"There's something in that," assented Adams.

In the meanwhile the subject of their debate kept making frantic but futile efforts to clear himself, and seemed entirely regardless of the jury who were determining his life or death. He was a very large animal, would weigh at least three hundred, and seemed anything but gentle. After talking over several different plans of getting their captive to the camp, it was decided that Maynard should return for the other three members of the party, and bring back with him a blanket and a coil of three-quarter-inch rope about fifty feet long that was in the store-tent, while St. Clair, Adams, and Le Roy should stay by the bear and frustrate any efforts he might make for escape.

Accordingly, Maynard, who was a fast walker, started for camp at as rapid a pace as the nature of the ground would permit, and reached the tents just as Claude and his companions came up from the boat. In a few hurried words he told the boys of the bear's predicament and his plans for getting the animal to camp alive. His friends were interested and excited at his story, and, getting the blanket and the rope, they started post-haste to return to Bruin, after Claude had written a note, and pinned it to a tree asking Norton if he came during their absence to await their return.

As they hurried along Claude charged them to say nothing to Norton and his friends about the bear, as the trap might belong to them, and he thought they would claim the bear and kill it if they knew of its capture, as the skin would be worth fifteen or twenty dollars, to say nothing of the bounty.

Urged on by their excitement, and stimulated by a prospect of sport, the boys covered the space of forest between the camp and the bear in an incredible short period of time, and, reaching St. Clair, Adams, and Le Roy, who anxiously awaited them, sat down a few moments to rest.

"Has—he—been—quiet—since—I—left?" inquired Maynard, puffing out his words like a steam-engine from the force of his exertions.

"He's behaved barely well," answered Adams, forcing a joke.

"How are we going to manage now?" asked St. Clair, looking at Maynard.

"I'll show you," returned his friend as he took the rope and made a large slip-noose at one end, and then, with a quick fling, threw it over the bear's head, and with a pull tightened it securely around his neck. "Now take hold and pull, fellows, and we'll choke a little of the mischief out of him;" and, suiting the action to his words, he pulled away on the rope, aided by the others, until the bear fell over on his side, his tongue lolling from his mouth. "Now, Adams, you and St. Clair hold the line tight, so he can't recover his breath, and we'll try and get the trap off of him."

Maynard then folded the blanket twice, and threw it over the bear's feet, as some protection from his claws, and asked Wingate and Phil to lay over Bruin to keep him down.

"I don't want any part of that job," said Phil, looking askance at the prostrate animal.

"Do you see anything green in the corner of my eye?" inquired Wingate, with a sly wink at the rest of his friends, which brought forth a roar of laughter.

"What are you afraid of?" queried Maynard, contemptuously. "The bear can't move as long as St. Clair and Adams hold the rope; he's half choked now. I'll be one to lay on him, if either of you'll join me, and the other three of you can spring the trap, only we must not be all day about it."

The cool manner in which Maynard spoke quieted, if it did not remove, the fears of Phil and Wingate, and they piled on top of the fallen bear. Then Maynard, Le Roy, and Claude sprang the trap, it taking every ounce of strength they had to do it. As soon as Maynard had cleared away the trap they examined the bear's leg and foot, and came to the conclusion that no bones were broken, although the skin was torn off some and the flesh badly lacerated.

"He'll be all right in a week or two," said Claude. "I owned a dog once who had his leg all chawed up in a fight, but no bones were broken, and his leg all healed up in less than a month, and was as good as the others. But how shall we get him to camp?"

"Lead him," replied Maynard as he folded up the blanket, and passed it to Phil to carry. "Slack up the line a little, fellows, and let him come to," and the director-general of the scrimmage put his hand on the knot and slackened it a little, not, however, without keeping a wary eye on the bear.

"What next?" inquired Adams.

"All hands take hold of the rope, and let Phil carry the blanket."

"That will suit me as well as a custom-made overcoat," and Phil, who hadn't much faith in leading bears, instantly put several rods between himself and his friends.

"Get clear to the end of the rope, boys," directed Maynard, "and if he makes a dash for us when he recovers his senses, keep out of his way; but don't give up the ship; in other words, hang to the rope. If he tries to run away from us we must shoot him, and if our united strength won't hold him, we'll take a turn around a tree with the rope."

The bear now showed signs of returning consciousness, and soon regained his feet. He seemed to know, in a moment, that the unwieldly burden he had been carrying was removed, for, without paying the slightest attention to the boys, he craned his head around, and began licking his wounded leg.

"Heave ahead, fellows! he's all right; let him do his doctoring later in the day," and Maynard gave a pull on the rope.

This did not suit Bruin at all, and he held back like a baulky horse, biting savagely at the rope, and growling discontentedly.

"Yank him along, fellows! It's three miles to camp, and I'm getting hungry," said Maynard, urging his friends onward.

I doubt if ever a bear was in such a fix before. At least this one was not, and he showed his disapprobation of the proceedings by every means in his power. Snarling and growling he would rush at the boys, who at such times would by a sudden turn fling him down, and then he would hang back for dear life, until forced to proceed to keep from choking. All this time the boys, in spite of their fears that he might get the best of them and injure some one of the party, were convulsed with laughter, and perpetrated some horrible puns at Bruin's expense, who, could he have understood them, would have lost all courage to have attempted further opposition.

Phil, who was well in advance, enjoyed the scene hugely, as he thought that, whatever trouble his friends might get into, his skin was safe. Although I have no doubt that, if they had called on him for assistance, he would have been prompt to render it. But this was his first trip in the woods, and he did not feel as much at home with the surroundings as the other members of the party.

"By Jove!" cried Claude, tugging at the rope, as the sweat rolled down his face, "this is better than a circus. How my father would laugh if he could see us for a moment!"

"Oh, hang your father! Now, I don't mean that; but let's get along, I am half-starved," and Adams tugged viciously at the rope.

"We are getting along as fast as we can," declared

Maynard, as the bear made another rush for them, compelling them to yank him over, to teach him better manners.

Before the boys reached camp their fun had degenerated into the hardest kind of work, which, added to the excitement they had undergone, and the length of time they had been without food, left them about used up, and no one was sorry when they had tied Bruin to a large spruce, a short distance from, and in sight of, the tent, and they could take time to sit down and rest.

Norton and his friends had been there, and Claude found in place of his note another, which read: "Waited as long as we could. Will see you to-morrow."

"They brought the boats," remarked Maynard; "I can see them down at the shore."

"Bother the boats! I wonder if they brought an axe?" queried Claude, as he arose and walked to the store-tent.

Much to his joy he found the two axes and hatchet, and tea, coffee, sugar, baking-powder, salt, matches, and a lantern.

"They skipped the blankets," he said to himself; "but no matter, we can get along one more night well enough."

"What did you find? anything we need?" asked Phil.

"Here are the axes, which we needed most," and Claude enumerated the other things.

"Coffee!" yelled Adams, smacking his lips. "Let's have some for dinner, or supper I guess we had better call it," glancing at his watch, and finding that it was after three o'clock.

The bear, which had been busy lapping his leg, now turned his attention to the rope with which he was tied, and tried to chew it off.

Maynard, however, had one eye on him, and, seizing a pole that lay on the ground handy, he gave Bruin a poke in the ribs that brought forth a growl, but which stopped his tampering with the rope.

"Now, fellows, let's proceed to business," said Claude. "If you are all as hungry as I am, you won't care how soon you eat. Phil, get a pail of water; Maynard, start a fire; Le Roy, wash a dozen potatoes, and put them in the iron pot, and put two quarts of water in it; St. Clair, come with me; take the other axe, and we'll cut two crotched sticks and a straight one, and put them in place, so we can hang the potatoes over the fire."

Claude and St. Clair soon returned and drove down the stakes over the fire about five feet apart, and placed the straight one on top. Then, taking an iron rod that they had brought with them for that purpose, turned up at each end, he put one end on the horizontal stick, and hung the potatoes to the other, and the water was soon boiling.

Although their stove had not been brought over, nor their cake-board, Claude contrived to make some biscuit, which were quite an improvement over the hardtack. While he was making the biscuit and coffee, St. Clair fried the trout, and, at quarter past four, the half-famished party sat down to a "good square meal," as Phil expressed it, and, with joke and laughter, they kept their places at the table until nearly five o'clock.

"What are you going to give us for supper, Claude?" asked Adams, with a grin, as he arose from the table as full as a tick.

"You say supper to me," laughingly replied Claude, "and I'll set the bear on you."

"Look here, fellows, we ought to feed the brute," said Phil. "I wonder what the skunk will eat."

"Fish," replied Claude. "Were there any left, St. Clair?"

"Eight, I believe."

"Give them to the old buffer, then," suggested Maynard, and after he eats them I'll get a pail of water, and we'll see if he's thirsty."

"Feed him yourself. I don't care to go fooling around him."

"Well, I can, if you are afraid of him," and Maynard went for the fish, and brought them up near the bear, and laid them on the ground, then, getting a pail of water from the lake, sat that down near him.

"What are you going to call that bear, Frank," asked Claude, as the boys stood watching him eat the fish.

"I don't know. What do the rest of you say?"

"Call him Squeezer," suggested Adams, with a chuckle; "he'll make his name appropriate if you give him a chance."

"Call him Growler," added St. Clair; "he's growling half his time."

"Call him Cuffee," put in Le Roy; "he's as black as a nigger."

"Call him too late for breakfast," said Phil, grinning, as if he had said something funny.

"That's what we'll call you, Phil," returned Adams, as he gave him a push towards the bear.

Phil jumped back lively, and made a rush for Adams, who eluded him by dodging about among the rest of the party, until St. Clair accidentally (?) stuck out his foot, and down went Adams, with Phil on top of him.

"What do you say to calling him Napoleon?" Or we might make it Nap, for short," and Maynard glanced at Claude, as if he had settled the matter.

"I suppose that will do," replied Claude. "You know Shakespeare says, 'What's in a name? A rose by any other name would smell as sweet,' etc. And then Napoleon was both a bear and a bull at times, so I think that will answer very well."

"Then Napoleon, or Nap, it shall be," asserted Maynard.

"Half-past five," remarked Claude, glancing at his watch. "We have loafed long enough. Come, St. Clair, let's clear up and wash the dishes. Wingate, you and Maynard cut up some wood, and Le Roy, Adams, and Phil, pick out such things as we shall not need here to-night and in the morning, and load them into one of the boats, and take them up to the other camping-ground. You will have just about time to get up there and back with one load before dark. Take one of the rubber blankets along with you to cover the stuff up with, and then if we have a shower in the night it won't get wet."

The boys now busied themselves about their separate tasks; but while Maynard did his share toward getting the wood, he kept an eye on Nap, to see that he did not free himself from his bonds. The bear, however, seemed to be sleeping after his meal, and gave no trouble.

After Claude and St. Clair had washed and cleared up the dishes they assisted Wingate and Maynard in procuring fuel, and at dusk had all that was necessary for use during the time they would be obliged to stay in their present quarters. Then they built a large camp-fire, around which to sit during the evening, and just as it was fairly ablaze the other boys landed from the boat and came up and joined them.

"Who's going fishing with me in the morning?" queried Adams, as the party disposed themselves around the camp-fire in whatever attitude best suited them.

"I'm your man," replied Phil, and Wingate and Le Roy both signified their willingness to accompany him.

"You had better take two boats, then," suggested Claude, and added with a smile, "You know we have another boarder now. Nap will stow away piles of fish."

"Nap be hanged!" exclaimed Adams. "Who's going to catch trout for him every day? I don't mean to, at any rate."

"He'll eat chub as quick as he will trout," said Maynard, "and there's plenty of them in the lake. Save what chub you catch for him, and keep the trout for ourselves."

"I'll bet that bear will eat swill," added Claude. "Anyhow, I'll try him on it to-morrow."

"Let's have a song, fellows; we haven't had a good

sing for a week," and Phil gave the fire a poke, and threw on several large sticks of white-birch, that sent the sparks dancing merrily into the air.

"What shall it be? I'm ready for anything," and Claude glanced around the circle of fire-lit faces for an expression of opinion.

"'Way down upon the Suwannee River,'" replied Adams, beginning to sing, and the others joined in with him.

The ice once broken, song followed song in rapid succession, and just as they had concluded "Home, Sweet Home," Maynard exclaimed, suddenly, "Look at Nap! What in thunder is the old sinner up to?"

The boys all glanced at the bear, and then gave a universal shout of laughter. The animal had crawled as near them as his rope would allow, and, seated upright on his haunches, had one ear turned toward them, his head slightly cocked over, and had been apparently listening to the singing with a great deal of enjoyment. The glare of the flames brought his black body out in strong relief against the forest behind him, and his little brown eyes twinkled like stars.

"Now, that's what I call an appreciative audience," said Phil, almost choking with laughter, as the bear, now that the singing had ceased, came down on four feet, and, drawing nearer the tree, stretched out on the ground like a large dog contemplating a snooze.

"'Music hath charms to soothe the savage breast,'" quoted Claude, recovering from his fit of laughter.

"Better make it 'beast' this time," suggested Adams, "it will suit the case better," and again their laughter echoed through the woods, causing the birds to flutter, while an owl, disturbed from his meditations, sent forth his peculiar note, as if in remonstrance of such gayety after dark.

"If we only had a fiddle now we could teach that bear to dance;" and Maynard hove another stick on the fire, glancing at his watch by the increased flame, and announced to his companions that it was ten o'clock.

"Then I am going to turn in," and Claude arose, stretching himself; but, suddenly turning to Maynard, said, "What are you going to do with Nap? Nobody is anxious to watch him all night, and he will chew that rope off and get away before morning."

"I can fix him," returned Maynard, "if you will all help me," and, going carefully to the tree, he succeeded after a few moments in unfastening the rope with which the bear was tied, and threw the loose end over a large limb of the spruce, about ten feet from the ground. "Now give us a pull!"

"What the dickens are you going to do now, — hang him?" queried Claude, as the boys, pulling away on the rope, lifted the forefeet of the bear off the ground.

"Not much. Only going to choke him, so I can muzzle him safely. Up with him a little higher;" and the boys, obeying Maynard's order, hoisted Bruin into the air till his hind toes barely touched the ground. Then Maynard, whipping a couple of pieces of marline out of his pocket, tied the forefeet of Nap together with one while he securely muzzled him with the other, so that it would be an utter impossibility for the captive animal to open his mouth until the line was taken off. "Now let him down, boys;" and, lowering away the line, the bear reached the ground and fell over on his side. Maynard loosened the rope around his neck, and secured the end to the tree; and then they left Bruin to regain his wind at his leisure.

"You would make a good showman, Maynard; you had better start a menagerie, when we get home," said Claude, laughing at the way Maynard had planned to secure the bear during the night.

"I will," replied his friend, with a smile, "and advertise you and the rest of the boys as 'Wild Hottentots,' à la Barnum."

"Dry up with your show business, and let's turn in, I am getting sleepy. A man who is going to get up at four o'clock to go fishing does not want to sit up all night;" and Adams started for the tent followed by the others, and soon all were quiet with the exception of Nap, who, having regained his senses, seemed indignant at the shabby trick that had been played on him, if one could judge from his actions, for he scratched and rolled, and tore around, all the time keeping up a subdued growling. But he soon found that Maynard's knots were not to be untied by any means at his command, and, becoming resigned like the Dutchman's wife, "who had to be," he soon became quiet.

CHAPTER V.

Early Fishing. — Moving Camp. — Getting to Rights. — An Inquisitive Guide. — Feeding the Bear. — A Trial at Jack Shooting. — Baking Beans. — Berrying. — A Caribou. — An Unsuccessful Chase. — A Visit to Flint's Camp. — Potatoes and Chains. — Teaching the Bear. — A Sunday Dinner. — Wild Lightning. — Looking for a Beaver Dam. — The Eagle's Nest. — The Big Pine. — Back to Camp.

As some of the mosquito-netting had been brought over during the day, the boys spread a piece over them as a protection in case they had another visit from the minges. But nothing interfered with their slumbers, and, a little after four, Adams awoke, and, punching Phil, who in turn punched Wingate and Le Roy, the quartette of fishermen arose, and went off to try their luck.

At five, Claude, St. Clair, and Maynard turned out, and, as soon as Frank had made his toilet, he took a look at Nap, and found him awake. Calling to his friends, the bear was hoisted up again, and relieved of his muzzle, and the rope taken off of his feet. Then he was lowered down again, and some ten feet of slack-line given him, so he could take a little exercise if he chose. While he was partly unconscious, the boys looked at his wounded leg, and found it was doing well. Then, leaving him to his own reflections, they built a fire, and proceeded to get breakfast, doing all they could

CAPTURING A BEAR.

until the return of the fishermen. While waiting for them, Claude and his assistants folded up the blankets, and took down the store-tent, packing them up ready for removal.

By the time they had accomplished this work the absent members of the party returned, bringing seventy-five trout, weighing on the average from a quarter to three-quarters of a pound each, and fifty-nine chub. Half of the chub were given to Nap at once, and the rest put away for his dinner, while the trout, under the skilful hands of Claude and St. Clair, were soon cooked to a crispy brown, and were smoking on the table. The boys then sat down to breakfast, and Phil told Claude that they saw a deer come down to the water, near where they were fishing. "And I think," said Adams, "that he intended to swim across the lake. But he saw us, and put back into the woods as if a pack of wolves were at his heels."

"There is game enough around here, no doubt," remarked Claude, "if we only have the good luck to find it."

"You must hunt for it if you want it," added Wingate, sententiously.

"Yes," laughed Phil, with a wink at Claude; "Ned Norton told me it was always good hunting up here."

"That means, I suppose," suggested St. Clair, "that greenhorns like us can hunt all day, and find nothing in the shape of game."

"Right you are, my boy," returned Le Roy, smiling.

"How shall we get Nap up to the new camp?" inquired Adams, casting a glance at the bear, who, having finished his chub, was now diligently engaged in lapping his wounded leg.

"Tow him up behind one of the boats, and let him swim," said Phil, jokingly.

"Not much!" exclaimed Claude, "he would capsize the boat. We must lead him up through the woods, and we must get him away, too, before Norton comes."

"Then I move he be muzzled again," put in Wingate; "his teeth are in pretty good order, I have noticed, and I don't want him to try them on me."

The morning meal over, the boys began work with a will. The living-tent was taken down and folded, the table packed up, and the goods at the camp equally divided among the three boats. Claude directed St. Clair, Wingate, and Phil to row the boats up to the camp-ground, while the rest of the party went through the woods, following the lake shore, with Nap.

As soon as the boats had left, Maynard and his three companions choked and muzzled Nap, and started with him through the woods. To guard against any trouble, Claude took his gun and Frank his rifle; but Nap followed much better than he had the day before, and the party were only two hours in making the distance. When they reached the camp-ground they found the boats already unloaded, and the things piled together near the site selected for pitching the tents. These were at once placed in position, the table set up, and the supplies put away in the store-tent, while the blankets were spread about to air. Nap was unmuzzled then and secured to a maple in the immediate vicinity, and, the party, at Claude's request, accompanied him a short distance away to where some good-sized cedars grew, and, hacking these down, — for all the boys were poor choppers, — they managed to split them up lengthway, and secured enough pieces from six to ten inches wide and seven feet long to lay in the tent where they were to sleep. These splits were then spread to the depth of three inches with cedar boughs, and over these three of their rubber-blankets were spread, topped by part of the woollen ones, thus giving them a soft and fragrant bed. By the time they had done this it was half-past eleven, and Claude said he must go back to the carry to meet Norton.

He ordered St. Clair to make preparations for dinner, and detailed Maynard and Adams to assist him, while, accompanied by the other three boys, he took the "Fairy" and "Water Witch," and rowed back to the carry. They reached there just as the three guides appeared with their loads, and Claude found they had brought the stove, the remainder of the blankets, and more canned goods. Norton informed him that they would get the balance of the things over the next day.

"Have you had a scrimmage with a bear here?" asked the hunter suddenly, whose quick eye had discovered the numerous bear-tracks in the vicinity.

"Not much of a one," replied Claude, blushing with the consciousness that he was not telling the whole of the story. "A bear came into the camp night before last, and awoke us. We turned out, blazed away at him as well as we could in the dark, and he went off into the woods."

"By thunder! I should think he had yarded here," exclaimed one of Norton's companions, as he examined the ground around the spruce where the bear had been tied. "Aint ye seen him since?"

"Yes," returned Claude, who now being directly questioned, would not lie about the matter.

"Wall?" returned the hunter inquisitively, waiting for Claude to go on.

But Claude, turning to Norton, told him that he would meet him there the next day and settle with him; and then, calling to his friends, began to carry the things that had just been brought over to the boats.

As the boys returned to take the last of the load, the guide tackled Claude again.

"What dy'e say become o' that bear, Mr. Emerson?" asked the guide, anxiously.

"I didn't say," returned Claude, dryly.

When a countryman's curiosity is once aroused — and it doesn't take much to start it — the only way I know to lay it is to kill him on the spot; but Claude was not prepared to go to such a length as that, and so hurried to his boat again.

But the guide followed him, and, as they shoved off, said, in a coaxing, wheedling tone, "I say, naow, what become of the bear?"

"Jumped into his skin and went off in it," returned Claude, as, dipping his oars in the water, he rowed away, enjoying the discomfiture of the native, who, having failed in attaining the information he so much coveted, returned, chagrined and crestfallen, to his companions.

"What dy'e 'spose become o' that bear, Ned?" remarked the defeated guide, as he joined his friends.

"I don't care what become of him," returned Norton. "Let's be moving, if we intend to get back to Tom's to night."

"Haven't eat my lunch yet, and I feel almighty peckish."

"Neither have I. We will eat it when we get to the spring. There is nothing but lake-water here to wash it down with;" and Norton started with his companions on the return trip.

It was one o'clock when the two boats reached the camp-ground, and Claude found the dinner about ready. Taking hold at once, and assisting St. Clair, he was able in a quarter of an hour to shout "Dinner!" which call was hurriedly responded to by his friends.

"What a place these woods are for an appetite!" remarked Adams, as they gathered around the table. "A fellow is always hungry here."

"You are at any rate," returned St. Clair.

"I don't believe I eat any more than any other fellow in the party," protested Adams, with his mouth full of trout.

"That may be," retorted St. Clair, "but the rest of us are not talking about it all the time as you are."

"Don't twit on facts, fellows," interposed Claude. "Pass me the potatoes, will you? Adams can eat all the time the week he cooks," suggested Le Roy.

"Oh, let up on Adams," expostulated Claude; then, turning to Maynard, "Did Nap eat all you gave him from the table this morning, Frank?"

"Yes, and looked over his shoulder for more. He's a good feeder," and Maynard threw a piece of bread at the bear, striking him on the nose.

Nap glanced with clownish severity toward the table, and then swallowed the bread.

"Give him the rest of these chub after dinner," said Phil, smilingly adding, "The better you feed him, the sooner you will tame him. That's my opinion."

"What are we to do this afternoon, fellows?" inquired Le Roy as they arose from the table.

"I think we had better put the camp to rights," answered Claude, "and then we shall have plenty of leisure. The stove ought to be set up, a crane rigged for boiling potatoes, and other things, the supplies properly arranged in the store-tent, and wood enough cut to last several days."

"I agree with you," remarked Maynard; "and as soon as I feed Nap I'm ready to do my share." Saying which he went for the chub, and, bringing them up near the bear, tossed them to him, one at a time, the rest of the boys applauding the dexterity with which Nap caught each fish with his fore-paws. Then Maynard took the refuse from the table, and, placing it on a tin plate, brought it along and set it down near the animal, who showed no disposition to molest him, but who opened his mouth and cleared out the platter with evident relish.

The work that Claude had spoken of was then begun, and by five o'clock all was finished. Then Claude and Phil went out fishing, the others amusing themselves in various ways about the camp. They returned at half-past six with thirty trout and as many more chub, and supper was soon after served.

While the boys were eating Maynard proposed that some of them should go out that night and float for a deer. Claude offered to go with him, and about dark they started off in the "Fairy," having rigged a jack in the bow of the boat. Claude paddled, and Maynard took his station under the light, ready to shoot. But although they heard several noises that they supposed were made by deer, they returned to camp about one o'clock in the morning, stiff, cold, and tired, without having fired a shot. Hoping for better luck next time, they crawled between the blankets with as little noise as possible, and were soon locked in slumber.

As none of the boys had thought of fishing that morning it was six o'clock before any one awoke. St. Clair was the first to turn out, and he soon had the others on their feet, Claude and Maynard looking decidedly sleepy.

"How many deer did you get?" inquired Adams, as the boys gathered about St. Clair and Claude, one of whom was starting an open fire and the other one in the stove.

"Nary a one," returned Claude, and then, as a thought struck him, "Did you put some beans to soak, St. Clair?"

"Yes, three pints."

"Then the country is safe," returned the cook, who, like all New-Englanders, had a genuine liking for baked beans.

"I must dig a bean-hole after breakfast. We'll cook them the same way the loggers do."

"How is that, Claude?" and Phil, who knew but little about lumbering or the ways of logging camps, turned with an inquisitive look to his friend.

"Simple enough. Dig a hole in the ground, put a

few rocks on the bottom; make a fire of hard-wood limbs over it, and when you have a good lot of coals, scratch them out, put your pot of beans in, with the top covered; then heap the coals around it, cover them up with dirt or sod, and let the beans stay ten or twelve hours. I can get ours ready for supper, and I will show you some beans that will make your mouth water."

"I don't think much of beans," said Phil; "we have them at home sometimes."

"I shouldn't think you would," cried Adams, contemptuously. "Who ever saw a New-Yorker that knew how to cook beans? You have to serve an apprenticeship in a Boston bakehouse to learn that piece of cookery, my boy."

After breakfast Claude dug his bean-hole, and put his beans to bake. St. Clair and Wingate took the "Fairy" and went down to the foot of the lake to the outlet, fishing, while St. Clair, Adams, and Phil tramped off in the woods, to see if they could raise any game. Maynard concluded to stop at the camp and keep Claude company, and render him any assistance he might need.

"I wish we had a chain to put on Nap," remarked Frank, after their friends had left the camp. "It's too bad to give the old fellow such a choking every night. I don't believe it helps his temper any."

"So do I. If you had a chain you would not have to muzzle him, and we should not have to watch him all the time. Perhaps we can find one down to Flint's Camp. If we do, we will try and buy it of him. We shall have to go down there to-morrow, and see if we can get some potatoes. We are about out."

"Suppose we go down to the lake and have a bath?" suggested Claude. "I can spare half an hour, now."

"I'll go with you, if you think there is no danger of Nap giving us the slip while we are gone."

"He'll be all right; besides, we can see him from the water, and keep an eye on him occasionally. The old fellow seems to be taking a nap, now. Come on," and Claude started for the lake followed by his friend, and a few moments more they were sporting in the water, finding it much cooler, however, than they had anticipated. A half-hour's bath refreshed and invigorated them, and they returned to camp and found Nap as quiet as when they had left.

About eleven o'clock the hunters returned with two rabbits, the only game they had seen, but reported that deer-track were numerous, the ground, in some places, being all cut up with them.

Claude took the rabbits, dressed them, and prepared them for a stew; and, at half-past eleven, took the "Go Ahead" and pulled down to the carry to meet Norton. He had to wait for him about fifteen minutes. The guides deposited their loads in his boat, and Norton asked him how they were getting on.

"First-rate," answered Claude; "but we are running short of potatoes. Do you think we can get any at Flint's?"

"Yes; he always keeps plenty on hand."

Claude now paid Norton the price agreed upon for his work, and, getting into his boat, pushed out from shore. As he dipped his oars into the water the inquisitive guide sang out:—

"Say, mister, seen anything o' that bear lately?"

"Yes," returned Claude, with a smile, as he sent his boat spinning through the water, " I shook hands with him this evening." An answer that was nearer the truth than his inquisitor had any idea of.

When Claude reached the camp he learned that the fishermen had not yet returned; and, as it was one o'clock, concluded to dine without them. After clearing up the table he proposed to his friends that they should take some dishes and one of the boats, and row to the inlet, and then ascend the river a short distance, where Norton had told him he would find some berries.

No one seemed very anxious for the expedition; but, finally, Maynard and Adams said they would accompany him, and the other two agreed to stay and look after the camp, as they were somewhat tired from their morning's tramp.

Launching the boat, the boys jumped in and headed for the inlet. Reaching the river, they ascended to a place where there had once stood some old lumber camps, the wreck of which yet remained. Near here they found raspberries very plentiful, and in two hours filled a six-quart pail they had brought with them. Then Adams and Claude, who had brought their guns, went off a mile or so up a logging road, while Maynard, declaring he felt too lazy to accompany them, lay down in the shade of some trees and went to sleep.

Half a mile from the river Claude and Adams found three partridges and secured two of them, and a little farther beyond they flushed a flock of ten, out of which they scooped in six. Being satisfied with their luck, they retraced their steps to the river, and awakening Maynard, whose eyes opened to their fullest extent when he saw their birds, they launched their boat and started down-river.

Just as they came in sight of the lake a noise on their left attracted their attention, and, looking in that direction, they saw a caribou just pushing his head through the underbrush and stepping into the water.

"Holy Moses!" exclaimed Claude, who was in the stern with the paddle, "a caribou!"

Maynard, who was rowing, dropped the oars, startled by the announcement, and Adams reached for his gun. Unfortunately for the boys, however, neither of their guns were loaded, and before they could get the shells in them and were ready to fire, the caribou had caught sight of them, and, with a frightened snort and whistle, turned suddenly and disappeared in the woods.

"We will chase him," cried Claude. "Put her for the shore, Maynard." A couple of strokes sufficed to do this, and as soon as the boat swung in to the bank, Claude and Adams grasped their guns, and, telling Maynard to secure the boat, leaped on shore, and started swiftly in pursuit of the animal they had so startled.

They had landed in a dense growth of young firs and spruces, and they soon found that locomotion was exceedingly difficult, and that unless they wished to lose their eyes they would have to travel very carefully. Ahead of them they could hear the caribou crashing through the underbrush; but the sound grew fainter and fainter, and after half an hour of as rapid progress as they could make, they lost the noise altogether, and were reluctantly compelled to abandon the chase. Turning about they met Maynard, who had been hard on their heels, and who wanted to know "What in thunder they were coming back for."

"Because the caribou has run us hull down," replied Claude. "I'll bet he is five miles from here by this time."

"And you didn't get a shot at him?"

"Nary a shot, confound him!" answered Adams, "and I'm tired to death."

"You look so," said Maynard, for the first time noticing their appearance, and then, bursting into a shout of laughter, added, "You both look as if you had been run through a thrashing-machine. Your faces are all scratched, and your clothes are torn in a dozen places."

"All we were thinking of was the caribou," remarked Claude, now looking at his pants, which showed several large rents, and wiping the blood from a big scratch on his right cheek. "This is the worse piece of woods I ever struck. I should have thought the caribou would have scratched his eyes out at the pace he must have travelled."

"There isn't much skin left on my hands," added Adams, lugubriously, as he glanced at his hands, which were marked up from one end to the other.

Pursuing their way more carefully, they reached the boat without farther mishap, and struck out for camp, reaching it at half-past five, where they found the "Fairy" and her crew, who had been there an hour.

Claude related to his friends the results of their excursion, and all the boys were sorry that the caribou had given him the slip. St. Clair told him that the fishing was splendid down at the outlet, and that he

Moose Shooting on the Magalloway River.

and Wingate had brought back over a hundred trout, besides some chub for Nap.

"Come, Claude," urged Adams, who was desperately hungry, "let's wash up, and pay our respects to those beans. Don't you think they are done?"

"I guess so," and, washing his hands and face, he, aided by St. Clair, proceeded to get supper.

The beans were found to be cooked just right, " done to a turn," as Claude expressed it, and with the berries, hot biscuit, and tea, made a supper that the boys were not backward in doing justice to.

After the meal was over, and things cleared away, a large camp-fire was kindled, and around this the party gathered, and talked and sang the remainder of the evening. As the friendly circle broke up, Claude announced that they would have to go to Flint's Camp the next day, and see if they could procure some potatoes. Then Phil proposed, that, it being Sunday, and as they could not go to church, they should all go down the lake, and pay a visit to Flint's Camp.

"I will stay and keep camp while the rest of you go," said Maynard. "Somebody will have to watch Nap, and I can go some other time."

"That bear is more trouble than he is worth," added Phil. "Better shoot him, and get rid of him."

"No, no," remarked Claude, who had begun to take a liking to him. "Let Maynard stay this time, and I'll see if I can't buy a chain, of Flint, to fasten him up with, and then we can all leave camp whenever we please;" and with the matter thus disposed of, the bear was compelled to submit once more to the choking and muzzling process, and the boys turned in for the night.

Sunday morning the boys slept later than usual, and it was eight o'clock before they were all up, and nine before breakfast was over. At half-past nine all hands with the exception of Maynard embarked in the three boats, and pulled down to the foot of the lake, making the distance without especial effort in a little more than an hour. The boats were taken carefully out of the water, and turned bottom up on shore, and then, striking into the carry road, the party headed for Flint's, reaching that camp in an hour, and were fortunate enough to find Mr. Flint at home.

He was surprised by so many callers; but he invited them in, asked them where they were stopping, and they passed an hour very pleasantly in listening to some of his yarns, he seeming to possess an endless number, on all sorts of subjects appertaining to hunting, fishing, and wood-craft. That he drew the long bow frequently was evident from the winks exchanged among the boys, whenever they were free from his observation. Finally Claude told him they wanted to buy some potatoes, and he offered them all they wanted. After consulting with his friends, Claude told him he would take three bagsful, about five bushels, and Flint harnessed an old horse, which he kept to do toting on the carry, into a sled, and hauled them over to the lake, a little over three miles distant. Before they started back to the lake, Claude informed Flint of the capture of the bear, and asked him if he had a chain of any kind he could sell them.

The old guide looked at the party in astonishment, after hearing Claude's story, and complimented them on their smartness, laughing heartily, however, at Claude's account of their manner of securing Nap nights, and after rummaging around for fifteen minutes, brought forth a pair of trace-chains, which he fastened together, making one chain twelve feet long, which he sold them for two dollars. When they reached the lake, Flint examined their boats admiringly, and expressed the opinion that they were beauties. He asked the boys what they cost, where they were built, what kind of wood they were made of, and wound up by offering to buy them when the party went home, if they would sell them. Then, bidding the boys good-by, and asking them to call and see him again, he turned his horse, and, jumping on the sled, rode homeward. The boats having been put into the water, a bag of potatoes was placed in each, and the flotilla moved northward.

In the morning, after the boys left the camp, Maynard amused himself by writing some letters home, and then took a book and read awhile. Becoming tired, however, of this way of passing his time, he turned his attention to Nap, who was lying quietly in the shade, near the tree where he was fastened.

"I wonder if old Nap is very ugly now," said Maynard to himself. "I'll see how he acts, and see if I can't teach him to do some tricks," and he walked up to the bear; Nap moved his head, and looked at him as he approached, not savagely, but rather inquisitively, as if saying to himself, "I should like to know what that fellow wants now."

"How are you, Nap, old fellow, — want a chub?" and Maynard poked him a little with a small stick he carried, causing the bear to stand up on his feet. Bruin looked at him, winking and blinking his eyes in a manner that made his captor laugh. "Pretty good fellow, Nap, aint you?" and the boy laid the end of the stick on the bear's nose, causing Nap to push it away with one of his paws.

Then Maynard brought four chubs, and two small trout to Nap, and said, "Now, old fellow, you will have to stand on your hindlegs, or you don't get a fish." He held out a chub to Bruin, who stepped toward him, and tried to secure it, but Maynard backed away, until the bear had reached the length of his rope; then, tapping him lightly under the chin with his stick, held the fish in the air, and said, "Sit up, Nap, if you want it." Nap did not seem to understand English very well, and made several comical but futile efforts to get the fish, causing Maynard to shout with laughter. Then he tapped the animal under the chin again, who tried, as before, to get the fish, and, after several attempts, sat down on his haunches. "Now, up, Nap, up," and, striking him again, the bear stood up on his hindlegs, probably more from accident than design, and Maynard gave him the coveted fish, which he ate with evident relish. When he had eaten it, Maynard tried again to make him stand up, and, after several efforts, was successful, and gave him another fish.. He worked away patiently with his pupil, and by the time he had given him the six fish, he had taught him to stand up and catch them every time. "I guess that will do for the present, Nap; but now you want something for them to swim in," and Maynard brought a pail of water and sat it down where the bear could drink his fill.

"It is rather monotonous staying here alone. I think

I will tackle my book again. Probably the boys won't be back until one or two o'clock;" and, turning into a hammock, he was soon deeply engaged in his story.

"What musical instrument does that guide remind you of, Claude?" inquired Wingate as the boats moved along, sufficiently near for conversation to be carried on from one to the other.

"Give it up."

"The lyre," and then a smile rippled over the faces of the boys.

"Oh, strike the lyre!" exclaimed St. Clair, with a chuckle.

"He'll strike you if you call him a liar," added Adams.

"I never call a man a liar," protested Wingate, "it's not polite. I always call him a musical instrument."

"What are you going to give us for dinner, Claude? I'm getting hollow," and Le Roy, who was rowing the "Fairy," looked at the cook, who was at the paddle.

"He ought to give us a regular tuck-out to-day," broke in Adams. "It is Sunday, you know, and most hotels give a better bill of fare Sunday than any other day."

"It will take too long to get up a fancy dinner. I'm starved now. It is half-past one at least," cried Phil.

"It will be past two o'clock when we reach camp, fellows," replied Claude; "but, if you will wait until five o'clock, I will give you the best dinner the camp will furnish."

"Wait until we get to camp and we'll vote on it," suggested Adams; "and as the wind appears to be breezing up ahead, suppose we row a little faster."

They reached the landing at quarter past two, and Maynard stood on the shore to receive them.

"The camp has not run away from you, I see?" said Claude, as he stepped on shore.

"No nor the bear either. But I am very glad you have come, for I am getting decidedly hungry."

"How many times have you been to the cupboard?" queried Adams, smiling.

"Not once, upon my honor. Pray don't judge me by yourself."

"I say, Frank, we are going to take a vote upon the dinner-question."

"A vote, Phil?"

"Yes. Claude says he will get us up a Young's Hotel dinner if we will wait until five o'clock for it, and we may as well settle it now. Those in favor of having dinner at five o'clock," and then adding, facetiously, "with a bill of fare consisting of turtle-soup, roast turkey, oysters on the shell, fricaseed humming-birds, ice-cream, roman punch, and champagne, will hold up their hands."

Adams, Maynard, Le Roy, and Phil held up their hands, and the matter was settled. Then the boys moved up to the tents, and Claude and St. Clair went to work, assisted occasionally by one of their friends.

About four o'clock Claude went into the woods, and obtained some birch-bark, and, cutting it into the proper size, made seven pieces, on which he inscribed with lead-pencil, and then placed one at each plate, the following : —

HOTEL DE FOREST.

SUNDAY, AUGUST 20, 1876.

MENU.

SOUP.

Chicken, Tomato.

FISH.

Baked Brook Trout.

BOILED.

Ham.

COLD DISHES.

Ham, Tongue, Canned Corn Beef.

ENTRÉES.

Baked Beans, à la New England.
Clams fried in batter.
Partridge, Fricasse, à la Parmachenee.
Rabbit Stew.

RELISHES.

Pickles, Chow-chow, Worcestershire sauce.

VEGETABLES.

Potatoes boiled, Green peas, String beans, Corn, Raw tomatoes.

PASTRY.

Plum-pudding, Lemon sauce. Currant cake.

DESSERT.

Raspberries, Apricots, Coffee.

The boys were amused with the birch-bark bills of fare, and each one declared his intention of keeping his for a souvenir of the occasion. The dinner, too, considering the place and circumstances, was beyond all praise, and that it was appreciated was shown by the repeated calls to Claude for the different dishes that comprised the menu.

After dinner, Maynard fed Nap with the refuse from the table, and, remembering that bears had a penchant for berries, gave him about a pint of raspberries, which he greedily devoured with a smile all over his face.

In the evening the boys had scarcely gathered around the camp-fire when a tremendous thunder-shower came up, and for an hour they were treated to such an exhibition of electricity as they had never seen before, while the rain poured in torrents, causing them to speedily seek shelter, and the wind blew so hard that at each moment they expected to see their tents blown away. By eleven o'clock, however, the storm was over, and then the party retired for the night.

When they arose the next morning everything was wet, and Maynard built up a rousing fire before breakfast to dry things around them. The woods being so wet, after breakfast the most of the party went to overhauling their clothing, mending rents and sewing on missing buttons, and, as there were plenty of fish in camp, they spent the afternoon in reading and writing letters home, trusting to luck to get them to a post-office.

Norton had told them of a beaver dam on a small stream, several miles above where they were encamped, and as the boys had never seen one, they started out after breakfast Tuesday morning to find it. As the bear was now chained it was not necessary for anybody to stay behind to watch him, and the whole party left the camp, taking a lunch with them, as they were uncertain what time they should return. Before leaving,

Maynard wrote the following notice in coarse hand on a sheet of paper and pinned it to the tree where Nap was chained, for the protection of any one who should happen to stray into the camp: "This bear is half-savage, and is not used to being fooled with. Let him alone, and keep out of his way."

The party struck into the woods north of the camp, and travelled in an irregular way for about three hours, stopping quite often to inspect deer-track, that were numerous along their route. At noon they had made about six miles as nearly as they could calculate, but without finding the stream they were in search of, and, becoming tired, sat down on a fallen spruce to rest and eat their lunch. Near them a dead pine towered skyward for a hundred feet at least, and near the top of this the boys descried the nest of some large bird. While they were speculating as to what it could be, an immense bald eagle came sailing through the air, and alighted in the nest, and to their surprise the boys found it contained several young eagles. All of the party had brought their guns or rifles with them, and Maynard could not resist the temptation to shoot, and, picking up his rifle, blazed away at the feathered monarch above him. He missed, however, and the huge bird, with a discordant scream, spread his wide wings and sailed away.

"I have half a mind to climb up to that nest," said Claude, "and see how much of a family the old fellow has."

"I will try it if you will," added Maynard.

Phil burst into a derisive laugh. "That nest is safe," he said, "from any harm you might do it by climbing up to it. Why, that tree is four feet through at the butt, and rises for forty feet without a limb. I should like to see you shin it," and again he laughed, the others joining with him.

Claude walked up to the tree, and found that he could not begin to meet his hands around it, and, after a few attempts at shinning it, he made up his mind that it could not be done.

"If we only had an axe," suggested Maynard, "we could chop it down."

"You could if you lived long enough," remarked Adams, with a provoking smile.

"Never mind their laughing, Maynard, we will try it some day."

"That's so, Claude. And we will capture all the young eagles."

"It is after one o'clock," said St. Clair, looking at his watch, and picking up his gun. "Hadn't we better be making tracks for camp?"

"I suppose we had," answered Claude; "we shall be hungry by the time we reach it."

The boys now turned homeward, keeping a bright look-out for game; but they only saw a rabbit and some squirrels, and these they did not meddle with.

"I wish some of us would be lucky enough to shoot a deer or a caribou. I should like some fresh meat," and Phil gazed at the others as if to ask their opinion.

"I will paddle you out to-morrow night if you'll agree to shoot one."

"Thank you, Adams. I won't guarantee to shoot one, but I'll do my best."

"Then we'll go."

It was half-past four when the party reached camp, well tired from their day's tramp. Looking about they found Nap all right, and could not see that anything had been disturbed. Claude and St. Clair prepared the supper, and, after it was eaten, Maynard fed the bear, and Phil and Adams started the camp-fire. When the work was over, the boys gathered around its cheerful blaze, and laid plans for future amusement. Wingate tried to start some singing; but his companions did not appear in the mood for it, and, after a few attempts, gave it up. The fact was that, although no one said anything about it, they were all quite fagged out, and one after another sought their bed, and by half-past nine every one was asleep.

CHAPTER VI.

Fishing and Berrying. — The Eagle's Nest. — Chopping the Pine. — An Interference. — Fight with the Eagles. — The Boys getting the Worst of It. — St. Clair to the Rescue. — Return to Camp. — A Visit to Chester's. — Evening Recitations. — A Trip to Moose Brook. — Discovery of a Deer in the Lake. — Its Chase and Capture. — Changing Cooks. — St. Clair's Speech.

THE next morning at the breakfast-table Claude announced that the berries and trout had all been eaten, and that if the party wished for any more some one would have to go fishing and berrying. Adams and Phil immediately volunteered to furnish the trout, and Wingate and Le Roy agreed to go for some berries. The members of both parties declared it their intention of making a day of it, and after breakfast Claude and his assistant were kept busy for half an hour in putting up lunches.

The fishing-party had concluded to go to the Outlet, as offering the most likely sport, while the berry-pickers were to go up the river; and just before nine o'clock the two parties, in the "Fairy" and "Go Ahead," pulled away from camp, one boat heading up the lake, and the other in the opposite direction.

After the four boys had left, Claude and St. Clair finished up their work, while Maynard fooled with the bear, who was now becoming quite tame. As soon as the work was done Claude came up to Maynard, and in a low tone asked him if he would like to go with him

A Hard-Fought Battle.

and try and capture the young eagles. The proposition was eagerly received, and telling St. Clair, if they were not back by noon, to get his own dinner, the two boys took Claude's gun, a dozen cartridges, an axe, and some lunch, and started off, telling St. Clair they would be back as soon as they could.

They knew quite well the route they had travelled the day before, but to avoid all danger of getting lost Frank carried his pocket-compass. They did not look for any game on their way, but made the best time they could to the "king pine," as the boys had called it; and at half-past eleven they stood beside it. The old eagle was nowhere in sight, and without loss of time Claude threw off his hunting-jacket, and, taking the axe, attacked the tree with all his strength. The chips flew merrily for a while, but, as he became tired, dropped slower, and then Frank offered to spell him, and Claude retired to rest, with the perspiration running down his face and body in large drops, which made him feel as if he had just gone through a heavy shower.

Maynard's courage was better than his judgment, and he hacked and banged away at the old pine with plenty of vigor, but little skill; and he was surprised to find how hard it was to strike twice in the same place, and how often his axe flew wide of the mark. The gap in the side of the pine, however, steadily enlarged, and at the end of three-quarters of an hour the boys had cut half through the tree, finding it, somewhat to their surprise, sound clear to the heart. Then, slipping on their coats, to avoid taking cold, they sat down and ate their lunch, procuring a little rest from their violent exertions.

They devoted twenty minutes to lunch, and then went on with their attack on the forest monarch. Frank had just begun to make the chips fly, when the eagle they had seen the day before came swooping down toward the tree, followed by another not quite as large, which the boys at once concluded must be his mate.

Claude picked up his gun, placed a shell, loaded with buck, in each barrel, and waited for the eagles to alight. This they did not do, but circled around the tree, giving vent to shrill cries, and Claude, watching his opportunity, blazed at them, giving one the contents of his right barrel, and the other the load in his left. From the way the birds acted he believed that both shots took effect, and he hastened to reload his piece. Before he could do it, however, with a shriller shriek than any they had yet given, the eagles swooped down on the boys; and then took place such a contest as the friends had never taken part in before, and hoped never to be compelled to again.

With their powerful beaks and sharp talons the birds struck savagely at the boys, each singling out an adversary, and Claude and Frank found they had their hands full, if not a little more.

Claude clubbed his gun and fought with desperation, for he knew he was fighting for his life; while Frank, with the axe, tried to cut down the female, who had attacked him, and who seemed more savage, if anything, than her mate.

The great wings of the birds flapped around the heads of the boys, like the fans of a windmill, and whenever the eagles struck them fairly, the blow would almost knock them off their feet.

For twenty minutes the fight waged fiercely, during which time the boys had nearly all their clothing torn off of them, while their bodies were bleeding in many places from the effects of the eagles' talons and beaks, and yet the birds appeared in no wise discouraged.

The matter now began to look serious. The boys were losing their strength; their breath came in quick, short gasps; and the blood and sweat commingled poured down their faces and bodies, while their arms ached from constant exercise. Claude began to think that his time had come, and most earnestly wished that he was back in camp; while Maynard wished his companion had been a thousand miles off before he had proposed the expedition.

Finally, in dodging a tremendous lunge that the old bald-head made for him, Claude tripped over a limb, and, in spite of the desperate efforts he made to recover himself, he went over flat on his back. For a moment he lost all courage, and really believed he never should see home again. His huge opponent lit on his breast, and it took every ounce of strength he had left to prevent the bird from tearing his throat. He called frantically to his companion. But as much as Maynard might wish to help him, he was in no condition to do so, for he had all he could do to successfully combat his own assailant.

At this critical state of affairs a new actor appeared on the scene, in the person of St. Clair, who, having become tired of loafing about the camp, had taken his gun, and followed them, having had a shrewd suspicion from the first as to their destination. This turned the tide of battle.

"Thunder and Mars!" yelled St. Clair, as he dashed toward them, "what kind of a circus is this?" and rushing to Claude he fetched the eagle, that was about getting the best of him, a crack over the head, that knocked him some two feet away, and then raising his gun, he gave him a charge of buckshot that effectually settled his warlike proclivities. He then turned his attention to Frank, who, notwithstanding his best efforts, had not succeeded in getting a fair clip at the eagle with his axe, and who by this time had also become about discouraged, and called to him to drop to the ground. The eagle, hearing the noise, seemed at once to understand that the tables were turned, and sought safety in flight; but he only went a few feet, as St. Clair, at that short range, poured a charge of buckshot into him that fairly riddled him, beside breaking both his wings, and he fell heavily to the ground.

"How did you happen here so opportunely?" and Claude, crawling to his feet, shook hands with St. Clair as if he had not seen him for a year.

"Give us a shake, Andrew," added Frank, before St. Clair could answer. "I was never so glad to see you in my life."

"The fact is, boys, I suspected where you were going when I saw you whispering together, and when you took an axe I was sure of it, from what I heard you say yesterday. After staying in camp a couple of hours I began to get lonesome, and so took my gun and followed you; and" — with a smile — "I should say that I arrived about the proper time."

"You are just right, — you did," replied Claude; "that was a close shave for us."

"I had no idea that eagles were so strong, and would fight so," remarked Frank.

"Nor I, either. I can believe a story I once read, now, about an eagle carrying off a child"; and Claude stretched out the wings of the one he had attacked, and the boys were astonished at their spread.

"I'll take a turn at this job now," added St. Clair, picking up the axe, "and both of you had better go to that little brook a few rods back, and wash your faces. You look as if you had been to an Irish wake"; and he laughed in spite of himself.

The boys went off to wash, and St. Clair went at the tree lustily, and had made considerable progress when his friends returned. Then Maynard spelled him, and when he had become tired Claude declared that he must have one more hack at it, and wielded the axe for a few moments, and then the tree began to crack.

"Look out, Claude; it is going," cried Maynard, running back.

Claude glanced up at the tall trunk, and seeing it begin to totter joined his companions, and in a moment more the king pine fell beyond them with a crash that awoke the echoes of the forest, and levelled beneath it everything in its path.

The boys, with some difficulty, made their way to the end of the tree, and found that the nest had been all torn to pieces and the young eagles thrown out. After some search, however, they found them, and then quickly left the locality; for the smell of decayed fish and offal, that came from the fragments of the nest, were too much for any sensitive stomach.

Putting on their coats, and picking up their guns

and the dead eagles, the party started for camp, walking as rapidly as the circumstances would permit, for it was now five o'clock, and they were afraid that their friends returning from the fishing excursion, and finding the camp empty, would be worried about them.

Claude took the two young eagles and the axe, and this was all he could attend to, as they were quite large, and struggled considerably. St. Clair and Maynard carried one of the dead birds and the guns. Thus loaded, it was half-past six when they reached the camp, and found their companions somewhat alarmed at their absence, and wondering where they could be.

When the fishermen saw them coming they gave a delighted cheer, which changed to exclamations of surprise on observing the kind of game they had brought back with them, and the appearance of Claude's and Frank's faces and clothing.

"What on earth have you been doing!" exclaimed Phil. "Been having a Don Quixote fight with a wind-mill?"

"Worse than that!" exclaimed Claude; and he proceeded to give them an account of the day's adventure.

They listened with breathless interest, while St. Clair built a fire, and busied himself about the evening meal, leaving all the talking to Claude and Maynard.

"What are you going to do with them?" queried Wingate, when Claude and Maynard had finished their recital of the day's sport.

"Why, have them preserved, of course. One of those eagles will measure nine feet from tip to tip of wing, and the other, eight. Have them set up and mounted nicely, and they will look nobby in the house."

"How are you going to get them out of here?" and Adams looked as if he had given Claude a hard one.

"I don't know. I suppose, however, we could carry them over to Chester's, and get Norton to fix them up. We could go over there and back in a day. What do you say, Maynard?"

"I'd laugh if we couldn't."

"It's only twenty miles," put in Le Roy.

"How is that supper getting along?" broke in Adams. "I shall not want any, if it isn't ready soon."

This reminded the other boys that their stomachs were also empty, and all hands turned their attention to forwarding the supper, which was soon ready, and despatched with a gusto that was foreign to them at home.

In the evening, around the camp-fire, the fishermen related their luck, and informed the others that they had brought in one hundred and twenty-five trout, beside about a peck of chubs for Nap. Claude and Maynard, who were very tired, went to bed early; and St. Clair, after relating the particulars of the battle with the eagles again, turned in, and the others soon followed him.

Thursday morning, after breakfast was over, Claude and Maynard went to work repairing their clothes, and the other boys lounged about the camp, reading and writing, and during the forenoon all took a bath in the lake. In the afternoon Frank and Claude took a large box that some of the stores had come in, and nailing slats over the top of it, tipped it up on one side, and used it for a pen for the young eagles, who took very kindly to the diet of fish, and bits of different food from the table, that their captors were able to provide. When they had fixed the box, and put the birds in, the two boys turned into the hammocks, while the rest of the party rambled off in the woods, to procure spruce-gum.

"I say, Claude," sang out Maynard, as he swung lazily in a hammock, a book in his hand, which he only made a pretence of reading, "shall we go over to Chester's to-morrow? Those birds will not keep a great while this kind of weather."

"Yes, I'll go if you will."

"We can start the first thing after breakfast, and you can let St. Clair take care of the dishes."

"Yes; and he can get the dinner and supper also, for we should not get back until night."

"There would be no need of our carrying a lunch, Claude; we could get dinner at Tom's."

"That's so."

"Two young eagles and a bear, Frank, — we shall collect quite a menagerie if we keep on."

"You are right. When we get them home we can start a ten-cent museum."

"And give the receipts to some charitable society," laughing at the idea.

"How much longer do you propose to camp here, Claude?"

"I don't know. I am not at all particular. Just as the rest of the fellows say."

"Suppose we move up the river next week?"

"I am willing."

"And camp somewhere in the vicinity of Rump Pond."

"It will be a nuisance getting Nap up there."

"Oh, no. I can take him through the woods easy enough. He is quite tame now; bet he'll lead as quiet as a lamb. He's becoming quite a civilized bear."

"Read awhile, will you, Frank? I want to take a nap."

"Call him up to you then."

"That joke's too thin. I'm sleepy. I want a snooze."

"Snooze away, then, old fellow, and I'll worry through a chapter of my book."

When the gunners returned, about five o'clock, they found both the boys asleep in their hammocks, and Maynard's book had fallen to the ground.

Adams and Phil, whispering to their companions to keep quiet, procured a couple of needles from a pine near by, and, softly creeping up to the hammocks, tickled the ears of the sleepers, first on one side, and then on the other, causing them to keep busy brushing imaginary flies away, on which they poured a shower of maledictions. Finally the victims of the pine needles caught sound of a subdued snicker from Wingate, and, arising to a sitting posture in the hammocks, they discovered the flies who had been so troublesome, and were greeted with a shout of laughter from the lookers-on and participants in the sport.

"What time is it?" asked Claude, when their laughter had ceased.

"Time you were getting supper," suggested Adams.

"Poor boy!—he was born hungry. I honestly believe there are only three periods of time for you in the calendar, and they are breakfast-time, dinner-time, and supper-time. You ought to be a cook, Adams, and then you could eat all the time." And Claude, having delivered himself of this panegyric, turned out of the hammock, and proceeded to mix up some dough for biscuit, while St. Clair built the fire, and set the table.

That evening, in the social circle, as the boys called their after-supper chats, Maynard spoke of changing their camping-ground to some point up the river on the following Monday; and, a majority of his friends being in favor of it, it was decided to do so.

Friday, as soon as they had eaten their breakfast, Claude and Maynard started for Tom Chester's, carrying the two dead eagles. As each of the birds weighed about twenty pounds they found it a tiresome tramp, and had to rest frequently. Claude carried his gun, and Frank his rifle, as they did not know what they might run across while on the carry. It was half-past seven when they left camp, and nearly twelve when they reached the shores of Second Lake. They were fortunate enough to find a boat at the landing, and, getting into it, rowed to camp. Tom was surprised and pleased to see the two boys, and while he was listening to the account of their fight with the eagles, Norton came in, and they had to begin the story again for his benefit. When they had finished, Claude asked Norton if he could mount the birds for them; and the taxidermist told him he could. The boys then arranged with him to set them up properly, and send them to their homes in Boston, by way of Colebrook, by express, and gave him their address.

Norton said the eagles were splendid specimens, and he wished he owned them, offering to buy one or both, but the boys would not sell them.

Claude had brought over all their mail from camp, and, giving it to Norton, asked him to send it out the first opportunity he had; and Ned promised he would. By this time dinner was ready, and the boys were not sorry to hear the call.

As they arose from the table Chester asked them if they did not want some caribou meat, and, Claude replying in the affirmative, the old man brought them two junks, weighing about ten pounds each. Norton procured some stout twine, and, making a hole in one end of each piece of venison, tied the string in, so they could carry it on their gun-barrels after they left the boat.

"Whose boat was that we took,— yours, Mr. Chester?" asked Maynard, when they were ready to start.

"No; it belongs to two explorers who went over there this morning to look up timber. You want to leave it where you found it."

"We shall," replied Claude, and then, bidding the two hunters good-by, launched the boat and rowed across the lake. Reaching the shore they hauled the boat carefully out, and Maynard, looking at his watch, announced the time as half-past two.

"Then we shall fetch camp by six o'clock," said Claude, as he threw his gun over his shoulder, with the piece of caribou dangling from it.

His companion shouldered his rifle and the other piece of venison, and, without further comments, started for the eastern end of the carry. Nothing unusual transpired on the way, and at quarter of six they reached the lake, and found the "Fairy" where they had left her. A moment later she was gliding over the placid waters of Parmachence, and at quarter-past six were at the camp.

They found the boys all at home, and supper all ready, only awaiting their arrival. After putting the meat in a safe place, and washing up, they told St. Clair they were ready to eat, and the boys took their places at the table.

"We will have a piece of roast caribou for dinner, to-morrow, boys," said Claude.

"And you can thank Tom Chester for it," added Maynard.

"Bully for Tom!" put in Adams.

"It is some time since we have tasted fresh meat," remarked Wingate.

"Confound your meat! Who cares for meat when you can get trout?" and Le Roy glanced around the table.

"The trout are nice," answered Phil; "but then a fellow don't want to eat them twenty-one times a week. Variety is the spice of life, you know."

"And life is the essence of existence," smiled Claude.

"Say that again, will you, Claude?" and then added, as he winked at the others, "Perhaps it will be too much of an effort for you."

"Is it copyrighted yet?" inquired Adams, with mock earnestness.

"What are we going to do to-morrow?" interrogated Phil, of no one in particular, as the party rose from the table.

"Eat!" declared Adams, with a laugh, in which his friends joined. "Give us a harder one, Phil."

AN OBSTACLE.

"Nonsense! You know what I mean. Where are we going?"

"Suppose we make an excursion to the other side of the lake; go to Moose Brook, and see if we can find anything to shoot," proposed Claude.

"I suppose the brook was called Moose Brook because there was never a moose anywhere near it," suggested Maynard.

"I am in for anything," said Wingate, "except loafing in camp all day"

"Suppose we have some recitations to night, fellows, to vary the programme," suggested St. Clair, when the camp-fire had been lighted.

"A good idea," agreed Adams; "seven recitations will fill up the evening nicely."

"Go ahead, St. Clair; you must break the ice, as you had the honor of making the proposition"; and Claude gave his assistant a punch in the ribs to help him on to his feet.

"No, no,—age before beauty. Lead off, Claude."

"If you are going to hang fire that way, I will. We don't want any of the girls' 'I never can play without my music' spirit developed in this crowd; and, without further circumlocution, Claude recited "Hamlet's Soliloquy."

He was followed by Adams in a humorous piece, which he announced as "The Hungry Man"; which was received with shouts of laughter from his friends.

Then Maynard, so to speak, "took the stage," and warmed himself and his hearers up with "Spartacus to the Gladiators."

St. Clair gave " Rollo's Address to the Peruvian Army."

Wingate repeated Whittier's " Slave Ships," in a very fine manner, and the boys applauded him lustily.

Phil improvised an address on temperance, which was really a good thing for a boy of his age, and Claude told him he ought to go on the lecture-platform.

Le Roy wound up the evening's circle by a parody on " The boy stood on the burning deck"; and as none of the boys had ever heard it, and it was exceedingly funny, caused them all to roar with laughter.

The company then broke up, and, retiring to the tent, were soon insensible to all of the mysterious noises of the night.

Saturday morning, after breakfast and the camp work were over, the boys launched the three boats, and, rowing leisurely among the islands at the upper end of the lake, gained the eastern shore, and followed it down to Moose Brook, a little below the outlet of which they landed. Each one had brought his gun or rifle, and, after lifting the boats carefully out on shore, they started into the forest, spreading out in a line about a quarter of a mile in width, all hands keeping a good lookout for game.

Small birds and squirrels were all that greeted their sight, however, and as they were of no use to them they would not kill them, and at one o'clock they reached the lake, not one of the party having fired a shot.

" A dry day this," remarked Claude, as the boys rowed homewards.

"Dry as an old toper who hasn't had a drink for a week," acquiesced Phil, who was in the same boat.

After all their poor success the day proved an eventful one.

As the boats rounded the northern end of the island, on which now stands Danforth's Camp, a large buck was seen to take to the water and swim toward the north-western corner of the lake, in almost a bee-line for their camp.

"A deer! a deer!" shouted Phil, who saw him first.

"Where?" demanded Claude, turning his head and looking in the direction where Phil pointed; "oh, I see!" and, quickening his strokes, sent the "Fairy" through the water as if she were a thing of life.

"Would you try him, Claude?" sang out Maynard from the "Go Ahead," that was close behind. "I think I can reach him with my rifle."

"Don't you believe we can overhaul him, and capture him alive?" suggested Claude.

"Let's try it," said Adams, from the "Water Witch."

"Yes, yes," added Le Roy, excitedly; "and if we can't catch him, then we'll shoot him."

"All right; I'll tell you my plan"; and Claude, who had rapidly thought the matter over, ordered Maynard and Le Roy, who were in the "Go Ahead," to follow the buck up, but to keep between him and the island, while he would try and get the "Fairy" between the deer and the shore where he was heading, and turn him away from it; and told St. Clair, who was rowing the "Water Witch," to get to camp as soon as possible and get the piece of rope with which they had captured Nap, and bring it out as quickly as he could, and close up on the deer with them if they succeeded in cornering him, and throw a noose over his head.

As soon as he had finished shouting his directions, Claude applied himself to the oars, and pulled for all he was worth, and soon had the satisfaction of hearing Phil, who steered with the paddle, say that they were rapidly gaining on the nimble ranger of the forest. In twenty minutes the "Fairy" shot by the deer, and the buck, seeing the boat between himself and the shore, turned for a point of land below him; but Claude headed him off once more, and, to get away from the boat, he turned toward the island again. Before he had gone any great distance, the "Go Ahead" checked him in that direction, and he headed squarely down the lake; but Frank, who was rowing, soon passed him on this tack, and again the "Go Ahead" hindered his advance.

Then he turned toward the west shore again; but Claude was too quick for him, and he was not able to effect a landing; and, becoming bewildered, he swam a short distance, first one way, and then the other, and sometimes would make a circle, while the boys excitedly watched his every movement.

The "Water Witch" was now discerned coming toward them; and as soon as Claude could make its crew hear him, he shouted to them to close in on the deer, while he and Frank did the same thing.

When the "Water Witch" was within a few rods of the buck, Claude and Frank turned him toward the other boat, where Adams stood in the bow with the rope, all ready to throw a noose over the deer's head.

His boat soon drew alongside the animal, and, with one well-directed cast, Adams lassoed him.

"Hurrah! Good for you, Adams! Bully boy!" exclaimed the other boys.

"Give him line now," directed Claude, "and let him put for the shore. But be careful he don't upset the boat. You had better row a little, Wingate, so he won't have to drag your boat; he must be getting rather tired, and we don't want to drown him."

The "Fairy" and the "Go Ahead" now closed up with the "Water Witch," so the boys could converse, "without bawling their heads off," as Claude expressed it.

The deer swam straight to shore, landing near the camp. As soon as he reached shallow water he waded fast, and, as he struck dry land, started on the gallop, hauling Adams head-first out of the boat. St. Clair dropped his oars, and, followed by Le Roy, jumped out of the boat, and caught hold of the rope; and the three boys prevented the buck from getting any farther away. The other boats' crews now landed, and Claude and Maynard took hold of the rope, and the deer was led to a tree near the tents, and the rope was fastened securely, leaving about ten feet of slack line. While this was being done Wingate and Phil secured the boats, and then joined their companions.

"Now, what shall we have to feed this fellow on?" inquired St. Clair, as the group stood looking at their new captive. "He won't eat fish; he needs a different kind of a diet."

"Feed him on grass and lily-pads," replied Claude.

"He's a large one," asserted Maynard. "What a splendid set of antlers he carries!"

"We shall have venison in camp all the time now," facetiously remarked Adams.

"We were lucky to take him alive," declared Phil; "I don't imagine that many deer are captured that way."

"Nor I, either," added Le Roy; "but, Claude, don't you think we had better have supper?"

"It is time we were getting it underway," remarked the cook. "St. Clair, see if the beans are all right, will you, and I'll set the table."

As they gathered around the table Adams ventured to say "that the day's sport had cost them deer"; but the remark was greeted with such a torrent of hisses and groans that he did not dare to joke farther on the subject.

"I resign my commission, my time is up," declared Claude, when the boys were seated around the camp fire. "Now, who is to be cook next week?"

"St. Clair!" they all shouted.

"Mr. Andrew St. Clair," said Claude, as he arose, with mock gravity, "I have the pleasure to announce that you are honored with a unanimous election to the office of cook to this party, and may you always be able to give us a square meal."

"Hurrah for the new cook!" cried Adams, taking off his hat and swinging it in the air, and three rousing cheers were given.

"Speech! speech!" shouted several of the boys.

St. Clair, thus called upon, sprang to his feet, and, bowing to the circle, said: —

"My friends, it is not within the limits of a Webster's Unabridged to furnish words with which I can express my sense of the high honor conferred upon me.

The New Cook's Speech.

In all ages and in all countries cooks have been exalted, and the best *chefs* have always been persons of influence and position. The cook everywhere is master of the situation. I might almost say that he makes the man. Let a cook give a king a poor dinner, and he is indirectly responsible for a multitude of woes; for if a king's stomach is out of order, or disgusted by an unsatisfactory dinner, all the tiger in him awakes, and he commits acts, which at the time he is scarcely responsible for. [Cheers.] But, on the other hand, under the influence of a well-cooked dinner, the better nature of the king is brought to the surface, and he pardons and rewards with a generosity most commendable. No, gentlemen, it is not the king who rules his empire, strange as this may seem; but his cook. [Great applause.] A man will sacrifice a great deal for his stomach. Vanderbilt is bound by a cook to whom he pays five thousand dollars a year, simply that the great man may get the right flavor to his tripe and liver, and have his hash served up minus hairs and collar-buttons. [Laughter.] Look at any lady in society. Is she the boss of her own house? Not much. The cook rules it with a rod of iron, and the mistress is as dependant on the cook as a week-old baby on its mother; while the master of the house, as compared with the boss of the kitchen, is a mere nonentity. [Cheers.] That cooks have their faults at times I will not deny. They have been known to get drunk on wine-sauce, and to even leave the home of their employers with all the silver ware done up in a table-cloth. It has been rumored that Ben Butler was cooking when he was accused of borrowing the spoons;

but, as the general is not here to conduct his defence, we will pass that part of the subject. [Laughter.] It is a well-known fact that cooks oftentimes have to undergo great sacrifices, in the interests of their employers, by eating the best of everything before a company dinner is placed on the table, and then suffer from the bellyache in consequence. [Laughter.] There are several kinds of cooks, I would have you know, gentlemen, — cooks known to fame, and cooks whose next-door neighbor don't bow to them on the street; restaurant cooks and hotel cooks; club cooks and private cooks; cooks on Pullman cars and cooks off of them; cooks on a vessel and cooks on shore; but, if I have not already exhausted the subject, I have talked myself hoarse, and will end by saying, that during my week's service it will be my pleasure to serve up the hash in as satisfactory a manner for this crowd as possible, having due regard for their digestive apparatus." [Cheers and applause.]

"St. Clair must have an assistant," remarked Claude, as Andrew sat down, "and I move that our friend Adams be elevated to that position. All in favor of it will please say Aye. Adams, you need not vote."

A chorus of "Ayes" followed Claude's remark.

The whole party felt rather tired after their day's excursion, and about nine o'clock adjourned to the tent, Claude and Maynard first taking a look at their new acquisition, — the buck, — to see if he was all right.

There was very little talk after the boys sought their blankets, and half an hour after they had retired there was silence in the camp, except when it was broken by the snore of some unusually tired sleeper.

CHAPTER VII.

A Rainy Sunday. — Moving up River. — A Tramp through the Woods with Nap and Lightfoot. — A Good Supper. — Around the Camp-fire. — A Mysterious Alarm. — A Bad Shot. — Plenty of Venison. — Claude and Phil visit Chester's Camp. — Visitors. — Tough Yarns. — Ascent of Camel's Rump. — Discovery of a Cave. — The Skeleton. — Frightened by a Bat. — Table-talk. — Return of Claude and Phil.

WHEN the camp awoke to life, Sunday morning, the boys found a cloudy sky, and the clouds low on the mountains around them. Hardly had they finished breakfast when it began to rain, and the water-shed continued until night, keeping the boys prisoners in their tent throughout the day.

The new cook met with some difficulty in preparing dinner amid a drenching rain, but did better than could have been expected, under the circumstances, and although the boys appreciated and applauded his efforts, he was none the less glad that the rain stopped at five o'clock, enabling him to get supper without taking a shower-bath.

Monday morning dawned bright and pleasant, and breakfast was eaten early. As the tents were wet from the rain of the day before they were left standing, and the three boats were loaded with the stove, the table, cooking utensils, blankets, the axes, lantern, some stores, and whatever they considered indispensable. The "Menagerie," to use Phil's words, was fed, and at eight o'clock they started up river. When they reached Little Boy's Falls everything had to be unloaded and carried around, including the boats; and it was not until noon that they reached the vicinity of Spruce Pond, but a short distance from Rump Pond, where they concluded to camp.

St. Clair cooked the dinner, and at three o'clock they started on the return, reaching the tents at seven, and found everything as they had left it. It was dark before supper was over, and the whole party retired to bed a little after eight, completely done up with the labors of the day. They slept later than they meant to Tuesday morning, and it was ten o'clock before they were ready to leave. The tents and everything else were taken this time, including the box containing the young eagles. The bear and deer now proved a decided nuisance, for there was no way to move them except to lead them through the woods, and that meant a hard tramp for some one. The boys were more than half inclined to kill them; but, after a long debate, concluded to take them to their new quarters. Maynard offering to lead the bear alone, if any one would lead the deer. As the buck was not so tame as the bear, Claude and Phil volunteered to try and get him up river, and the other four boys started in the boats.

It was agreed that whichever party reached the camping-ground first should come back and meet the other, and help them, if necessary. Claude told his friends who were going in the boats, that the shore party would follow the west bank of the river until they reached Little Boy's Falls, and crossing near there would continue on up the east bank. With this understanding the boating-party rowed away.

Before starting with the deer Claude and Phil gave him a handful of salt, and Nap was also treated to a biscuit well covered with molasses, of which latter article he was very fond. The boys were armed, not knowing what emergency might arise.

They started off in good spirits, the animals behaving better than they had expected. Indeed, Nap marched like an old soldier, and kept close on Maynard's heels, without offering to molest him. The deer, however, was a little nervous, and would start occasionally at some noise, and show a disposition to break away; but Claude and Phil were patient with it, and the party made fair progress.

At eleven o'clock they reached the river, and at one crossed it, a short distance below Little Boy's Falls. The deer crossed it without trouble, and both the animals were allowed to drink here. Bruin, after drinking, showed considerable reluctance to enter the stream, and it was not without considerable coaxing on Maynard's part that the bear finally waded to the other side.

Just beyond Otter Creek they met Wingate and Le Roy, who had come back to assist them, and who informed them that they had reached camp all right, that the tents were set up, the things stored away, and that St. Clair and Adams were busy getting supper.

"That is the best news I have heard for a month," declared Claude. "I believe for once that I am as hungry as ever Adams was."

"Hungry!" echoed Phil; "I could eat a handspike."

"How have the animils behaved?" inquired Wingate, mimicking Tom Chester's pronunciation of the word.

"Very well," replied Maynard. "Nap set out to get up on his ear when we crossed the river, but I coaxed him out of it."

"Where did you cross?" queried Le Roy.

"A little way below Little Boy's Falls."

"I'd like to know how those falls obtained their name," remarked Claude.

"Give it up," returned Phil.

"It's three o'clock," said Wingate, consulting his watch; "we had better be moving."

Two hours more brought them to the camp, and Nap and the deer were securely fastened.

St. Clair told them that he could have supper any time they were ready, and the boys washed up, while the food was being put on the table, and at half-past five they sat down to a pretty fair spread for the woods. St. Clair had not been satisfied with his Sunday's dinner, although the storm was to blame for its deficiencies, and he regaled them on fried trout, broiled caribou, fried and mashed potatoes, canned peas, hot biscuit, raspberry short-cake, and canned plums.

"There's nothing bad about this," declared Claude, who, having eaten half-a-dozen small trout, now helped himself to some of the caribou. "I think my mantle has fallen upon a worthy successor."

"I agree with you;" and Maynard, with his mouth full, winked at St. Clair in a very appreciative manner.

The boys sat long at the table that evening, and thoroughly enjoyed the meal; and when they had finished, St. Clair told them that neither Adams nor himself had found time to cut up any camp-wood; and while the cook and his assistant cleared up the dishes and fed the menagerie the other boys supplied the fuel.

"It's about time that deer was christened," remarked Claude, as the boys drew up to the camp-fire, and each settled himself in the most comfortable position.

"So say we all of us," sang Phil.

"Call him Steamboat," suggested Maynard; "he snorts like a Mississippi steamer when he gets frightened."

"Call him Rusher," laughed Adams; "he rushed me out of the boat pretty lively the day we caught him."

"Call him Venison," said Le Roy, with a chuckle.

"Call your granny Venison," sneered St. Clair. "What kind of a name do you call that?"

"You can call her that, if you wish," retorted Le Roy; "anyway she is old, deer meat."

A roar of laughter greeted this sally, while Wingate began to look about for a club.

"Suppose we call him Lightfoot. I am sure that would be appropriate"; and Phil glanced around him for an expression of opinion.

"You have it," nodded Claude. "That's a good name for him;" and, there being no dissenting voice, the deer was known in the future as Lightfoot.

"Say, fellows,"— and Adams looked from one to the other,—" can you tell me who was the straightest man in the Bible?"

"What do you take us for,—a minstrel troupe?" queried Wingate.

"I take you for all you are worth, as the man said when he married a rich wife; but can you answer my conundrum?"

"Give it up," cried several voices.

"Joseph was."

"Why?" asked Claude.

"Because Pharaoh made a ruler of him."

The boys all smiled, and St. Clair, who sat next to Adams, patted him on the back.

"Let me alone," cried Adams. "I've got another one for you."

"Put him out," shouted Wingate, from the farther end of the circle.

"Put some ice on his head, and keep him quiet, can't you?" laughed Phil.

"Can you tell me"—

"Of course I can," broke in Maynard.

"Can you tell me why an infirm old man is like a musical character?"

"Because he's a sharp."

"Because he's a flat."

"Because he is sometimes found near a bar."

"Because he takes a rest."

"No, you are all wrong. It is because each requires a staff."

A chorus of groans greeted the answer.

"If the rest of you are not tired I am, and I'm going to bed," and Claude arose with a yawn, and went into the tent.

The boys sat a short time longer, and then feeling

sleepy and tired, for the work of the last two days had been the hardest they had experienced since leaving home, left the camp-fire to snap and flicker itself out, and throw fantastic shadows on the dark woods around.

In the middle of the night they were awakened by a terrible racket, and starting up, alarmed, they rushed out-doors without waiting to dress.

The deer showed considerable excitement, and snorted and whistled like a steam-engine, while Nap growled and walked about uneasily, as if something or somebody had interfered with his dreams.

" What's the row? "

" What was that noise? "

" What is it? " cried the boys, peering into the darkness. But the questions were easier asked than answered. Nothing unusual was in sight, and Claude and Maynard dressed, and, lighting a lantern, made a tour of the camp; but nothing could be found in the way of tracks or other signs that any wild animal had been near the camp, and the cause of that night's disturbance was always a mystery. As the two boys returned to the tent, and undressed again, Maynard remarked, that he guessed Nap had been troubled with the nightmare.

The next day Wingate and Le Roy carried one of the boats over to Rump Pond, and spent several hours in fishing, catching a large number of small trout. When they returned to camp they left the boat behind them, thinking that some others of the party might also like to try the fishing there.

Claude, Maynard, and Phil took some lunch with them, and their fire-arms, and made an excursion to

Caribou Pond, about two miles distant from the camp. They followed the base of the hill, just behind their tenting-ground, keeping near a small brook that emptied into the river near their camp.

They saw abundant signs of deer and caribou, as they walked along, and many of the tracks appeared fresh. Reaching the pond they threw themselves down behind a fallen tree, near where a small point jutted into the water, and lay patiently awaiting what Dame Fortune might bring them. For an hour or more they kept quiet, only conversing in whispers, and at the end of that time a noise, as of some heavy animal coming through the forest, startled them, and, peering over the prostrate tree, they beheld two moose, that they judged to be male and female, come out on the point, and wade into the pond.

"Holy mackerel!" exclaimed Maynard, — "two moose!"

"That is game with a vengeance," added Claude. "The distance is a little long for my gun; you and Phil had better try them. Each single out one."

"You take the one on the right, and I will the one on the left," whispered Frank.

"All right"; and Phil brought his rifle to his shoulder, and both boys fired simultaneously. Neither of the moose dropped, however, but both, turning toward the woods, started on the shambling trot peculiar to them. As they left the water Claude fired, impartially giving one barrel to each of the animals; but it did not stop their progress for a second.

"Well, if that isn't provoking then kick me for a jackass!" groaned Frank, as the boys arose to their feet and slipped fresh cartridges into their pieces. "A fellow who couldn't hit one of those moose with a rifle from where we lay couldn't hit a barn-door at forty yards."

"Come along and see if we can find any indication of their being wounded;" and Claude leaped over the tree and ran for the point, his friends close at his heels.

Reaching the place where the moose had left the water they examined the ground carefully, as well as the bushes and small trees in the vicinity, but could find no marks of blood, and were forced to believe, what was an evident fact, that all their shots had been futile.

"I guess we had better practise shooting at a mark to-morrow," observed Phil, dryly, as the boys looked discontentedly at one another.

"Better luck next time, I hope," remarked Claude, cheerfully, rallying from the disappointment; "now let's go back to the old tree and eat our lunch. There may be some deer come in here by and by, and if any do we will see if we can't shoot straighter."

"I should say so," added Frank, as he followed his two friends back to their hiding-place.

They eat their dinner, and then talked in whispers, while they lay waiting for something to put in appearance. At the end of a couple of hours their quiet had become monotonous, and they were just talking of returning to camp, when they heard a rustling in the bushes, and, peeping noiselessly over their bulwark, beheld a medium-sized deer coming out of the forest, and taking the water between them and the point.

"For Heaven's sake, don't miss this time," urged Claude to the riflemen.

"If I do, send me home to-morrow," whispered Frank, and he with Phil, taking careful aim, fired. The next moment the deer was seen to drop, but, struggling to his feet, made a few uncertain steps that brought him just clear of the water.

Claude brought his gun to his shoulder, but as he was about to press the trigger the animal fell again, and this time remained motionless. Putting his piece at half-cock, Claude rushed for the deer, accompanied by his two friends, who gave vent to their satisfaction by shouts of triumph. Reaching the fallen animal, which they discovered to be a buck, with a fair set of horns, they stooped down and examined him. One bullet had gone through his neck, the other had struck him just behind the fore-shoulder; and the blood was pouring from both wounds, either of which would have been sufficient to kill him.

"Now we shall have some fresh meat," remarked Phil, as they finished their examination of the deer, and, putting his hand in his pockets, brought forth a piece of line, with which he tied the animal's feet together. Meanwhile Claude found a young maple, which he hacked down with his hunting-knife, and, trimming it to the right length, run it between the buck's feet, and he and Phil shouldered it, and then turned homewards.

With one end of the pole on one shoulder, and their guns over the other, the two boys had all the load they cared to carry, and after walking about fifteen minutes Frank spelled Phil at his end of the pole. Taking turns in this manner, they arrived at camp about five o'clock, where they found the other four members of the party, who cheered lustily when they saw the venison, causing

Lightfoot to dance around the tree where he was tied up, as if a hound was at his heels, and making Nap watch them with wide-open eyes. They were not sorry to drop their burden and take a rest.

"Where have you been, fellows?" inquired St. Clair.

"Up to Caribou Pond," returned Claude.

"Get the deer there?"

"Yes."

"We also saw a couple of moose that we didn't get," remarked Maynard.

"Get a shot at them?" asked Adams.

"Yes," replied Phil; "we all fired, and all missed."

"I never was so provoked in my life," added Frank. "They were just the right distance away, and how we all missed them is more than I can account for. If only Claude and Phil had missed them"— with a smile, —"I should not have thought so much of it; but that *I* should fire at an object as large as a moose at that distance, and miss, it was a caulker on me."

"Great I," laughed Le Roy.

"Tell us all about it, Claude," urged Wingate. "I will, if St. Clair and Adams will hurry up the supper, for I'm half starved;" and he gave his friends a detailed account of their trip from the time they left camp until their return. As he finished his story St. Clair yelled "Supper!" in a tone that could have been heard half a mile away, and the boys rushed for the table.

They had been blessed with a good appetite from the time they had left home, and could eat three meals a day without any urging. In fact, they all declared that they eat three times as much in the woods as they did at home, and from personal experience I know they were right in the matter; hence a call to meals was always hailed with satisfaction.

After supper the deer was dressed, and the hide and head put carefully away in the store-tent. Phil expressed the desire to have the head set up and the skin tanned, and asked Claude if he would accompany him the next day to Chester's, so he could leave it there, and have it sent down to Norton, at Colebrook, if they did not find him at camp.

"It strikes me, Phil, that will be a pretty hard tramp."

"Not very hard. Take one of the boats down river, and walk across the carry."

"It would be nearer to start from here and walk through the woods," suggested Wingate.

"Don't know the way," and Claude shook his head doubtfully. "The farthest way round is the nearest way home sometimes, and I think it would be so in this case."

"We could keep the right course by compass," added Phil.

"That may be; but it would be a thundering hard tramp, all the same."

"You can't go over there and back in less than two days," said Adams, while St. Clair was of the opinion it would take them four.

"I should not hurry any if we went," declared Claude, "and should rather be four days than two doing it."

Phil was very anxious, however, to get the head and hide out, and, after talking the matter over the most of

Parmachenee Lake, looking West.

the evening, Claude agreed to go with him, and the boys retired to rest.

They left camp Friday morning at seven o'clock, wishing to get fairly on their way before the sun was too hot. Claude had his gun, and Phil his rifle, and both took twenty-five cartridges. An axe, a drinking-cup, a pocket compass, some matches in a small phial, and rations for six good meals, completed their outfit.

"I suppose you'll be here, Claude, when you get back."

"I guess I shall, if the bears don't eat us, St. Clair."

"I shall not look for you before Sunday."

"I guess we shall get back surely by Saturday night," said Phil, as they started into the woods in a south-westerly direction, followed by the "good lucks," and "good-byes," of their companions.

"Anybody want to take a cruise up river?" inquired Maynard.

"I'll go with you," said Wingate.

"Suppose we all go," added St. Clair. "Perhaps we can get as far as the Forks. They can't be more than six or eight miles above here. We can take lunch with us, and then we needn't hurry any."

Le Roy expressed his willingness to make one of the party; but Adams concluded to stop in camp, and finish a book he had just begun reading, that he was very much interested in.

About nine o'clock the exploring party, as St. Clair called it, left camp with two boats, Maynard and St. Clair in the "Fairy," and Wingate and Le Roy in the "Go Ahead." The sail up the river was beautiful, the banks being for the most part high and fringed on either hand by a thick forest. The Camel's Rump towered skyward west of them, while northward the boundary mountains barred their vision in that direction. They found the river above the camp as crooked as it was below, and it was turn and twist, and twist and turn, the entire distance. Muskrat were plenty along their way, and they shot two, but did not pick them up. Frank hoped to get an otter; but they did not see any. They noticed a number of red-headed woodpeckers, kingbirds, and blue-jays, and, much to their surprise, several robins, who seemed out of place in such a wilderness.

They reached the Forks at one o'clock, and, taking out their boats, built a fire and warmed a pot of coffee they had brought along with them, and then eat their lunch. Having satisfied their hunger they launched their boats and turned homeward. As they floated down the river they noticed more particularly the height of the Camel's Rump, and made up their minds that the view from its summit would well repay anybody for the climb, and, after some talk about the matter, concluded to try and make the ascent of the mountain the next day. About six o'clock they reached the camp, and found that Adams had company.

Spoff Flint, of whom the boys had bought the potatoes, and an old hunter by the name of Nay Bennett, were on their way to Arnold's Bog, and had turned out of their course to pay the boys a visit. They were invited to stop overnight, and signified their willingness to, and after supper paid St. Clair's cooking a high compliment.

In the evening, around the camp-fire, the two old

hunters entertained them with hunting adventures until eleven o'clock. Spoff began with a bear-story, and Nay followed with an account of a moose-hunt. Then Spoff reeled them a yarn about a deer that he had captured one winter in the snow, and Nay continued with a hair-breadth escape he had once had from a wild-cat. Story followed story, each narrator trying apparently to see who could tell the largest one. Knowing that the boys were green, the hunters imposed upon their credulity in the most barefaced manner; but they were so used to spinning large stories that they probably forgot they were not telling the truth more than half the time. The hunters were good talkers, however, and, in spite of occasional doubts, the boys enjoyed the stories hugely. In the morning, after breakfast, the hunters took another look at Nap and Lightfoot, and Spoff telling the boys to stop and see him when they went down river, bade them "Good-by," and, calling to Nay, stepped into their canoe and paddled away. Nay told the boys they were going up the East branch, a short distance, to where a trail began that led to the bog.

After their visitors had departed, Maynard told Adams that they were going to climb the Camel's Rump, and asked him if he wanted to go. He replied in the affirmative, saying he had passed one day alone, and that would answer for him for some time.

They fed the menagerie, put up some lunch, and then, taking their fire-arms, crossed the river and waded towards the mountain. They found the travel exceedingly difficult, the growth being very close, and, as the route was up-hill all the way, they found the tramp a tiresome one.

Three weeks of out-door life had hardened their muscles, and put them in good condition, so that the walk was nothing for them compared to what it would have been a month previous.

The entire distance, until they were quite near the summit, lay through a thick forest that effectually secured them from the hot rays of the sun. But still it was very warm travelling, as but little air was stirring in the woods. Occasionally they sat down to rest, and at such times they would speak of Claude and Phil, and wonder how they were getting along.

They finally reached the summit, and were greeted with a grand view of an unbroken forest, stretching away without limit, broken by silvery threads and spots, designating the rivers, ponds, and lakes by which they were surrounded. When they had viewed the grand landscape from every point of the compass they sat down and took dinner.

"It does not look as if the forests of Maine were going to be all cut this year," remarked St. Clair, as he gazed around on the immense wilderness spread out before them.

"All that stuff you read in the newspapers about the forests of Maine becoming cleared up in a few years is all bosh. Probably the special correspondents who write those things were never up here in the wilderness in their lives. I'll bet if you should climb this mountain one hundred years from to-day, the view from its top would not be changed a particle, unless a destructive fire should occur in the meantime."

"That is my opinion, too, Maynard," said Le Roy, "and ever since we made our trip to the Richardson

Lakes, I have laughed at those newspaper accounts you speak of. Why, one of the guides told me, and I have no doubt but that he spoke the truth, that he knows a number of pieces of land that were cleared up for farms twenty-five years ago that, having been deserted, have grown up to woods, and returned to the original forest."

" Don't you remember that farm on the Richardson Lakes, near the Narrows, where we were? That is all grown up to bushes now, and in ten years longer it will probably be woods," added Adams.

After eating their lunch the boys wandered about the top of the mountain, and came across some surveyors' marks, for the boundary line between Maine and New Hampshire runs directly across the top of the Camel's Rump, north and south.

" This is the State line," declared Maynard as he noticed the marks; " I suppose we could follow this clear to the Connecticut river if we chose."

" Don't start until after supper, Frank," said Le Roy; " you might get hungry before you reached the river."

" I think we had better be getting down this mountain; it's a good three hours from here to camp, and it's two o'clock now."

" Right you are, Wingate," answered Frank; " so here goes ! " and the party began the descent.

They went down a little to the west of where they had come up, and, when about half-way to the bottom, Maynard, who was in advance, stumbled and fell, and, as he scrambled to his feet, was surprised to see, a little to his right, a hole, about the size of the top of a flour barrel, that looked like a tunnel into the mountain. A well-worn path led to it from the forest, and, peering into the entrance, he tried to see what lay beyond, but the darkness prevented him.

"What have you found now?" inquired St. Clair, as the boys hastened to him, to see if he had been hurt by his fall.

"I'll be hanged if I know! A hole certainly, — a bear's den possibly, but it is so confounded dark in there I can't see six feet beyond my nose."

"Let's explore it; perhaps it's a cave," cried Adams, excitedly.

"You are not in a cave country, my boy. If we were down in Western Virginia or Kentucky it might be one, for you can stumble on one there most any hour in the day. But these granite hills are not like limestone, and it is seldom you find much of a cave, at least a natural one, in New England. If we had a lantern we might see what it amounted to; but we can't get into it without light; and then if we should find a bear or some other wild animal inside, it might be awkward."

"Oh, hang your lantern!" retorted Wingate. "There's a big, white birch a little way ahead; let's peel off some bark, make some torches, and have a look at it. With three rifles and two double-barrel guns, we are good for any animal that turns up, from a skunk to a moose."

It needed but little to stir the spirit of adventure in the boys, and Wingate's words found an echoing response in his companions' hearts, and, starting for the white birch, by aid of their knives they had soon peeled a sufficient quantity of bark, and, going back to the hole in the mountain, they quickly made a dozen torches.

Lighting one of these, and putting their pieces at half-cock, they started into the hole on their hands and knees, Wingate leading the way. For the first six feet the passage was straight, and then turned sharply to the left, the grade being downward all the time. As they crawled along, the tunnel became higher and broader, and they could soon walk upright. There were a great many pieces of rock scattered along the path, of different sizes, from an egg to a foot-ball. The sides of the passage were rough, showing veins of mica, that glistened under the light of their torch.

When they had accomplished about thirty feet their torch was burned nearly out, and they lighted another, the passage now turning toward the right. At this point it was about seven feet high, and three feet wide, and continued so the rest of the distance, some forty or fifty feet more, when it suddenly brought them into a cave, or apartment, about sixty feet square, but of irregular shape. The floor of this cave was smooth and hard, and, lighting another torch, one being insufficient to pierce the Cimmerian darkness, they went on a tour of inspection.

The first discovery they made (a startling one to them) was the fact that the cave had been made wholly, or in part, by human hands, as they found marks of drills on the walls, and evidences that blasting had once been done there. Here was something to speculate on, and the boys began carefully to examine the walls, to see if they could find traces of silver or gold. After ten minutes' careful examination they found a thin streak of silver, and near it a large vein of lead, pronounced so by Le Roy, who knew a little about geology.

They were looking along the left-hand wall, as they had entered from the passage-way, and, as they reached the farther corner, were surprised and shocked to find the skeleton of a man lying on the floor, a fleshless mass of bones, without anything suggesting clothing.

"Heavens and earth!" exclaimed Maynard; "what is this?" and he held his torch nearer to the hideous skull after a moment's hesitation, for his sudden discovery had startled him.

"The skeleton of some man, perhaps an Indian," added Wingate.

"It must have been here an awful time" said Adams; "there isn't a vestige of clothing left about it."

"Nor anything else to show what he was, or what he was doing here," declared Le Roy, looking carefully about.

While they were speculating and theorizing over the dead man's bones, a large bat, that had been disturbed from its slumbers, dashed over to them with a whirr, and alighted on Adams' head, causing that young man to shout, "The devil!" and frightened them so in the semi-darkness, not seeing or knowing what had attacked their friend, that, without a thought of their fire-arms, they turned and rushed for the passage-way.

But every one was in the other's way, and they all sprawled head over heels on the floor, struggling and yelling, half-frightened to death, as their torches became extinguished, leaving them in a gloom that could be almost felt, from its denseness.

Maynard was the first to recover from the panic, and suddenly thinking what it must have been that caused their fright, he began to laugh.

"What a set of fools we are!" he cried, as he drew out a match, and, lighting it, found one of the unburned torches; "it was nothing but a bat"; and, lighting the torch, he held it up, and beheld a tremendous bat with outspread wings, clinging to a jutting rock on the wall over the skeleton, and then he roared again to think of the ridiculous picture his friends and himself must have presented when they tied themselves up in a knot on the floor. His laughter was contagious, and his companions, all but Adams, joined with him.

He, however, was thoroughly frightened, as the bat, in trying to alight on his head, had scratched his hat off, and, recovering this, and his gun, which he had dropped during the rush, he exclaimed, as he lighted another torch from Maynard's, "Bat or no bat, let's get out of here. We shall not reach camp to-night at this rate."

"I suppose we ought to be moving, Frank; we must have fooled away an hour in here."

"All right, Charlie," replied Maynard, turning toward the passage-way, Adams hastily skipping on ahead; "we'll come up here again when Claude and Phil come back."

On their way down the mountain the discovery of the cave and the finding of the skeleton was the one topic of conversation, and each of the party wearied their brains in trying to account for them in a satisfactory manner.

The cave was supposed to be either a mine or a dwelling, and the skeleton to have been a miner, Indian, smuggler, hunter, trapper, or possibly a wild man.

It was as bad as a Greek puzzle to them and they could not solve it. The fact that Norton, nor Chester, nor any of the hunters or guides they had met in the country had mentioned it to them, naturally led the boys to believe that none of them knew of its existence; and the more they thought the matter over the more mysterious it appeared.

It was a little after six when they reached camp, and all helped in preparing supper. When it was over the camp-fire was lighted, and the boys returned to the subject of the cave and the skeleton, which seemed to possess a wonderful fascination for them, and fairly tortured themselves in their anxiety to solve the mystery.

"Will any fellow answer me one thing?" queried Wingate as he gazed around at his friends. "What became of the rock that was taken out of that cave? for you will all allow that there must have been a good deal of it disposed of somewhere."

. "That is easy enough," declared Maynard. "It was carried out-doors, and is now overgrown with moss and bushes. Didn't you observe how uneven the ground was around the entrance? It was all dumped below that hole, and I'll bet that if you pull up the bushes, and dig around there with a crow-bar, you'll find a large pile of small stones. You see that job must have been done years ago, and all traces of the work outside have been hidden by the cunning hand of Nature."

"Anyhow I should like to know whether the skeleton is that of an Indian or a white man," declared Le Roy.

"And whether he died a natural death, or whether he was murdered," suggested Adams.

"I guess he died for want of breath," smiled Maynard.

"So will you if you talk much more," retorted St. Clair.

"Let's go to bed, the last stick of wood is on the fire, and I don't intend to cut any more to-night," and with this decided statement from the cook the party broke up and sought their couch.

After breakfast Saturday morning St. Clair announced that the berries and fish were all gone, and that, if they wanted any more, the boys would have to get them, as he and Adams had all they could do that day to do the cooking and get a supply of long camp-wood chopped for the evening fires.

Wingate and Le Roy offered to procure some trout, and Maynard said he would go down river and get some berries. The boys took a lunch and left camp about nine, Wingate and Le Roy going over to Rump Pond to fish, and Frank down the river to some of the loggers' clearings, where the raspberries grew in great profusion.

Both parties returned within a few minutes of each other, about five o'clock, Maynard with ten quarts of raspberries, and the two fishermen with over a hundred trout, and about half a pound of spruce-gum that they had found all on one tree on their way home.

"Claude and Phil come yet?" inquired Maynard, as he turned his berries over to St. Clair to take care of.

"Not a sign of them yet, and it is so late now I shall not look for them much until to-morrow."

"They ought to go over there and back in less than four days," said Wingate.

"I don't know about that," returned Le Roy. "It is quite a distance ; and then the travelling in some places is pretty bad. See what a hole we struck the other day, up the river. If they get back here by to-morrow noon I shall think they do well. I don't believe they reached Chester's before last night."

"Then they had to sleep out Thursday night," put in Adams.

"That won't hurt them any," remarked Maynard; "we have not had any real cold nights yet, and with a fire they could be comfortable enough. The only danger I can think of for them is of their getting lost."

"They won't get lost," said Wingate laughing, "Claude is a pretty level-headed fellow. I have no doubt of their going over there and back safely."

"I don't propose to borrow trouble on their account, any way," declared St. Clair, cheerfully. "If they are not here by to-morrow night then it will be time enough to worry. They probably did not start on their return until this morning, and I don't believe that any of us could come from Tom Chester's camp across through the wilderness that we saw from the Camel's Rump, yesterday, in one day, and have to make our course by compass at that."

"They should have spotted a line going over," suggested Le Roy.

"How is supper getting along, Adams?"

"First-rate, Frank, it will be ready as soon as I take up the beans."

A moment later and St. Clair called supper, and the boys dropped the subject of their absent friends' return for the present.

"By gracious! these beans are the boss," declared Maynard after eating two or three mouthfuls.

"So are these trout, simply immense," and Wingate helped himself to half-a-dozen.

"Not in size," laughed Adams.

"No, but in taste they can't be beat."

"Give me a good, strong cup of tea, to-night, Andrew, will you? I want a regular eye-opener. I became rather tired picking those berries.

"You deserve it, Frank; you must have kept very busy to have picked ten quarts."

"I wasn't laying around in the bushes a great while, I tell you."

"Say, suppose I sample some of those berries that you are making such a row about?" and Le Roy passed his plate along. "Put another biscuit on it at the same time. I don't feel hungry to-night."

"I shouldn't think you did," and Adams grinned as he helped him.

"Now that we have helped these three hungry cormorants, let's you and I sit down, Adams. We shall be getting left if we don't look out."

"Yes, pitch in," advised Maynard, as he speared a biscuit, "or it will be a cold day for you."

And thus the talk ran on until even the hungry boys could eat no more, and arose from the table, feeling at peace with themselves and all the world.

The evening was spent around the camp-fire, talking of their absent friends, and at an early hour they went to bed.

Sunday forenoon was passed in various ways by the party, with the exception of Maynard, who amused himself by giving Nap lessons in a new trick. St. Clair and Adams made preparations for dinner to include Claude and Phil; and about one o'clock they came in, looking as if they had been on a tramp from Boston to Chicago, and walking as if they were thoroughly tired out.

CHAPTER VIII.

Claude's Story. — An Unpleasant Adventure. — Oversleeping. — A Foggy Morning. — "Quack! Quack! Quack!" the First Ducks. Phil's Story. — An Excursion to Little Boy's Falls. — A Hot Day. Maynard and the Bear. — Building a Shanty. — Roast Duck for Supper.

"You look as if you had been having a hard time, fellows," remarked Maynard, as Phil and Claude laid aside the axe and their fire-arms, and turned into the two hammocks that swung just outside of the centre of the camp.

"I should rather remark," answered Claude, dryly.

"Did you get over there all right?" queried Adams.

"Yes," replied Phil.

"Who did you see?" said Wingate.

"Tom Chester, a couple of Pittsburgh guides, and a party of three men from Concord"; and Claude turned in the hammock to get an easier position.

"Are you hungry?" inquired St. Clair.

"I think I could eat anything from old boots to raw skunk-meat, if you call that being hungry," and Phil took several long sniffs at the dinner that was now nearly ready, and smacked his lips in anticipation of the coming feast.

"What makes you so quiet, Claude? Give us an account of your trip, will you?" and Le Roy walked over to the hammock.

"Let me alone, Tom, until after dinner, and then I'll talk to you. I'm as tired as a tramp and as hungry as a wolf," and Claude cast longing glances toward the table.

During the fifteen minutes that intervened before St. Clair announced the dinner, Claude and Phil went sound asleep, and Maynard, who noticed it, told the others that he guessed the boys were pretty well played out.

When dinner was ready Adams awoke them, and, taking their places at the table, they lost no time in sampling the viands before them. While the dinner was in progress, Maynard and Wingate related to Claude and Phil their adventure of the day before, to which the boys listened with marked attention, laughing heartily as they described the panic among them caused by the bat.

After dinner Claude and Phil went to the river and took a bath, then returned to camp, and changed their clothes. By this time St. Clair and Adams had finished their work, and, like the rest of their friends, were itching to hear an account of the trip to Second Lake; for they all knew from the appearance of Claude and Phil that something unusual had occurred during their absence. Their two tired comrades having sought the hammocks again, the rest of the party gathered around them, and Claude began his narration of what had transpired during the three days and a half they had been away from camp.

"When we left camp Thursday morning, after crossing the river, we took a westerly course by compass, after consulting the map I carried with me.

"The travelling was good most of the time during

the forenoon, except when we struck into logging works, which we did occasionally, and then we would have to go out of our course some distance to clear the tops and brush.

"About eleven o'clock we crossed a stream, which we took to be the Little Magalloway, and then changed our course a few points farther south, to avoid crossing a high mountain. At one o'clock we were to the westward of this, and reached a small stream that flowed south-west, and which probably emptied into Second Lake.

"By this time we were tired enough to rest, for the deer's hide seemed to weigh about fifty pounds, and the head and antlers about a ton. During our walk we had changed burdens with each other, and that had made it a little easier.

"Sitting down by the side of the brook we eat our lunch, washing it down with the sparkling water before us, and at two o'clock, feeling rested and much better, we crossed the stream, and continued our way.

"After leaving the brook the character of the woods changed considerably. Before dinner the growth had been larger, — spruce, pine, and fir among the soft woods, and maple, white and yellow birch, and occasionally ash, for hard-wood timber, while the underbrush had not been bad at all.

"But half a mile from where we had eaten we ran into a swamp, or bog, with clusters of small firs, cedars, and, once in a while, some spruces. These grew so close together that at times it was simply impossible to force our way through them, and we were compelled to make a detour.

"The ground here was treacherous,—soft and wet, and full of holes; and quite often we would sink down over the tops of our boots. It was very tiresome, I tell you, and after half-an-hour of it, I told Phil we had better keep farther north, and see if we couldn't clear it, and find drier ground.

"We changed our route accordingly, and, after an hour's hard tramp, reached firmer land and higher ground, a ridge running nearly east and west.

"By this time it was four o'clock, and I knew that all chance of reaching Chester's camp that night had gone. However, we pushed on, and at half-past five came to another stream, which, by consulting the map, we found must be the outlet of Third Lake.

We waded across this, and, selecting a suitable place, prepared to camp. We cut up a stack of camp-wood, made us a bough tent, and at seven o'clock built a fire, and took supper. Before turning in, we dried our stockings, which were wet through, and bathed our feet and legs in the brook, for we both felt sore and stiff. Having piled a lot of large hard-wood sticks on the fire, that threw out a generous warmth for a distance of ten feet, we laid down, and after a while went to sleep.

At first the stillness was oppressive, but a breeze sprang up, making a gentle murmur among the treetops; and, soothed by this woodland music, I soon lost all consciousness, and knew nothing more until a yell from Phil brought me out of a sound slumber, and, sitting upright, I found in my lap the cause of Phil's outcry."

"What was it?" broke in Le Roy.

."A fearful great adder, of the spotted variety, larger round than my thumb, and about four feet long, had crawled on top of me during the night, and, liking the warmth of my body, had coiled himself up on me, and snoozed away in the most comfortable manner possible."

"Blast such a bedfellow as that!" cried Adams, decidedly.

"My sudden waking and moving frightened the snake, and he uncoiled and wriggled away before I could get a crack at him. We tried our best to kill him, but he went in under the root of a spruce near us, and that was the last we saw of him."

"But I shall not forget him very soon," added Phil. "I was lying close to Claude, and threw my arm over him, I suppose, in my sleep, and my hand came down on the snake. The touch of his cold, clammy body, ran through me like an electric shock, and awoke me in a second, and, seeing the snake, I gave a yell that would have awakened an Egyptian mummy."

The boys laughed at the expression of disgust in Phil's face, at the remembrance of the reptile, and Claude continued: —

"After the adder had given us the slip, I looked at my watch, and found it was half-past four, and thinking that it would not pay to turn in again, I scraped the coals left from the fire together, hacked some slivers off of an old pine stub near us, and soon had a good fire under way.

"At that time in the morning the air was decidedly chilly, and the fire felt first-rate, I assure you. After taking a wash in the stream, we eat our breakfast, cleaning our larder completely out, and at half-past six we started, after scattering our fire so that it would do no damage.

"We felt a little stiff from Thursday's tramp, and walked slowly at first, increasing our pace, as we limbered up.

"Being perfectly well convinced that the stream by which we had camped was the upper Connecticut, we concluded that the best thing we could do was to follow it south until we sighted the lake, and then follow that to Chester's camp, which we did, arriving there a little after nine.

"Tom was at home, and was glad to see us, and urged us to have some breakfast; but we concluded we could wait until dinner-time, and asked him what was going on.

"He gave us the news, and told us all that had happened at the camp lately that was worth relating. He said that Norton had gone down to Colebrook with a party who were on their way out, and that he would send the head and hide to him the first opportunity.

"We met the Concord gentlemen at dinner, and they told us they had shot a moose the night before near the foot of the lake, and showed us the skin. I tell you, boys, it was a large one.

"After dinner we told Tom we were going to return; but he would not hear of our going; said that if we left then we should be out over night, and, added that if we would wait until the next morning he would take us in a boat, after breakfast, and carry us to the head of the lake, and up a stream a mile or two, so that from where he would land us we could easily reach our camp before dark ; and, on the strength of his promise, we concluded to stay.

"In the afternoon we went out with him about three miles from camp to a small stream, where he showed us a beaver dam; and, I tell you, boys, it is worth seeing. Men could not have built it any better, and the trees were cut off by the beavers as smooth as if done by a saw.

"In the evening the two Pittsburg guides, who appeared to be pretty good fellows, related some of their experiences in driving river, and told us how a friend of theirs lost his life while trying, with others, to start a jam of logs one spring on the Connecticut. According to his telling, river-driving must be a very exciting business.

"We had a good sleep Friday night, and felt first-rate yesterday morning. After breakfast Tom took us in a boat, and rowed up the lake.

"On the way he asked me if we had seen any Kanucks around our camp, and I told him no ; and, as I scarcely knew what he meant, I asked him if they were Indians.

"'Dog-gone them! no; but a darned sight worse. They're French Canadians. They come down this way every fall, and they're the lyingest, drunkenest, thievingest set of cusses you ever saw. Why they'd steal the hole out'n a grin'stone, and if any of 'em come foolin' around yer camp, order 'em ter leave, and if they don't, put a charge 'er shot inter 'em.'

"I expressed a hope that we should not be troubled by any such visitors, and admired the beauty of the lake, as the boat shot through the still water, propelled by Tom's sturdy arms, sending the little ripples out from under the bow, which floated astern in the shape of silver bubbles, and were lost in the wake behind us.

"Reaching the mouth of the stream he had spoken of, Tom poled the boat up it for a couple of miles, until we reached some shallow rapids.

"He told us that he could not go any farther, and landed us on the east bank.

"He asked us particularly as to the location of our tents, and, after we had answered him, said he knew the place well, and told us we were not more than ten miles from our camp, in a bee-line.

"He said if we travelled east-north-east from where we then were we should strike the Magalloway but a short distance below our camp; and, telling us not to get lost, bid us good-day, and we struck into the woods, having no doubt but that we should eat supper with you.

"Feeling almost as if we were at home we started onward with good courage, talking and laughing, and on the lookout for anything in the shape of game.

"Soon after this we came upon some deer-tracks that looked so fresh that we concluded to follow them a short distance, and see if we couldn't get some venison.

"We followed the tracks, I guess for an hour, but saw nothing of the deer, and finding, upon consulting my watch, that it was eleven o'clock, we gave up the pursuit, and turned our steps once more homeward.

"But now we were at a loss as to the proper direction in which to travel, as, while trailing the deer, we had paid no attention to the compass, and the sun, being so nearly overhead, did not help us much.

"After quite a consultation we decided upon what

we thought was the proper course, and pushed on. After travelling an hour we caught sight of the mountain we had seen going over, a long way to the north of us, and, changing our course to a more northerly direction, tramped for an hour longer, which brought us near the base of the mountain, we judged a little south of where we had passed it before.

"As we felt easy as to our whereabouts now, and had began to get decidedly hungry, we sat down on an old windfall, and eat the small lunch we had brought with us, consisting of a piece of corn-cake, and some doughnuts and cheese.

"Being anxious to reach camp by supper-time, we only made half an hour's stop, then once more continued our journey. We reached the Little Magalloway about three o'clock, and, as we came in sight of the river, stumbled on to three rough-looking fellows sprawled out around a fire, one of whom was just taking a drink from a black bottle as we reached them. Hearing our footsteps and voices they sprang to their feet and confronted us, and three more villanous looking vagabonds, I never saw in my life."

"You can bet your bottom dollar on that," echoed Phil, heartily.

"We looked at each other a few seconds, and then the largest one said, 'Where you go?'"

"'Over to Parmachenee Lake,' I answered, for it dawned upon me suddenly that perhaps it would be as well not to let them know just where our camp was located.

"'Where you come from?' he asked.

"'Second Lake.'

"'What you do up here?'

"'Hunting and fishing.'

"'Alone?'

"'Yes.'

"'No guide, you have?'

"'No.'

"'How long been here?'

"'Just come.'

"'Have a drink?'

"'Don't use it.'

"While this conversation was progressing, Phil stood close beside me and we did not pay much attention to the other two men.

"It would have been better for us, however, if we had, for suddenly they stole up behind us, and while one grasped my gun, and gave me a crack behind the ear, that knocked me flat, the other grabbed Phil by the throat and choked him in such a manner that he could not use his rifle, and soon dropped that, and the axe which he was carrying.

"When I came to, I found Phil rubbing his throat, and I picked myself up, feeling as if my head was half broken. The three villains stood near us examining our watches that they had robbed us of, which they slid into their pockets as they saw me get up.

"Pointing my gun at me as I regained my feet, while one of the others levelled his rifle at Phil, the one who had talked with me, and who now had my gun, told us if we did not leave he would blow our brains out.

"'Do you intend to keep our things?' I asked, indignantly, 'you have robbed us.'

"'They're our things now. You get out! if you don't I help you!' and the fellow advanced towards me, as if to put his threat into execution.

"'Come on, Phil,' I called; 'this is no place for us;' and I walked off in the direction we had come.

"'Let's pitch into them,' said Phil. 'The beggars have taken my watch and rifle, our axe, and everything else.'

"'Nonsense!' I replied. 'Follow me,' or you'll get your head broke.'

"'See here you fellars,' remarked the one with my gun, 'you come back here, we kill you.'

"We started off lively after this threat, the scoundrel following us for perhaps a quarter of a mile, when he returned to his companions.

"As soon as he was out of sight we stopped, and looked at each other with woe-begone faces.

"I wish the rest of us had been there," spoke up Adams; "we would have made those fellows sick."

"How did you get out of the scrape, Claude? I see you brought your gun back," said Maynard.

"And our watches, too," laughed Phil.

"I had no intention of returning to camp without our property, if I could help it; and Phil felt the same as I did.

"After waiting a few moments, and talking the matter over, we made our way carefully back to the scene of the robbery, and discovered the three thieves just starting off, following the bank of the river.

"We crept noiselessly after them for an hour, as near as I could judge, and then they crossed the river, and made preparations for camping.

"They built a fire, and cooked some pork and potatoes in a frying-pan and, after eating, all pulled out short clay pipes, filled them with tobacco, and began to smoke.

"Then each one produced a bottle, and took an occasional drink.

"Several times they examined our watches, and the gun and rifle, and then would jaw away to themselves, but we were too far away to distinguish what they said, although we could hear the buzz of their voices plainly."

"Confound the scoundrels!" broke in Maynard, "I should like to have been there, and put a bullet through the whole of them."

"I should rather have put a charge of peep-shot into them," laughed Wingate, "a fellow would not want to be hung for killing such trash as that."

"There's where you're right," said Phil.

"I noticed," continued Claude, "that the smallest one of the party did not drink near as often as the others, and, after a while, this excited our suspicions, and we concluded that he was trying to put up a job on his companions, and later it turned out so.

"By dark the two largest were pretty drunk, and, crawling up near the fire, lay down with their feet toward it.

"The small man then arose to his feet, threw some more wood on the fire, and looking carefully around, as if he was afraid somebody was watching him, drew near to his companions, and bent over them.

"Then Phil and I crawled up to within about fifty feet of the scoundrels, and watched the operations of the sober one.

"While making our way on our hands and knees, I came across a stout maple stick, about four feet long, and two inches through, as handsome a club as you ever saw.

"I could see our gun and rifle standing against a spruce on the opposite side of the fire from us, but too near the scamps for us to think of getting them, until after we had disposed of the sober rascal, who seemed now about to rob his friends.

"As he kneeled down, we were horrified to notice that he had a wicked looking knife held between his teeth by the blade, and we wondered if he was going to murder as well as rob them.

"Watching his proceedings, however, we came to the conclusion that he had taken out his knife as a matter of precaution, not intending to use it unless his companions should awake.

"It appeared in this case that there was no 'honor among thieves,' for the small villain deliberately robbed the larger ones in plain sight of us.

"While he was rifling their pockets, we crawled up to within twenty feet of him, and stopped behind a large pine-stump waiting our chance to make a rush on him.

"We saw him get both the watches and my pocket-compass, and then rising slowly to his feet, stood for a moment watching them, with his back toward us.

"This was our chance, and whispering to Phil to follow me, we arose silently to our feet, and made a rush for the double thief.

"In front of us the ground was clear of bushes and sticks, and we were nearly up to him before he heard us.

"Turning with the knife in his hand, he faced us, but before he could utter an outcry, or use his weapon, I brought the club down on his head with a crack, that was music to me, and he dropped like a log at the feet of his companions.

"I took his knife and flung it into the river; and while I secured our watches and compass, Phil scooted around the fire, and captured our gun, rifle, and axe.

"Being afraid that the one I had struck would soon recover his senses, I pulled out a piece of string from my pocket, and, taking the fellow's greasy hat, which had fallen from his head, I shoved it into his mouth, and tied the string around it, securely gagging him. Then taking some marline that we had with us, we tied his hands securely together, as well as his feet, and picking him up carried him behind the stump from which we had watched his operations.

"The blood was flowing slowly from a cut where my club had struck him; but I didn't have any sympathy for him, and leaving them we struck up river.

"Talk about hard travelling, you don't know anything about it, boys, until you undertake to travel through the woods in the dark.

"The moment we had gone beyond the fire-light the darkness seemed intense. We dared not leave the river, as we might have wandered around in a circle and gone back to the scoundrels whom we had so signally defeated.

"With one hand outstretched we groped our way along, stumbling, tripping, and falling, our only guide the river, whose whispering current on our right seemed like a faithful friend to us.

STEAMER DIAMOND ON CAMBRIDGE RIVER, LAKE UMBAGOG.

"Fears of pursuit hurried us on at the best pace it was possible to take under the circumstances; and, although we barked our shins, tore our clothes, and scratched our faces and hands, there was no stopping."

"Must have been pleasant walking," broke in St. Clair; "don't you wish your girl had been with you?"

Claude smiled at the idea; but, taking no further notice of the interruption, continued: —

"We travelled in this manner until daylight, so tired we could scarcely stand, and sleepy as dogs, in spite of the excitement we had passed through; and at half-past four concluded that we had travelled, as near as we could judge, about six miles.

"We were half frozen, as well as tired and hungry, and, cutting some wood, built a fire, and sat over it awhile, until we recovered from the chill that was on us.

"But the heat made us so drowsy, that the first thing we knew, as the Irishman said, we did not know any-thing, and dropped off asleep.

"When we awoke it was ten o'clock; the sun was shining in our faces, and only a few coals of the fire remained.

"Rising to our feet with an effort, we compared notes, and then struck eastward for camp, and, under the guidance of a divine Providence, were fortunate enough to reach here without any farther trouble, and when we came in, I tell you, I did not feel like talking much."

"Nor I, neither," chimed in Phil.

"Well, you have had an adventure," declared Maynard; "I would like to know how those scoundrels felt when they discovered you had recovered your things. I'll bet they swore some."

"Shouldn't wonder if they did," chuckled Phil.

"Suppose they should happen to stray over here," Adams said with a slight tone of alarm in his voice.

"I should like no better fun than to have them," declared St. Clair, rubbing his hands; "I don't think they would want to visit us again in a hurry."

"I don't wish to see anything more of them," said Claude decidedly. "They are a worse crowd than we struck at Mosquito brook two years ago, and there is no fun in fighting with such scoundrels. If they were to get over here they would not come into camp, but would hang around until some time when we were away, and then steal all we had. They're a bad lot, and I want nothing to do with them. Isn't it most supper-time, St. Clair?".

"Five o'clock. I guess we had better be getting it ready, Adams."

"How far is that cave from here, Maynard?" asked Claude, "where you went yesterday."

"About four miles, I should judge."

"We must go up there some day, I would like to see it."

"So should I," added Phil.

Although Claude and Phil had eaten a large dinner, they were not backward in coming forward when the call to supper was given.

"Did you warm up any beans, St. Clair?" inquired Claude, as the party gathered around the table.

"Yes, I thought you would want some."

"You're a brick, well baked."

"So are the beans well baked," added Adams, as he passed them to Claude.

"Wouldn't some of those beans have gone well about six o'clock this morning?" queried Phil, as he winked at his friend.

"Don't mention it; I was as hollow as a bass-drum."

"Well, fill up! fill up!" cried St. Clair, as he passed the biscuit.

"I don't suppose you and Claude will sit up a great while this evening, Phil," said Frank, smiling.

"Not much," replied Claude, "I'm going to bed as soon as it is dark under the table."

"I'm with you," and Phil gaped as if even then he could scarcely keep his eyes open.

"Adams, you'll be boss cook to-morrow," said St. Clair; "I finish to-night."

"Who is to be my assistant?" gazing around the table for a volunteer.

"I will," offered Maynard, after a few seconds' silence.

At dark, Claude and Phil retired to the tent, and in a few moments were oblivious to all around them, but the other boys sat around the camp-fire until ten o'clock, and talked over the exciting adventure that had befallen their two companions.

"We are going to have a cold night," remarked Maynard, as the circle broke up. "I wouldn't wonder if we found frost on the ground in the morning."

"It don't matter," replied St. Clair; "we have plenty of blankets, and can keep warm."

"Suppose Nap and Lightfoot will be warm enough?" inquired Wingate, as the boys went to their tent.

"I'll risk them," declared Maynard. "Nature has provided them with warm clothing."

The boys undressed as silently as they could, not wishing to disturb their tired companions, and everybody went to sleep without making any talk, and, either out of sympathy with Claude and Phil, or from some other unknown cause, not a soul awoke until eight o'clock the following morning.

Adams was the first one to get up, and when he looked at his watch, he could scarcely believe his eyes. He found upon going out that a thick fog enveloped everything and he could scarcely see a dozen feet from camp. The wood and everything else was almost as wet as if rain had fallen, and he was compelled to go into the store-tent to get some dry birch-bark and kindlings that were kept there for an emergency of this kind.

After he had started the open fire he stuck his head into the tent, and called out.

"All hands on deck! It is eight o'clock. Do you intend to lie all day?"

"Eight o'clock!" repeated Maynard, arising to a sitting position, and rubbing his eyes.

"Yes, eight o'clock. Turn out and start the fire in the stove if you want any breakfast. You're a pretty assistant!"

"Why didn't you call me?" remonstrated Frank, as he sprang up and hurriedly began to dress.

"Because I just awoke, myself," returned Adams, laughing.

"What makes it so dark, Jack?" inquired St. Clair, as he half rose up and peered out of the tent.

"Fog. It is thick as mud. You could cut it

with a knife," and he withdrew to attend to the breakfast.

The other members of the party at once arose, and, after attending to their toilet, gathered around the open fire, for the air was quite chilly.

"We shall have a hot day to-day," remarked Claude, "after the sun eats this fog up."

"That is so," replied Maynard. "I remember, when we were at the Richardson Lakes, that foggy mornings always gave us very hot days."

"I wonder that we have not seen any ducks, yet," said Wingate.

"Perhaps they don't get way up in here," hazarded Le Roy.

"Nonsense," replied Claude, "with all these ponds about here they should be very plenty. I think it is a little early for them yet."

The words had scarely left his mouth when "Quack! quack! quack!" was heard coming from the river a little below them.

"What do you call that?" cried Phil, excitedly.

"Ducks, by thunder!" and rushing for his gun, Claude was out of sight in the fog before the rest of the party had recovered from their surprise.

A little below the camp there was a pool of deadwater in the river, and toward this Claude directed his steps, as noiselessly as possible.

When he picked up his gun, which was loaded with buck-shot, he had taken a couple of shells containing duck-shot, and, as he walked along, he substituted these for the buck-shot cartridges.

As he approached the pool he could hear the ducks

splashing in the water, and, stealing up to the bank of the river, he peered through the alders, and beheld seven black ducks not thirty feet distant. Bringing his gun to his shoulder, he took aim and fired his right-hand barrel; but his foot slipped on a rock as he pulled the trigger, and he never raised a feather.

At the noise of the report, which echoed, and reëchoed through the forest, the ducks gave a startled "Quack!" and, rising in a body, flew directly past him up river.

Growling at his awkwardness, he covered the flock with his left-hand barrel, and let them have it, and had the satisfaction of seeing three of the flock drop. Two of these were dead, and one badly wounded.

He rushed back to camp for a boat, and met all his friends but Adams and Maynard, with gun and rifles, ready for the sport.

"Did you hit any, Claude?"

"Yes, killed two, and wounded another, that I guess we can get. Come with me in the boat. The flock flew up river after I fired; didn't any of you see them?"

"No," replied Phil. "They must have been out of sight in the fog."

"You may as well return to camp; there are no more on the river!" and Claude, accompanied by Le Roy, jumped into the "Water Witch," and pushed down river, while the others returned to the tents.

Reaching the still-water, the two boys soon discovered the dead ducks floating in the middle of the river, but the wounded one was nowhere to be seen.

"Confound that little nigger! he has hid," said Claude, as he picked up the two dead birds.

"Let's search the banks," suggested Le Roy; "he cannot be a great ways off."

After hunting up and down both sides of the pool for about fifteen minutes, Le Roy caught sight of the duck's head just as it rose along-side of a clump of lily-pads, about two rods distant, and, taking quick aim, fired, making a splendid shot, the bullet going directly through its neck almost cutting its head off.

"By Jove! Tom, that was a good shot!" exclaimed his companion, and, paddling up to the dead bird, they secured it, and then turned toward the camp just as the cry for "breakfast" came floating down the river.

"Roast duck for dinner," said Claude, as the boys reached their friends, and he passed the three ducks to Maynard to take care of.

"Any beans left?" inquired Claude, as the party took seats at the table.

"Nary a bean," replied Adams. "You fellows eat like all possessed, yesterday. There are fried venison, baked potatoes, hot biscuit, coffee, and berries."

"Pass the venison, then. I'm not at all particular, as the horse-thief said when the regulators asked him whether he'd be hung or shot."

"Have a potato, Claude?" and Maynard passed the dish.

"Thank you, I don't care if I do."

"This is a rousing cup of coffee, Jack," remarked Phil, as he slowly sipped the aromatic beverage that was steaming before him.

"Yes, I made it extra strong this morning," replied Adams. "It was so cold and foggy I thought we would need something to brace us up."

"This fog is beginning to rise," said Phil, as he helped himself to the second biscuit, and looked anxiously around the table to see how many were left.

"Yes, it will be all clear, by ten o'clock," answered Claude.

"Those ducks were mighty fat," asserted Le Roy, as he harpooned another potato in the dish, and transferred it to his plate.

"Yes, they were," acknowledged Maynard, "and I must pick them after breakfast."

"Save the feathers to make a pillow of," suggested Wingate, laughingly.

"Speaking of ducks," laughed Phil, as if he had something funny on his mind, " reminds me of the story of the Irishman and his hens."

"Let's have it," said Adams.

"Reel it off," cried Claude.

"An Irishman in New York, who dabbled somewhat in politics, and who, like most of his countrymen, was conceited enough to think the machine could not be run without him, went down to City Hall one day to make a complaint about the sewerage. Going up to a clerk in one of the departments, he said, —

"'Me name is Muldoon. I lives in the sivinth war-r-d, and the water is in me cellar, and me hins will be drowned.'

"'Well, I can't help it,' returned the clerk.

"'I tell yees me name is Muldoon. I lives in the sivinth war-r-d, and I controls fifty voates, and the water is in me cellar, and me hins will be drowned. Ye moind that now, I controls fifty voates.'

"'But I can't help it; I have nothing to do with it,' protested the clerk.

"'But I tell yees I controls fifty voates,' continued Mr. Muldoon, earnestly, 'and the water is in me cellar, and me hins will be drowned.'

"'Bother your hens!' returned the clerk, 'we can't do anything for you here; the mayor is the man you want to see.'

"'The mare, is it?'

"'Yes.'

"'Faix, I'll go to him.'

"In about two weeks Mr. Muldoon turned up in the clerk's office again, and walking up to him began: —

"'Me name is Muldoon. I lives in the sivinth war-r-d, and I controls fifty voates, moind, and the water is in me cellar, and me hins will be drowned. Now just yees remimber that I controls fifty voates.'

"'Haven't you been here before with this complaint?' inquired the clerk, an amused smile playing across his face.

"'Faith, I hav.'

"'And I sent you to the mayor.'

"'Be gobbs, ye did.'

"'Did you go?'

"'I did that.'

"'And what did the mayor say?'

"'Faix, he said,' replied the Irishman, after a few moments' hesitation, 'he said, *Misther Muldoon, why doant yees kape duks?*'"

A shout of laughter rolled around the table as Phil concluded his story, and the boys left their seats.

It was now half-past nine, and the fog had all disappeared, with the exception of a few light banks that here and there clung to the lower part of the mountains.

A gentle breeze had sprung up, which scattered it far and wide, some of it ascending in spiral circles, and some stringing out into long lines of white, delicate mist that was driven before the wind, and breaking up, assumed a hundred eddying shapes. The sun was now shining brightly, and already its heat was beginning to be felt in a manner that suggested as hot a day as the boys had predicted.

"What is the programme for to-day?" inquired Phil, glancing from one to the other of his friends for an expression of opinion.

"You had better go fishing," replied Adams, who had heard the inquiry; "the trout are all gone; I just gave the last to Nap."

"Are there any berries left?" inquired Claude.

"Not one. We finished them this morning."

"If it were not for those roast ducks, we might go down to Little Boy's Falls and make a day of it."

"We can keep the ducks until evening, and have a late dinner," suggested Maynard.

"That is so," replied St. Clair. "Let's go, Claude. We can take a lunch with us, and get back early, and have a five o'clock dinner."

"We can get some berries down there, also," said St. Clair.

After talking the matter over a little longer, the boys came to the conclusion to go down to the falls, and try their luck with the trout, and also pick some berries. As it was barely possible that the three scoundrels who had attacked Phil and Claude might possibly stumble across the camp, both Adams and Maynard stopped at home, and agreed to have dinner ready at five.

Claude told them to load their fire-arms, and have them where they could lay hands on them quickly if they had occasion to use them.

At ten o'clock the expedition started, Claude, St. Claire, and Wingate in one boat, and Phil and Le Roy in the other, the boys carrying their guns and rifles, as well as their rods, and two pails, and some dishes in which to pick the berries.

They took it easy going down river, the heat discouraging any uncalled for exertion. They kept a sharp lookout for ducks or other game, but the only thing they saw was an otter. Claude and Wingate fired at it, but did not hit it, and, the animal diving, they did not see it again.

"You orter have hit that otter," declared Phil, calling out to Claude whose boat was ahead.

"How can you find courage to make such a miserable pun as that, Phil, this hot day?"

"His breakfast don't set well," answered Le Roy.

Floating along with the current, aided occasionally by a stroke of the oars or dip of the paddle, it was noon when they reached the falls, and drew out their boats.

"It is too hot to have very good luck fishing now," remarked Claude, as they took their things from the boats, "and we may as well eat our luncheon, then pick berries awhile. What do you say, fellows?"

"His friends expressed their willingness to adopt his suggestions, and, dipping up a pail of water from a spring near the river, they withdrew to the shade of a large spruce, and tested the lunch, which they declared was "about the cheese." Then they went to picking berries, and, although the sweat stood in great drops on their faces, they kept diligently at work for a couple of hours, securing fifteen quarts. The berries were large, and very plenty, and it did not take a great while to pick a quart.

"Phew! isn't it hot! I've had about enough of this kind of fun," declared Phil, and, looking at his watch, found that it was half-past two.

"Come, Claude, we've picked berries enough. Let's try and get a few trout," added Wingate.

"All right!" and Claude and Phil, who had the two pails of berries carried them to the boats, and their friends brought along the dippers in which they had been picking.

"We shall have to leave here by half-past three, if we are going to get to camp at five," said Claude, as he made a cast, and dropped his fly in the white water, near the foot of the falls, and let it float down to an eddy on the opposite shore.

"That is so," returned St. Clair, who was a short distance below him, "and we shall have to make a little more exertion than we did coming down this morning."

Just then a half-pounder rose to Claude's fly, and he struck him fairly, and soon had him on the bank, and popped him into his basket, shouting as he did so, "First fish!"

For an hour the boys kept up the sport with varying success; but in that time, only captured forty fish, the heat, and the bright glare of the sun being against them. Then, launching their boats, they rowed up the river, wading in the stream, and dragging the boats after them where the water was not deep enough to row.

"Morning and evening are the time to fish, if you want to take many," remarked St. Clair. "I'll get up early to-morrow morning, and go over to Rump Pond with you, Claude, if you say so?"

"I'll go with you if it is not foggy. They won't take hold a foggy morning. Will you go, Charlie?"

"Yes," replied Wingate, "if you and Andrew go. But I doubt if you wake up at four o'clock."

"I can if I charge my mind with it," replied St. Clair, decidedly.

After their friends had left them in the morning, Adams and Maynard did up the camp-work, and then Maynard taking two or three pieces of cold biscuit covered them with molasses, and walked up to Nap, who was rubbing his side against a tree, and, judging from the way he grunted, was having a most enjoyable scratch.

"Come, Napoleon, leave off scratching, and attend to business; sit up there now, like a little man," and Maynard motioned him to sit up on his haunches.

The bear, seeing the bread and molasses, stopped rubbing, and standing up on his hind legs, put his fore-paws on his teacher's shoulders, almost knocking him over, while he stuck out his tongue, and fairly laughed, as he tried to possess himself of the coveted sweet morsels in Maynard's hands.

"Down, Nap, down; you are taking too much liberty," said Maynard, as he rapped him under the chin.

"Look out, Frank!" called Adams from one of the hammocks, where he was sitting; "that bear will leave his marks on you one of these days. I wouldn't fool around him the way you do for fifty dollars."

"Pooh! he's as harmless as a kitten, if you only treat him decently"; then turning to the bear, "Now, Nap, sit down. There, that is right. Now lift up your fore-paws and straighten up," and Maynard took hold of one of his paws as he would that of a dog, and made him take the same position as a dog does in begging. "Now keep quiet," and he placed one of the pieces of bread, molasses-side up, on the bear's nose. The moment Nap smelt it, however, he tossed it on the ground and gobbled it up before Maynard could prevent him.

A shout of laughter from Adams, who was an interested spectator, greeted this performance.

"Confound you, you villain! What do you mean? Take that!" and the teacher gave his pupil a rap on the side of the head. "Sit up there, now! if you don't I'll give you a taste of an alder stick."

The bear resumed his former position, running out his tongue, and winking his little brown eyes, and looking at Maynard with a comical glance, as if he understood what he had done, and gloried in it.

"He's laughing at you, Frank," said Adams, who had caught the look on the bear's face, and was chuckling at his friend's discomfiture.

"I'll make him laugh the other side of his face, if he don't face the music," declared Maynard, laughing a little in spite of himself at the bear's droll appearance.

"'If at first you don't succeed, try, try again,'" chanted the cook from the hammock.

"Now then, make ready," said Maynard, as he placed another piece of bread on Nap's nose. "Take aim, fire!" and he made a quick upward motion with his hand in front of the bear's face.

This time Nap came to the scratch, and tossing the bread from his nose into the air, caught it handsomely in his mouth as it came down. Then Maynard patted him on the head, and rubbed his nose, while Nap reached for another piece of his favorite food.

But the boy made him sit up as before, and throw the bread from his nose, and catch it, the bear repeating this performance several times without once making a miss.

"There, old man, you've done well," said Maynard, "and when the fellows come back I'll give you a pint of berries, if they bring any"; and he patted Nap on the head, and left him to his own diversion.

"I tell you what it is, Jack, that bear will do credit to his training by the time we get him home said Maynard, as he walked over to the hammock, and dexterously tipped his friend out of it.

"Yes, if you ever get him there," returned Adams, as he picked himself up. "I want you to understand, young man, that you are showing disrespect to your superiors when you turn the cook out of a hammock," and Adams regained his place, this time keeping a wary eye on Frank.

"It's a thundering hot day," remarked Maynard, as he threw himself into the other hammock, and began idly swinging to and fro.

"I haven't heard any thunder," replied Adams.

"Well, you may before night."

"I don't believe the fellows will catch many trout, do you?"

"No; I should not think they would bite worth a cent to-day."

"I wish we had something to do," said Adams. "It is dull business staying in camp all day."

"I'll tell you something that ought to be done, and that is, build a shanty over that stove, and let's set about it," urged Maynard as he left his hammock and picked up an axe. "It is very disagreeable cooking in that stove on a rainy day, and we shall not always have such fine weather as we have been having. Why, there have only been two or three rainy days since we left Colebrook."

"How shall we do it?" queried Adams.

"Make a skeleton frame of poles, and then cover it with birch bark and cedar splits."

"All right; you boss the job, and I'll help you do the work."

"Take the other axe, then, and follow me."

The boys went a short distance from camp, and cut eight small maples, and trimmed them off, leaving a crotch at one end of each; four of these sticks were eight feet long, the others six. Adams carried these to camp, while Maynard cut four more about seven feet in length, leaving on two of them a short piece of limb about two inches long.

Joining his friend they set the four long, crotched sticks firmly in the ground, driving them down a foot. They were set two together, the crotches at right angles, and seven feet apart. The other four were then set the same way, and the same distance from each other, and in line. These constituted the posts, and the back ones being a foot shorter than those in front gave a pitch to the roof. Maynard then took the four he had cut last, and laid the two straight ones at the front and back in the crotches left to receive them, while the other two, with the little limb or hook on them, he placed on the sides, the bit of limb catching in the crotches, and preventing them from slipping back, these four sticks being the plates.

The boys now cut five straight spruce poles, seven feet and a half long, for rafters, and placing them on the plate, a foot apart, tied them firmly into their places with marline.

"The sides and back will be the worst part of the job," remarked the boss carpenter, as he stood scratching his head and wiping the perspiration from his brow, while he gazed at the frame of his building with evident satisfaction.

"What next?" inquired the assistant.

"We must cut a lot of small poles, about three inches through, and bring them here, and make them the right length, then we can sharpen an end of each, and drive them down, setting them just as close together as they will stand. Then we can get some birch-bark, and cover them."

"But how can we fasten the bark on?"

"Stick your knife blade through it into each post, then drive in a wooden peg."

"Yes, I guess that will do it, Frank. But look here, old fellow, what is going to hold the top of those posts, or pickets, or whatever you call them in line? They will be all wabble-jawed."

"You notice the rafters project over the plate?"

"Yes."

"After we close up one of the sides with a row of posts, we will lay a stick outside of them on the rafters at the top, and tie it to the plate. By letting the posts run three or four inches above the rafters we can do it. Don't you see?"

"Yes, I do now. You are quite a genius, Frank."

The boys then busied themselves for the next two hours in cutting and trimming their posts, and, when they had carried them all to the camp, they were surprised to find it was two o'clock.

"I thought there was an aching void in my stomach," declared Adams, when he had looked at his watch; "let's have something to eat, Frank"; and the boys sat down to their lunch.

"I find I am hungry myself," said Maynard, as they began to eat.

"I can only help you until three o'clock," observed Adams; "I shall have to get those ducks in to roast then."

"That is so. However, I will do the best I can alone after you leave me, until you want me to help you. We can't finish it to-day, anyhow, but we can to-morrow."

After lunch the boys finished one side, and then Adams had to attend to his cooking. At four o'clock he called Maynard to assist him, who, in the meantime, had finished the other side of the shanty, leaving the back and roof to complete.

The cook and his assistant now turned in earnest to the dinner, and had the table set and everything ready to serve at ten minutes past five, at which time they heard voices, and a moment later the fellows appeared with their trout and berries.

"Have some of those berries for supper, will you, Adams? By Jove! we worked hard enough to get them"; and Phil passed the pails to the cook, while the assistant took charge of the trout.

"All right!" replied Adams; "supper is ready as soon as you are."

"We will be there as soon as we wash"; and in five minutes the party were seated at the table intent upon demolishing the good things that Adams and Maynard had prepared for them.

"What in Jerusalem is that?" queried Claude, as he caught sight of the shanty; "a house for Nap and Lightfoot?"

"Not much," replied Maynard, and he explained to his friends what he and Adams had been doing.

"That's a good idea," asserted Claude; "we are liable to have three or four rainy days in succession before the month is out, and it will be much more comfortable cooking under cover such days than it will out doors; and, although I am out of the cooking for the rest of the trip, I appreciate your thoughtfulness, and you deserve the thanks of the crowd."

CHAPTER IX.

An Early Turn-out. — A Visit to Rump Pond. — Phenomenal Fishing. — Two at a Time. — A Whale. — A Sudden Dive. — Quick Retribution. — The Two Bathers. — Capture of the Large Fish. — Return to Camp. — A Visit to the Cave. — The Storm. — Buried Alive. — Short Rations. — A Hard Bed.

It was scarcely light Tuesday morning when St. Clair, awaking suddenly, sat up, and began rubbing his eyes to get them wide open. After a moment he reached over and shook Claude and Wingate, who were lying near him.

"Come," he called, "it is daylight, and we must be moving, if we are going over to the pond."

"Confound the pond! I'm as sleepy as a night-watchman. What is the use of starting so early?" and Wingate stretched and yawned as if he had half a mind to turn over and go to sleep again.

"Don't be lazy, Charlie," said Claude, as he arose and began dressing; "you know we promised to go; and Andrew has kept his word in waking up, and I shouldn't be surprised if we had some fine fishing this morning."

Thus importuned, Wingate made a virtue of necessity, and the three boys were soon dressed and out-of-doors. They found the air cool and bracing, and the sky bid fair to give them a pleasant day.

Taking their rods and nets, they went through the woods to the pond, following a line the boys had spotted when they were over there before. The weeds, bushes, and trees were wet with dew, and the walking, on that account, was very disagreeable, and when the party reached the pond and launched the boat they were nearly wet through in some places, from pushing against the damp underbrush.

Rowing to the outlet they stopped the boat and began casting. Almost as soon as their flies touched the water several trout arose, and simultaneously the three friends struck their first fish. All of them, however, were small, neither one running over half a pound. These were successfully landed, and again the flies were dropped on the water, and again the trout rose; Claude this time hooking two, one being about a quarter of a pound in weight, while the other would go fully three-quarters of a pound.

The boys now began to get excited, as the sport continued to increase. Trout after trout was captured, and still there was no diminution in the biting.

"Great Scott! I've hooked a whale!" suddenly exclaimed Wingate, with a flush of excitement, as his line ran rapidly out, and the slender rod bent almost double.

"Be careful how you play him!" cried Claude, who just then brought in a pound fish, and, laying aside his rod, took the dip-net, and anxiously watched his friend's movements.

St. Clair also became too much interested in the battle to fish himself; and, reeling in his line, and two small trout at the same time, deposited the fish in the boat, and laid his rod alongside of Claude's. Then, taking the paddle, he sat ready to give the boat a turn should an emergency require.

"Great Cæsar's ghost! the water is alive with them!" exclaimed Claude, as he noticed several follow up the two fish that St. Clair had hooked, while others were breaking all around them.

"Look out, old man!" yelled St. Clair. "Reel in lively now; your fish has turned and is heading for the boat."

"I know it," responded his friend, "you keep the boat clear of him, if you can; if he goes under it I shall lose him."

The trout came in a bee-line toward the centre of the boat, Wingate reeling in as fast as he could. Just as the fish was about to pass under the light craft St. Clair, with a dexterous movement of the paddle, swung the boat around, and the fish passed by the end of it, and Wingate was obliged to give him line once more.

And now a still more exciting scene in the act was introduced. The fish already hooked was on the lower fly, and as he shot by the boys, another trout, larger than any they had yet seen in the pond made a snap for the upper fly, which was dangling along on the surface of the water, and securely hooked himself. This complicated matters considerably, and the lucky fisherman was in an agony of fear, thinking his rod was gone up for a certainty. Both trout were lively, and full of game, and would sometimes make a rush in opposite directions, and if his leader had not been an unusually good piece of gut, it would certainly have parted in the frantic struggles of the frightened fish to free themselves.

After St. Clair had swung the boat to all points of the compass to keep the trout from going under it, they stilled down a little, and Wingate reeled in gently, and had nearly coaxed them within reach of the landing-net, when they started off again, like a whale who has just been struck by a harpoon, and reeled out seventy-five feet of line with such celerity, that the boys thought they would take it all. This disaster did not happen, however, for the trout suddenly stopped, and went to bottom, where they sulked for half an hour, before Wingate was enabled to bring them to the surface again.

They were not so vicious now, and, after fifteen minutes of good management on the part of the plucky young fisherman, whose arms and wrists ached so badly he could scarcely hold his rod, he worked them near enough to the boat for Claude to pass the landing-net under them. His friend reached out with the net, and had it fairly under the fish, and was just about to lift them out of the water, when St. Clair, who had become too excited to sit still, arose to his feet, and, as he did so, tipped the boat, with a jerk that threw him back into his seat, and pitched Claude head-first into the pond, still holding fast to the net.

"What in thunder are you up to?" exclaimed Wingate, who had come very near following Claude, surprised by his friend's disappearance.

"It was an accident—I didn't mean to—look out for your trout!" replied St. Clair in a breath, as the fish, frightened by the splash near them, started off again with a rush, evidently thinking some leviathan of their own species was about to swallow them.

In a moment Claude came to the surface, sputtering and blowing the water from his mouth and nose, and struck out for the boat.

"I hope you haven't lost those trout," he called, as soon as he could speak.

"No, they are on yet," replied Wingate, who was trying to check them.

"Take this landing-net, will you, St. Clair?" called Claude, swimming to the boat.

St. Clair swung the stern of the boat around towards his friend, and grasped hold of the landing-net. Just as he obtained a good grip on it, Claude gave his end a sudden jerk, and in a second St. Clair had also taken a header into the pond, while the violent rocking of the boat caused Wingate to take a seat in the centre of the craft a little harder than he meant to. As he dropped, his knuckles struck so hard on the gunwale of the boat that he involuntarily loosened his grasp on the rod, and a second later the trout were towing it around the pond.

"Now you are as wet as I am!" cried Claude, gleefully, as St. Clair rose to the surface, puffing and blowing like a grampus.

"That was a mean trick, Claude!" responded Andrew with a laugh, as, still grasping the net, he swam with his friend toward the boat.

"I don't see anything mean about it," retorted Claude; "I owed you one, and I paid it, — that was all."

"I should think both of you were crazy," called back Wingate, who had picked up himself and the paddle at the same time, and was chasing his rod. "If I lose these trout I'll make you both swim ashore."

"That wouldn't be any hardship," responded Claude.

"Not a bit," echoed Andrew.

A few moments' paddling enabled Wingate to overtake, and secure his rod, and, as the fish were now quiet, he put a little strain upon them, and found they would bear it.

"Hurry up, fellows!" he called to his friends; "I think we can net the trout now."

"Coming as fast as possible," returned Claude. "It's heavy swimming with your clothes on."

The two swimmers soon reached the boat; and, while Claude and Wingate steadied her, St. Clair passed in the landing net, and climbed in over the bow, then assisted Claude to get in.

Wingate now succeeded in getting the two trout within reach of the landing-net once more, and Claude slipped it under the fish, and a moment later they were in the boat, — a prize that any angler might well be proud of. Taking a pair of small scales from his pocket, Wingate weighed each fish separately, and found that one weighed two pounds, and the other two and three-quarters, making four and three-quarters pounds of trout at one catch, and the boys cheered at the result.

"The fun is over, fellows," remarked St. Clair, "and we must be getting back to camp. I begin to feel chilly."

"So do I, and the sooner we get on some dry clothing, the less likelihood of taking cold," and Claude, seizing the oars, gave a few vigorous strokes that sent the boat spinning to the shore.

They had left their baskets at camp, and, after taking the boat carefully from the water, cut some sticks, and strung their fish, and then started at a brisk pace for their tent.

It was eight o'clock when they walked into camp, and found their friends waiting breakfast for them. Beside the two large trout, they had brought in ninety small ones, a few of which, however, run as high as a pound each, and their companions first congratulated them on their success, and then shouted with surprise, as they caught sight of the two larger trout.

"Jupiter and Saturn!" exclaimed the cook, "you did not find those trout in Rump Pond, did you?"

"Nowhere else," retorted Wingate.

"How much do they weigh?" asked Maynard.

"One weighs two, and the other two and three-quarters."

"They are beauties," said Phil, as he stepped up to admire them.

"What is the matter with you and St. Clair?" inquired Adams, addressing Claude. "You look wet."

"No, only a trifle damp," laughed the leader of the party.

"Been into the pond?" queried LeRoy with a smile on his face.

"Ask Wingate," returned Claude. "I am going to change my clothes, and then I'll be ready to eat as much breakfast as any fellow in the party."

"You were always ready to do that," responded St. Clair, as he followed Claude to the tent, also anxious to exchange his wet clothes for dry ones.

"Did your boat capsize, Wingate?" asked the cook, as his two wet friends disappeared in the tent.

"No," with a laugh as he recalled the comical circumstance; "but it came pretty near it."

"How did they get wet, then?"

"I'll tell you"; and, still chuckling at the remembrance, Wingate related the story, and when he reached the point, where Claude caused St. Clair to quickly take such a header, they roared until the woods resounded with their laughter, and causing Nap to turn his head toward them and listen, while Lightfoot gazed in their direction with astonishment.

"Come, Adams, bring on your breakfast," called Claude, as he and St. Clair emerged from the tent in their dry clothing; "I feel fairly faint, I'm so hungry."

"It gives a fellow an appetite to turn out at four o'clock in the morning," added St. Clair, as the boys took seats at the table, where they were immediately joined by the rest of the company.

"What is the order of the day? what are we going to do?" queried Phil with a comprehensive glance around the table.

"Eat," replied Wingate, with a grin, as he sweetened his coffee.

"Nonsense; I mean where are we going?"

"Why, don't you say what you mean, then," bantered St. Clair.

"Haven't I?"

"I don't know what you fellows are going to do," said Adams; "but Maynard and I have concluded to stay at camp, and finish our shanty."

"A good idea," returned Phil.

"I'll tell you what I propose, fellows," said Claude. "An excursion to that cave which you visited when Phil and I were away."

"Yes, boys, let's pay it a visit, and see if we can't find

another bat," and Phil laughed at the remembrance of the bat incident.

"That will suit me," added Wingate, "as well as anything. It's going to be a little cooler to-day, and it will be a good time to take it in."

"I should like to go there again, first-rate," declared Le Roy.

"And I too," said St. Clair.

"How pleasant it is, eating out-doors!" remarked Maynard.

"Yes, it is," returned Claude; "and we may as well enjoy it while we can, for we shall have some rainy days before long, when we shall be obliged to eat in our tent."

"I suppose you will take a lunch with you?" and Adams looked inquiringly at his friends.

"Yes," answered Claude; "as soon as breakfast is over, put it up."

"And remember," added Phil; "you have five hungry fellows to provide for."

"We had better take a lantern with us this time," suggested Le Roy.

"Yes, we'll take two," added Phil, "the more light we have, the better."

At half-past nine the exploring party, as Claude called it, started. Each one carried their fire-arm, and, in addition to these, an axe, two lanterns, and a pail of lunch were distributed among them.

Adams and Maynard ferried them across the river, and the party struck out for the mountain, following, as nearly as possible, the same route that the boys had passed over in their former visit.

About half-way to the cave, while crossing a logging-road, they were fortunate enough to flush a large flock of partridges, and they secured seven of them. Not wishing to be bothered with the birds on their tramp, they tied them together, and hung them to the limb of a spruce, to await their return.

They reached the cave at half-past twelve, and took their lunch at the entrance. Then, lighting the lanterns, they crawled into the passage, and worked their way along until they reached the point where they were able to walk, and then rose to their feet.

As they strode along, the gleam from their lanterns penetrated the darkness ahead of them, while the walls of the passage echoed to their voices and tread.

"I wonder who could have done this," remarked Claude, "it must have been a long, hard job."

"Some miner I think," replied Le Roy. "We found a thin vein of silver in one of the walls," and several croppings of lead.

"A lead mine would not pay way up here in the woods, even if a large amount of it could be found. The transportation of the ore out to where it could be marketed would eat up all the profits of mining," said Phil.

"Probably the men, whoever they were, expected to find gold," added St. Clair.

"Suppose we should find a bear in here?" and Wingate looked a little uneasy at the thought.

"Bah! We shall not have any such luck," declared Claude. "It is not time for bears to begin to den up yet. They are roaming about the country now, subsisting on berries, and hunting for bee's nests. A month or six weeks later, I should think, there might be some likelihood of it, but not now."

"Well, here we are," said Le Roy, who was in advance, as he entered the cave, and flashed his lantern around the apartment.

"Why, it's a large cave!" and Claude glanced about. "It must be fifty feet square."

"It is not very high, though," added Phil. "It can't be over ten feet."

"Just about that," replied Claude, glancing at the roof.

St. Clair, who held one of the lanterns, now paced across the cave, and, returning, said he made it just sixty feet.

"I would like to know if that confounded bat is here?" queried Le Roy, peering around at the walls.

At this the boys laughed, and, flashing the lanterns about, looked in every direction, but could see no sign of life.

"I guess you frightened the bat as badly as he frightened you," chuckled Phil.

"Where is the skeleton?" inquired Claude.

"In this corner," and St. Clair led the way to the mass of bones.

The boys inspected and theorized over them for some time, and then Le Roy called the attention of Claude and Phil to the silver and lead.

"Let's have some souvenirs of this place, fellows," proposed Claude, and, taking the axe, he knocked off some pieces of the ore containing both silver and lead. He distributed these among his companions, and also pocketed two pieces for Adams and Maynard, thinking they might like to have them.

"When we get home we ought to form a company, and call it the Parmachence Silver Mining Company, and come up here and work this mine," said Le Roy.

"Yes, and starve to death in the attempt, as perhaps yonder poor fellow did," retorted Claude.

"There is one good thing about this cave," asserted Phil; "it's clean and dry."

"Yes," replied Wingate; "it would make a splendid home for some dime-novel brigand, if there were only any people up here for him to rob."

"Right you are," returned Claude, "and with two or three well-armed companions he could 'hold the fort' against a whole regiment."

As the boys had not examined the whole of the walls carefully on their former visit, they now did so, and were rewarded by finding several other places where thin veins of silver and outcroppings of lead were discernible.

Wingate excited them all by shouting that he had found some gold, and the boys rushed to where he was sharply examining a place in the wall, holding the lantern close to it and trying to dig out some with his knife.

"Where's your gold?" asked Le Roy, as the party gathered eagerly around Wingate.

"Here! Don't you see it?"

Le Roy gazed at the yellowish rock and smiled as he said: —

"You won't get rich out of that stuff, Charlie. Its nothing but iron pyrites. Many a green miner has been sold by that same article."

"It's time we were getting out of here," asserted Claude, holding his watch to the lantern Wingate carried; "it's three o'clock."

"By gracious! how the time flies up here!" remarked Phil. "The days slide away as if they were greased."

"Go ahead, Wingate, with your lantern," said St. Clair, "and I'll bring up the rear with mine, and then we can all see."

"How far do you suppose it is from the top of the cave to the outside of the mountain, Claude?"

"I don't know, Phil. The path we came in by has a pretty heavy descent all the way, and the mountain slopes upward. It may be a hundred feet for all I know."

"Come along, fellows," cried Wingate, as he started up the passage-way.

The boys made good progress until they reached that part of the tunnel where they had to crawl on their hands and knees, and then their advance was necessarily slow. They finally reached the sharp turn before spoken of as being about six feet from the entrance, and, swinging around this became aware that a frightful tempest was going on outside, and which they now heard for the first time.

The rain poured in torrents, the lightning flashed into the entrance with a brilliancy that momentarily blinded them, and the thunder reverberated above them like the roar of cannon, and seemed fairly to shake the mountain.

"Phew!" cried Wingate, as he crawled within three feet of the hole, and felt the rain blown into his face, "there's an awful row going on outside, I think we

View of Kennabago Lake from Snowman's Point.

had better stay where we are awhile, and see if the storm don't let up some presently. It's raining cats and dogs now."

"That is the best thing we can do," replied Claude, who was next behind Wingate. "Probably this is only a shower, and will pass over in a half an hour or so."

"We shall have to get back around the turn in the passage; the rain is coming in here," and Wingate called Claude's attention to a small stream that had begun to form under him, and was running down the path.

Just then a furious gust of wind swept into the passage with a howl, and extinguished Wingate's lantern, beside drenching him with rain.

"Tell the boys to back down the path, Claude, I can't stand this," and Wingate made a lively backward movement to get out of the reach of the rain and wind, which seemed raw and chilly, in spite of the thunder and lightning.

Claude did as Wingate asked, but the backward movement of the party was suddenly stopped by an unusual heavy clap of thunder, accompanied by another flash of lightning that fairly seemed to burn them, it was so sharp. At the same moment a roar and crash, that sounded above the din of the tempest, startled and frightened the boys, and it seemed to them as if the mountain was being torn in pieces. The roar and crash were followed by a grinding and thumping noise, and immediately after the entrance of the cave was darkened.

"For Heaven's sake, what was that?" shouted Le Roy, who, being around the turn, had heard the noise, but could not guess the cause. "Claude, Wingate," he called, "are either of you hurt?"

"No, we are all right," cried Wingate; "but, O boys!" and there was a tremor in his voice, "a fearful thing has happened; we are buried alive!"

"*Buried alive?*" cried the boys with a shout that echoed and reëchoed down the dark passage-way behind them.

"*Yes, buried alive!*"

For the second time Wingate made this appalling announcement, and then a most painful silence ensued, in marked contrast to the horrible din outside.

For a few moments the boys were completely overwhelmed with the bitterness of the situation. Then they rallied from the shock, and began thinking how they could best extricate themselves from the most unfortunate dilemma in which they found themselves placed. Finally, Claude broke the oppressive silence.

"What do you think has happened, Wingate? Has there been an earthquake?"

"The Lord alone knows, for I don't. Wait a moment until I light my lantern again, and I will try and find out what the trouble is. All I know now is the entrance to the passage is closed."

Lighting his lantern Wingate crawled as near the entrance as he could get, closely followed by Claude. After a few moments' investigation he became convinced that a large boulder had been loosened from its bed by the storm, and had rolled down the mountain, lodging in a hollow in front of the entrance of the cave, and completely covering up the hole, with the exception of two small places each side of the passage-way, perhaps four inches in circumference, and through these a dull streak of daylight appeared.

He announced his discovery to his companions, who sent up a wail of regret at the apparent hopelessness of their position.

"Let me take a look at things, will you?" said Claude, and Wingate backed on his hands and knees to a place where Claude could pass him, the entrance to the passage being so narrow that only one could enter at a time.

Claude took Wingate's lantern, and crawled to where the boulder lay at the mouth of the passage, and examined the surroundings thoroughly. He found the bottom and top, as well as both sides, composed of solid ledge, that did not offer the slightest chance for excavation.

Setting the lantern down he passed his hands through the holes each side of the passage, and felt about on the outside to see if there were any broken rocks under or near the boulder that imprisoned them.

He found quite a number of loose stones, but they were all too heavy for him to move with one hand, and any hopes that he had formed of being able to dig themselves out from the inside were thus nipped in the bud.

"A bad egg!" he muttered to himself. "By Jove! we are in a tight place, and no mistake about it. I'd give a hundred dollars for a keg of powder!"

"What do you think of it, Claude?" asked Wingate, who had crawled up to his friend just as he had finished his soliloquy.

"It looks bad. I don't see as we can help ourselves a particle."

"That was the way it struck me."

"Crawl back, will you, Wingate? and we'll return to the cave and talk it over."

The boys retreated to the apartment they had lately left, with very different feelings from those with which they had entered it, and Claude blew out the lantern he carried, as they grouped around him, remarking that they had better save what light they could, and that one lantern would do to talk by.

"Well, Claude, how are we going to get out?" inquired Le Roy.

"That's a conundrum that I don't know whether I can answer or not. Of one thing, however, I am convinced, — that whatever help we have must come from the outside. We can do nothing toward freeing ourselves."

"True as gospel!" echoed Wingate.

"This is a nice kettle of fish!" added Phil. "Don't I wish I was at camp?"

"We may as well take it easy, fellows," said Claude, as he sat down on the floor of the apartment and leaned back against the wall, the other boys seating themselves near him. "Things are not so bad as they might be, for the cave is dry and warm, and the air here is not bad, and that is so much in our favor."

"That's all very well," remarked St. Clair; "but how are we going to get out of this coop? — that is what I should like to know."

"I can see only one way," returned Claude, "and that is, to stay here until Adams and Maynard come to look us up, which they probably will do to-morrow morning."

"That's a charming prospect!" responded Phil; "nothing to eat, and a stone floor for a mattress!"

"Who has the lunch-pail?" inquired Claude.

"I have," answered Le Roy.

"Anything in it?"

"Hold your lantern, St. Clair, and I will see."

St. Clair did as directed, and Le Roy reported that there were three doughnuts, two biscuit, and a slice of meat.

"We shall have to divide that as fairly as we can at supper-time," said Claude, "for it is all we shall get until sometime to-morrow. It is four o'clock, now," glancing at his watch, by the aid of St. Clair's lantern, "and we can wait until seven before we eat."

"But, suppose we don't get anything to eat to-morrow?" and Phil gazed at Claude anxiously.

"Then we shall have to do without it, and draw our belts a little tighter," replied the leader, forcing a smile.

"What troubles me most," said Wingate, who had been thinking over their position, "is the fact that after the boys come here, as they undoubtedly will, to-morrow forenoon, they may not be able to get that rock away from the mouth of the passage-way. It may weigh two or three tons for all we know, and if they can't move it, we *are* in a nice pickle."

"I don't imagine they can wink it by main force. They will have to try science. If there are loose rocks outside of it, or under it, they will have to dig them away in front, and from underneath, until it will roll down the mountain of itself, or pry it away with levers. Anyhow," continued Claude, brightening up, "we shall not starve, for there are two small holes,—one each side of the rock,—and through these the boys can pass us some grub."

"Suppose they can't move it at all," remarked St. Clair.

"Then one of them will have to go down to Flint's camp, and get help enough to come up here and get the stone away, while the other keeps us from starving."

"Don't you suppose they will look us up to-night?" inquired Phil.

"No, sir; I don't. In the first place they would not give us up at camp before nine or ten o'clock; and in the second, we have both the lanterns, and they could never find their way here in the dark."

"That's so; I forgot we had both the lanterns."

"And, speaking of lanterns," continued Claude, "we had better put this one out. We can talk just as well in the dark, and we can light it when we eat. We may need the light more to-morrow than we do to-night."

The lantern was extinguished, and the boys sat talking in the midnight gloom, their voices echoing strangely through the stone vault. Several schemes for releasing themselves were proposed, but each one was given up as impracticable, and, after talking for several hours, Claude lit a match, and found it was quarter to seven.

"Let's have our supper, fellows," he remarked, adding jocosely, "it won't require much time to eat it;" and, taking the lunch-pail he divided its contents as evenly as possible among his comrades.

"By gracious! Shouldn't I like a drink of water? I'm half choked!" cried Wingate as he munched a piece of dry biscuit.

"And so am I," echoed his friend. When they had eaten the little food that remained from their dinner Claude announced his intention of going up to the entrance before he blew out the lantern, and see if the weather had cleared up.

His friends accompanied him, and, when he reached the big boulder that formed their prison door, he listened with his ear to one of the holes on the side, and found the rain was still coming down hard, while the wind blew a gale. The thunder and lightning had stopped, however, but the air that came in through the cracks seemed a great deal colder than it had during the day. As he backed away from the rock he was delighted to find a little stream of water, that trickled down on the back side of it, filling a small hollow on the bottom of the passage, and then flowing down the path. Although he had not mentioned it he was fully as thirsty as his companions, and, lying flat, he put his lips to the small, cup-like orifice, and soon appeased his thirst.

"Is it storming?" asked Phil, a short distance behind him.

"Yes; the wind is blowing hard, and the rain is coming down lively. It don't thunder or lighten any. But let me get back; I have found some water here, and just had a good drink, and you had better all fill up, for it is only surface water, and we shall lose it as soon as the rain is over."

His friends required no urging, for they all felt as if

their mouths were parched, although they had only been without water about six hours.

Claude left the lantern so the next one could see, and backing down the passage to where two could pass, Phil went by him, and took a drink, and one after another the remaining three boys assuaged their thirst, when all returned to the cave.

The light was once more extinguished, and the boys amused themselves in various ways for the next three hours, and then Claude remarked, "that he did not know if he could sleep any, but he was going to try it, anyway," and, stretching out on the hard floor, with his head pillowed on his arm, he tried to woo the drowsy god, but with indifferent success. The rest of the party concluded they would try it also, and a deathly stillness reigned throughout the apartment, the sound of the storm not reaching the cave, embowelled as it was in the mountain.

"Call me in time to build the fire in the morning, will you, Claude?" said Phil, as he shut his eyes, and tried to pick out a soft place in the rock on which to lay his bones.

"I will if you want me to," and, with a laugh, "if you build the fire, I'll get breakfast."

"What good Samaritans, you are! You won't leave any work for the rest of us," and Wingate, who was lying on his right side, reached under and picked out a stone the size of an egg, that had been digging into his ribs for two or three minutes, and then drew himself into a heap and quieted down.

And in these snug quarters — I might say too snug — we leave them, and return to the camp.

CHAPTER X.

The Kitchen Finished. — A Terrible Storm. — Thunder and Lightning. — Killing Time. — The Two Strangers. — Pork and Hardtack. — Building a Fire Under Difficulties. — A Rainy Night. — Where are the Boys? — Determination of Maynard to Seek them in the Morning.

AFTER their friends had left them, Adams and Maynard cleared up the dishes and attended to their other camp duties, and about eleven o'clock began to finish the shanty. They worked on it hard, stopping only a few moments at noon to take a cold lunch; and at two o'clock, when the first mutterings of the storm reached them, they had it completed, and the stove set up in it.

Before the tempest broke upon them they succeeded in getting all of the cooking utensils under the shanty, with several armfuls of dry wood, and then moved the dining-table into the tent.

The prelude to the storm was a mass of black clouds driving rapidly across the sky, dropping down so as to cover the mountain tops. Then a heavy roar of thunder, at first distant, but gradually nearing them, accompanied by occasional flashes of lightning. Then came the rain. Slowly at first, in large drops, then swifter, until it resembled a flood, and the thunder and lightning became almost continuous.

The boys moved swiftly around the camp, putting

different articles under shelter, and getting things in order until the force of the rain compelled them to suspend operations, and they took refuge in the tent, where, throwing themselves on their blankets, they listened to the storm that howled through the trees with a fury that threatened to level some of them before it was over.

The first onset of the storm was the worst, because the wind came in gusts, some of which tried hard to upset the tents; but the boys had them well secured, and, although the canvas shook and flapped, the numerous pins firmly driven into the ground held them in place.

After fifteen or twenty minutes had passed the wind settled down into a steady blow; but for an hour or more the lightning flashed with an unearthly brilliancy, and the thunder roared with a noise that was almost deafening. There was no hold-up to the rain, however, if we may except an occasional slackening, when Adams would remark, "that it had merely let go for a moment to get a better hold."

The thoughts of the boys naturally turned to their friends, and, after sitting silent for some time, Maynard glanced at his watch and said, —

"Half-past two; it's about time the fellows were starting for camp."

"They are fools if they start in this rain," declared Adams.

"That cave is dry and warm, and they'll stay in it until the storm is over. The rain will probably stop in an hour or two."

"Don't look much like it now. By Jove! that flash

of lightning made me cringe. I don't like this fireworks part of the business"; and Maynard turned a shade paler as the thunder crashed apparently directly over their tent.

"No, sir," responded Adams; "you won't catch them frogging it through the woods in this storm. I shouldn't mind the rain so much, but this thunder and lightning is terrific."

"A ducking won't hurt anybody; but, as you say, I don't like the lightning. It seems to me it is a great deal sharper than any I ever saw at home."

"Let me see, — how long were we coming from the cave the day you and I went?"

"About three hours."

"Then we may look for the fellows about three hours after the rain stops."

"I suppose so."

"But suppose it don't stop?"

"Then it will be doubtful what time they will return. But I don't believe it will rain all the afternoon."

"Nor I."

"I tell you what it is, Jack, this is kind of rough on Nap and Lightfoot."

"Right you are, Frank. But we can't help it any, and I suppose they are used to getting wet."

"The eagles are all right. Their box will keep the most of it off of them."

"That's so."

"Lucky we finished that cooking-shanty before this storm. It would have been a nice job getting supper out-doors to-night if this rain holds on."

"We should have looked like a couple of drowned rats before we had finished."

"Let's play dominos, Jack. I don't feel like reading, and that will help us pass away the time."

"All right, Frank, I'll play awhile, although, to tell you the truth, I don't care two cents for the game."

"Don't you? I like it pretty well."

Maynard took a box of dominos from his valise, and, sitting up to the table, they began to play. An hour passed by in this manner, the games being quite evenly divided, and then Adams concluded he had played as long as he wished; and the boys left the table, and peeked out of the tent to see how things looked.

The thunder and lightning had stopped; but the rain still continued to fall, and the wind blew hard, but not quite as strong as when the storm began.

Pools of water had gathered on the ground near the tent, and the sullen roar of rushing water told the boys that the river was fast rising.

"It's going to be a nasty night if this storm holds on, and don't you forget it," said Maynard, with emphasis, as the boys gazed at the dismal prospect outside.

"Yes, and it's after four o'clock, now. I'll bet the fellows are on their way home. They wouldn't stay there all night, for they will not have anything to eat."

"I don't believe they would stay if they had. Claude knows we should be expecting them, and would feel worried if they did not put in an appearance."

"That is so. No doubt they will come; but I shall not look for them before seven o'clock. Had we better wait until they come before we eat our supper?"

"I say not. Let us eat ours about six o'clock, and then we will do what we can, when they come, to make them comfortable. I tell you it will be a mean tramp for them."

"You are right, my boy!" and Adams threw himself down on the blankets once more, where he was joined by Maynard, and they laid and talked for some time about their absent friends.

"I'm getting tired of this. It is slow work, doing nothing," remarked Maynard, after a while. "I guess I will try and build a camp-fire, and then, if the rain holds up, by the time the boys get back they can dry their clothing!" and, rising with a yawn, he put on his rubber-coat, and went into the store-tent for some bark and kindlings.

Left alone, Adams picked up a book; but he found it too dark to read in the tent without straining his eyes, and, after a few moments' trial, he cast the volume impatiently aside, and, with a smothered growl at the persistency of the rain, made a dive for the "kitchen," as he and Maynard had named the shanty, and started a fire in the stove, and busied himself with preparations for supper.

If you ever tried to build an open fire in the woods during a pouring rain, you have some idea of the difficulty under which Maynard labored. If you have not tried to perform this task, you don't know anything about it. Several times he had the fire fairly started, as he thought, and as often it would disappear, sending up a few fitful sparks, and a few tiny columns of smoke. But Frank had a good grip on the two twin brothers, Perseverance and Patience, and finally his efforts were crowned with success. To be sure, the fire snapped and sputtered some, but it triumphed over its opposite, water, and each stick added to the pile increased its hold on life, until it grew to be a huge column of flame, that shot into the air with crackle and roar, sending out its cheerful light and genial heat to the most remote corners of the camp.

"You are a genius, Frank, — a regular fire-king, — to get such a jolly blaze as that in this heavy rain. I didn't think you would get it burning."

"Nothing like trying, Jack. 'I'll try,' never was beat but once, and that was when old Cowley tried to shin a greased pole feet first."

"He had to cave then, did he?"

"You are right, he did. He was only fairly started, when he came down with a run, struck on his head, and turned himself inside out. He was the most demoralized specimen of a man you ever saw."

"I should think he must have been," and Jack laughed at the monstrous statement.

"Better make coffee and tea both, hadn't we?" queried Maynard, who now joined Adams in the kitchen to assist about the supper.

"Yes, I would, and make them both strong."

"Trust me for that. I'll give them a regular cap-hoister."

The kitchen stood within ten feet of the living-tent, and the boys dodged from one to the other without getting very wet.

"I tell you, Maynard, this kitchen is a big thing. It would have been almost impossible to have cooked a hot supper to-night without it."

"Right, my boy. You stumble on the truth by accident once in a while."

The supper progressed as favorably as could be expected under the circumstances, and they had everything on the table, and were about to sit down at six o'clock, when suddenly two strangers appeared to them.

They were tall, rugged-looking men, dark-complected, and both wore full beards. They each had a heavy knapsack strapped to their shoulders, and both carried an axe.

"Well, young men, you are pretty comfortably fixed here, I should say," spoke up the eldest, as he glanced around the camp.

The boys were so much startled by their appearance that they stared at the strangers for some moments without answering. The noise of the storm had kept the boys from hearing the coming of the men until the strangers were within a few feet of them, and their first feeling was one of alarm. But, as they gazed into the faces of the men, they became reassured, and finally Maynard found voice to reply, —

"Yes, sir, very well for a rainy day."

The youngest, who had been exploring the place with his eyes, now caught sight of the bear and deer, and laughingly observed, —

"I snum, Dan'l! we've stumbled onter a menagerie. I guess I'll get a pole, and stir up the animiles."

"Don't meddle with the bear," added Maynard, quickly; "he is not partial to strangers."

"No, I 'spose not. I aint going ter touch him. I was only jokin'."

"Can you accommodate us with lodgings for to-night?" asked the eldest of the strangers, as the two men slung their packs to the ground.

"Who are you?" inquired Maynard.

"Surveyors," again replied the eldest. "My name is Daniel Parker, and this is Russ Goodman. We are up here looking out timber chances."

"All right, sir. We were just about to sit down to supper. Will you take some with us?"

"I guess not," returned Mr. Parker, who acted as spokesman, and who seemed to be the one in authority. "We have pork and hard-tack and tea, and, if you will let us use your stove, we shall get along nicely."

"Pork, hard-tack, and tea!" repeated Maynard, his nose unconsciously turning up a little as he mentioned the bill of fare; "and is that all you live on while tramping in the woods?"

"Yes, with the exception of a little game and fish that we procure occasionally; what more do you want?" and Mr. Parker gazed with surprise at the youth.

"You don't come any of the pork and hard-tack business in this camp. But we are standing here in the rain. Come in out of the wet, as the whale said to Jonah when he swallowed him," and Adams passed into the tent, followed by the others.

"Pull off your rubber-coats, and sit up to the table," invited Adams, as he laid a couple of plates, knives, and forks, and added two more cups and saucers, "and we'll see if we can't give you something as good as pork and hard-tack."

Mr. Parker said they had not expected to eat with them, and only wanted a chance to sleep; but the boys would take no denial, and the two woodsmen drew up to the table.

"Now, help yourselves, gentlemen," remarked Maynard hospitably; "here are baked beans, roast venison, fried trout, baked potatoes, corn, peas, hot biscuit, raspberries, and cake. We can give you tea or coffee, whichever you prefer."

Mr. Parker took tea without milk or sugar, and his companion, coffee in the same manner, and they helped themselves to the edibles, gazing about the tent as they did so.

"Are you boys keeping a hotel up here in the woods?" queried Russ, as he glanced over the nice supper spread before them.

"No, only camping out," returned both the boys with a smile.

"Yer live pretty well, and yer know how to cook. Whar do ye belong?"

"In Boston," answered Adams.

"I take it there are more in your party," observed Mr. Parker, his examination of the tent having convinced him of this fact.

"Yes," responded Maynard, "there are seven of us. Five of our companions went off to visit a cave on Camel's Rump this morning, and they have not yet returned."

"A cave!" exclaimed Russ with interest; "I didn't know thar was any cave on the Rump, did you, Dan'l?"

"No, I never heard of any. On what part of the mountain is it, young man?"

Maynard told him, and gave them an account of his visit to it with his friends.

"Wall, that beats me," observed Russ. "I thought I knew this country about as well as any man of my years, and I've been all over Camel's Rump many a time, but durn me, if I ever saw anything of a cave."

"You would not be likely to notice it unless you were hunting for it, or tumbled on to it accidentally, as we did, for the entrance was partly concealed by bushes."

"And yer friends went up there to-day, yer say?"

"Yes."

"Isn't it about time fur them ter be back?"

"I should think it was."

"They'll find it pretty rough travelling in the woods after dark."

"They have both of our lanterns with them, and we shall have to see by firelight until they return."

"I don't believe they'll come back to-night."

"Yes, they will," put in Adams, "for they only took a lunch with them."

"Pooh! They can stand it till to-morrow mornin', easy enough. Why, Mr. Parker and I have been without grub several times for forty-eight hours on a stretch."

"We are not used to living that way," responded Maynard. "You won't find any fellow in this crowd going without eating for forty-eight hours, if he can get where there is any grub. It will take something more than rain to keep him away from it," and Maynard laughed at the idea.

"What are your names, young gentlemen?" inquired Mr. Parker, when Maynard had recovered from his laughing fit.

"Mine is Frank Maynard, and my friend's is John Adams."

"John Adams? You have good blood in you, my boy, if you descended from the presidential family."

"I don't claim any relationship with them," declared Jack with a smile. "The fact of it is, I have never had time to study our genealogical tree, and whether I came from that branch of the family or not I can't say. However, I don't mean to disgrace the name."

"A good intention, and I hope you will keep it," asserted Mr. Parker, kindly.

"Wall, boys, if yer'll excuse me, I'll have a smoke!" and Russ rose from the table, and producing a short-stemmed clay pipe, filled it with plug tobacco, and, lighting it, went out to look at the weather.

Mr. Parker also arose, and the boys cleared the table, and carried the things to the stove to keep warm for their friends, and then washed up the dirty dishes.

Maynard then replenished the camp-fire which was burning low, and, as they could not sit out-doors without getting wet, they gathered in the kitchen, which was brilliantly lit by the camp-fire, and found it very comfortable around the cooking-stove.

The boys asked their guests more particularly in regard to the business of lumber surveying, and Mr. Parker gave them a great deal of useful information on the subject, beside telling them many exciting experiences of his tramps through the woods, in which he was ably seconded by his companion.

In return, the boys told the men about their trip since leaving home, and also about their former visit to the Maine woods, and gave them sketches of each of their companions. The time passed very pleasantly, and when Adams observed that it was ten o'clock, and that the fellows would hardly come then, Maynard could scarcely believe it. But a glance at his watch, assured him that his friend was right, and he now began to feel very much worried about the party who had gone to visit the cave.

"I can't account for it," said he; "I don't believe they would stay in that cave all night without anything to eat, and only a stone floor to lay on, just from fear of getting wet. They are not that kind of fellows."

"I am afraid they they are in trouble," assented Jack. "I think they would have put in an appearance before this unless something more than the rain had prevented them"; and a sigh welled up from the deepest recesses of his heart as he thought of the many good times he had seen with his friends, — "the best set of fellows," as he told Mr. Parker, "that ever lived."

"Oh, you'll see 'em in the morning!" asserted Russ, who saw that the boys felt badly, and wished to cheer them up. "You may depend upon it, that they were afraid of getting their jackets wet, and concluded to stay in the cave all night. You'll see 'em before breakfast in the mornin', I'll bet."

"I don't believe it," returned Maynard gloomily, as he sprang to his feet. "Something has happened to them, I know; and if they are not here by the time we are done breakfast in the morning, we must go up there. Will you and Russ go with us, Mr. Parker?"

"Certainly, if you desire. But I hope and trust that no misfortune or accident has befallen your friends. I am of Mr. Goodman's opinion that they disliked the long tramp through the woods in the rain, and concluded to stay all night, in spite of the fact of their having no food. It is daylight by four o'clock, and I should look for them here to camp by seven, sure."

"If they are not here by that hour," asserted Maynard, "I shall look them up without farther waiting, for, while I am willing to acknowledge that the rain might have detained them a few hours, I am positive they would not have let it keep them away over night. They all have an abundance of dry clothing in camp, and could have peeled off their wet garments as soon as they reached here. But, as we can do nothing for them to-night, I suppose we may as well turn in, for I suppose you are both tired and sleepy," and Maynard led the way to the tent, followed by Adams, and their guests, and without farther talk sought their blankets.

The two woodsmen dropped off to sleep without any trouble; but the thoughts of the two boys kept them awake for a long time, and it was after midnight before they found the sleep they coveted.

CHAPTER XI.

Troubled Sleepers. — The Nightmare. — The Rescuing Party. — Removing the Boulder. — The Prison Doors Opened. — Back to Camp. — A Jolly Supper. — A Quiet Night. — Departure of the Woodsmen.

"WHAT was that?" and Le Roy raised himself on his elbow, and peered around trying in vain to pierce the darkness.

"What's the row?" and Claude, who slept next to him, awakened by the outcry, turned drowsily over to find a softer place in his hard bed, if that were possible.

"I thought I heard something."

"So you did. It is Phil snoring," and, with a chuckle, Claude pulled Le Roy down again. "Now, go to sleep, before you wake the rest of the fellows up."

"How in creation is a fellow going to sleep in such a hole as this? My bones are about pulverized now."

"I'll swap mattresses with you, if you think mine is any softer," returned Claude, laughing softly.

"What are you grinning about, confound you? I suppose I can stand it till morning."

"I don't doubt it. It takes a good deal to kill such a fellow as you are, Le Roy."

"It's my opinion, if we live through this we shall be able to survive anything," and Le Roy once more closed his eyes and tried to go to sleep.

Quiet reigned again for several hours, but was suddenly broken by Phil jumping to his feet, and crying "Help! murder! the skeleton! where am I?"

"Down in a coal-mine, underneath the ground," droned Wingate, awaking just in time to catch Phil's last words, and trolling this sentence out in such a comical voice that all the boys, with the exception of Phil, burst into a shout of laughter that echoed through the cave with a noise that was startling.

"It's no laughing matter," cried Phil indignantly, who, having now become wide awake, sat down again among his companions.

"That's what the nigger said when the mule kicked him," remarked St. Clair, dryly.

"What's the trouble, Phil? Have you been dreaming," inquired Claude.

"Dreaming! I should say I had. I'm all perspiration from my head to my feet."

"Don't work so hard in your sleep," suggested Le Roy.

"What was after you, Phil, a ghost?" inquired Wingate.

"I thought I was in a dungeon, something like this cave, only smaller, and a grinning skeleton"—

"Grinning skeleton is good!" broke in St Clair.

"Oh, let him finish his yarn, Andrew!" urged Claude.

"With his long, fleshless arms advanced to me, and, pointing downward, said, 'Come with me!'

"I backed away from the hideous apparition; but suddenly it grasped me by the throat, and, with an infernal yell, exclaimed, 'Now I have you!' With a shudder of affright, I cried for help, and broke away from it, and that awoke me."

"You must have drank something stronger than water yesterday," bantered Le Roy.

"Your brain is too active, young man," laughed St. Clair; "carry a brick in your hat in future."

"His mind is too imaginative," observed Wingate.

"Too what ative?" queried Le Roy.

"I'd like to know what time it is," remarked Claude. "Where are the lanterns?"

"Strike a match," suggested Wingate; "it will answer just as well."

Claude followed his friend's advice, and, consulting his timepiece, found it was ten minutes past four.

Then it must be daylight, outside," observed St. Clair. "If I was only out of this cave, wouldn't I bounce for camp? Perhaps not!" and he sighed as he felt the clamorous wants of his stomach, and thought of the bountiful supply of provisions in the store-tent.

"Let's shake up our pillows and turn over our mattresses," said Wingate facetiously, and take another nap. We don't want to turn out yet. It will be dull waiting when we do get up, for the boys can't get here before ten o'clock."

"That is so," agreed Claude. "They will be looking for us this morning, and will get their breakfast before they start, and they will not be likely to leave before seven o'clock. As Charlie says, we may as well get a little more sleep, if we can."

After this the boys quieted down again, and in a little while dropped asleep, and when they awoke the next time it was nine o'clock. Lighting one of the lanterns, and taking the other, as well as the axe and the lunch-pail, they made their way as near as they could to the entrance, to await with what patience they could the expected arrival of their friends.

They had hoped to get another drink where they found water the day before, but it had all disappeared, much to their regret.

Claude who was in advance told them that the rain was over, and that he believed the sun was shining.

Mr. Parker and Russ, who were early risers, awoke at five o'clock, and called the boys, as Maynard had told them the night before he wished to get up early.

The boys were soon dressed, and, taking hold with a will, had breakfast on the table at six o'clock. As soon as they had eaten, Adams packed some meat, biscuit, and doughnuts in a pail, and at seven o'clock, as their companions had not appeared, started for the mountain accompanied by the two woodsmen, carrying their axes, Russ remarking "that they might come kinder handy."

On their way, they found the partridges hung up in the tree, as the boys had left them the day before; and this convinced them to a certainty that their friends had made no effort to return.

"You are sure there were no wild animals in that cave?" asked Mr. Parker as they hurried along.

"There were none when we were there before, I'll stake my life," answered Maynard.

"It ud be a bad job for the youngsters, ef they had happened ter tumble onter a bear or wild-cat in there."

"They were armed. I'd risk them on that tack," declared Adams. "Why, we shot a panther when we were at Dixville Notch."

"Yes, but you were out-doors, and had a good

chance at the critter. In that cave a cat would have the advantage of 'em, because it could see in the dark, and they couldn't."

"But they have two lanterns," observed Maynard.

"Yes, I know. But they would probably get broke in the scrimmage, and then they wouldn't dare ter fire in the dark, for fear o' hurtin' each other."

"I guess we shall find them safe," said Mr. Parker.

Without running, the party covered the ground at a rapid pace, and at ten o'clock reached the entrance to the cave. But the boulder at the mouth bothered Maynard and Adams, and they could scarcely tell where they were, until a voice that sounded hollow in their ears, coming from underground, hailed them.

"I say, out there! Who are you?"

It was Claude's voice, and the two boys jumped as if they were holding the handles of an electric battery.

The voice told them the exact position of the mouth of the passage, and the presence of the boulder readily accounted for their friends' long absence from camp.

"Some scoundrels have rolled that big stone down into the mouth of the passage-way!" declared Adams, excitedly, and he glanced around as if it would be a pleasure to him to strike somebody.

"Nonsense!" ejaculated Maynard, and then, getting down on his knees, on the left-hand side of the boulder, he shouted, "Claude!"

"How are you, Frank?"

"Are you all in there?"

"I should say we were."

"Alive and well?"

"Yes."

"Thank God for that!"

"Amen!" returned Claude, fervently.

"Are you hungry?" queried Adams.

"I rather guess. Did you bring any grub, Jack?"

"Yes, plenty of it."

"You are a brick! Pass it along."

"How can we get it to you," inquired Maynard.

"Here, through this hole," and Claude stuck out his hand as far as he could. "Pass it to me, and I'll pass it back to the other boys. We are in single file here, you know."

The meat, biscuit, and doughnuts, were now passed to Claude in small quantities, and he distributed them among his companions, reserving an equitable share for himself.

"How large is that rock, Frank?"

"It's a bouncer, Claude."

"Do you think you can get it away?"

"Yes, sir. It would have given us a hard one if Jack and I had come alone; but we have two gentlemen here with us, who stopped at the camp last night, and we will have you out of that trap shortly. They are coming with two big levers now, that they have been cutting while we were passing you the grub. How do you think the rock came here? Of course it was not here when you went in."

"I guess, not," replied Claude dryly. The thunder or lightning started it from somewhere above, and it rolled into the hole. Wingate was within two or three feet of it when it dropped in there, and we cannot be too thankful that he escaped unhurt."

"That's so, by Jove!"

Mr. Parker and Russ now arrived with two stout maple sticks, and, placing these behind the back corners of the boulder, with the assistance of Jack and Frank they tried to pry it out. But the stone was too heavy, and, although they tugged and lifted until, as Russ expressed himself, "he could hear his backbone snap," they couldn't start the rock a hair.

"It is too much for us, Russ," said Mr. Parker; "we shall have to attack it from below. We must take away some of the small stones in front of it, if there are any, and make a channel for it to roll in. Then, by picking a few out from under the front part of it, it will start of its own accord."

"Yes, and it will make things snap when it strikes inter those small spruces below us, I tell yer."

The two men now cut away the bushes from in front of the boulder, so that they might have a good chance to work, and then, with the aid of the boys, began to remove a number of small stones, which they found very plentiful, thus proving the assertion of Maynard that the *debris* from the cave had been dumped near the mouth of it.

In half an hour's time they had removed all the stones necessary in front, and then began to pry out a few small ones that the boulder rested on, and which acted as a trig to it.

This they found to be by far the most difficult feature of the job, but they kept steadily at work until they had dug out all the stones that seemed in any way to hold the boulder but one, and that held its position with the tenacity of a balky horse.

"I snum, Dan'l, I don't believe we can git that one

out!" exclaimed Russ, as he stopped a moment to rest, and wiped the perspiration from his forehead. "Yer see it is three-cornered, and one picked end is just drove solid inter the ground. We shall have ter block up under it behind, and make some wedges, and rise her up that way. You and I can drive the wedges, and the boys can trig under the boulder as fast as we lift it. And if we can get her up far enough ter get one o' these big pries under the middle o' ther stone, I believe the four of us can throw it over. What do yer think?"

"We can try it, and see; but we need some heavy hardwood wedges."

"There's a beach down yender, that'll be just the thing."

The two woodsmen felled the beach, and made four good heavy wedges, and then returned to the rock.

From where Claude sat, he could hear all that was going on outside, and repeated the most of it to his companions. When he told them about the new method the men were going to try, the boys began to feel worried, for fear it would not succeed.

"I tell you, Claude, its lucky Jack and Frank brought those men with them. They never would have been able to have extricated us alone."

"Right you are, Wingate, and we should have had the pleasure of passing another night in this hotel, and, for all I know, two more. Flint's would have been the nearest, or, at any rate, the easiest place to get to, that they could have visited for help; and as they would have worked here about all day, trying to get the rock away themselves, it would have been late the next day, if not the following morning, before they could have returned."

"I should like to know what brought those men to our camp?"

"A divine Providence!" returned Claude, seriously, "and it won't hurt any of us to look at it in that light."

"I agree with you," and Wingate offered up a silent prayer that their delivery was so near.

Mr. Parker and Russ now placed a stone on each side of the boulder, close to it, and, placing the sharp ends of the wedges between, began driving the heavy blocks.

Adams and Maynard stood by, one on each side the boulder, and threw in small stones as fast as the large rock moved upwards.

The wedges were six inches thick at the butt, and, when they had been driven to the head, had raised the rock about four inches. Larger stones were now procured for baits, and, taking the second pair of wedges, the first having been about used up by the pounding they had undergone, the two men drove them in as before, raising the boulder about four inches more.

"I believe we can tip it over now, Russ," observed Mr. Parker, as he examined the situation.

"We kin try, anyway. If we only had a couple o' cant-dogs here, we could turn it right out o' there; but perhaps the pry'll do, and, picking up one of the levers, Russ placed it in position under the boulder.

"Now, then, all together," cried Mr. Parker, as they took hold of the lever.

"Jist let me git my shoulder under that stick, I kin lift twist as much that way," and Russ, having placed himself to advantage, added "now give it to 'er."

They lifted, all together, and the huge rock, tottering a moment on its balanced edge, flopped over, and rolled down the mountain side, sweeping all before it for at least a quarter of a mile, when, its force having become much diminished from the many obstructions it had met on its flight, it was finally brought to bay by a tremendous yellow-birch, which it struck with a shock that tumbled several large dead limbs from the upper part of the tree to the ground.

A shout of triumph went up from Adams and Maynard, and, as Claude and the others appeared, one by one, their hands were grasped by Jack and Frank, and shook with a heartiness that told their joy at their friends' escape from their prison.

Then Maynard introduced the cave party to Russ and Mr. Parker, and the boys shook hands heartily with them, and thanked them warmly for their very opportune assistance.

"And now," said Claude, "it is one o'clock, and the sooner we get back to camp the better; and if we don't have a good dinner or supper, whichever you have a mind to call it, to-night, it will be because we can't cook it."

"I should like to take a look at your cave before we return," remarked Mr. Parker.

"Certainly, of course you would. I didn't think of that. Maynard, light the lanterns, and you and Jack go in with the gentlemen. We are about choked, we are so thirsty, and, jf you'll excuse us, we will go down the mountain until we strike that first brook, where we can get a drink, and wait for you there."

"All right," returned Maynard, and he and Jack went with the two woodsmen to look at the cave.

"I snum! this is snug quarters," observed Russ, as they crawled on hands and knees along the passage.

"The path is larger as soon as we turn the corner just ahead," answered Adams.

When they entered the cave, the two men examined the skeleton first, of which they could make no more than the boys, although they had theories enough upon the matter. Then they looked at the veins of silver and lead, and inspected the whole of the walls and the roof sharply, but were forced to confess that there was not enough of value in the mineral deposits to pay for working the mine.

After half an hour's stay they returned to the outer world, and then hastened to join the rest of the party, whom they found at the brook.

"Did you see anything of our partridges, Maynard?" queried Le Roy, as the parties joined, and started for camp.

"Yes we found seven partridges hung to a tree, and that settled our opinion as to your whereabouts."

"I guess they were pretty well soaked," added Claude, laughing.

"We ought to give that cave a name," suggested Maynard, as they hurried along.

"Call it 'Skeleton Cave,'" proposed Phil. "How is that?"

"A good name, I say," acquiesced Wingate.

"'Skeleton Cave' be it, then," declared Maynard.

"I guess it will take Frank and I sometime to-night to get supper for all you hungry mortals," laughed Adams.

"We will all help you to-night, Jack," observed Claude.

"Too many cooks spoil the broth."

"They will not in this case."

It was half-past four when the party reached camp, and a fire was lighted in the cook-stove, and all the boys took hold to forward the supper. Three of the partridges were plucked and dressed by St. Clair. Wingate sliced some venison, and stuffed the two large trout for baking. Phil washed some potatoes for baking and boiling. Le Roy picked over some berries and set the table. Claude, who was the best pastry-cook in the party, made a couple of raspberry-pies and the biscuit, and Maynard and Adams found their hands full in attending to the cooking. Russ saying "that he must do something to get up an appetite," was chopping wood as if his life depended upon it, and Mr. Parker was engaged with his field notes, making memorandums of his lumber surveys.

For an hour or more the camp had the appearance of a beehive, the boys darting here and there about their work, while a buzz of joke and repartee filled the air, and everybody was as happy as a clam at high-water.

The last thing, Adams made the coffee and tea, and fifteen minutes afterward announced that "supper was ready," and, with a cheer from the boys, they and their guests gathered around the festive board.

"And what a supper that was, especially for the party who had been imprisoned in the cave, who had been for thirty hours without a solid meal!

The two baked trout, ornamented with small, square, crisp, thin slices of pork, flanked on one side by fried venison, on the other by fricaseed partridges, and supported by baked and boiled potatoes. Then they had canned beans, peas, and tomatoes for vegetables. Two pyramids of biscuit, baked with a delicate brown tint, and as light as a cork, occupied each end of the table, while the berries and pies were to the more substantial viands what the fragrance is to the rose.

Claude did the honors of the occasion, and, after serving their guests, helped his friends, Adams pouring the tea and coffee.

There was little talking at first, for all were too hungry; but, after the sharper pangs of hunger had been quieted, the boys found their tongues, and the air was filled with their jokes and laughter. Their guests entered into the spirit of the feast, and told their stories and cracked their jokes with as much zest as the younger members of the party. Before the meal was over they had to light their lanterns, and it was eight o'clock before they arose from the table.

The dishes were cleared away and washed up, and they gathered around the camp-fire to continue their conversation, Russ bringing forth his old T.D., at which he pulled incessantly, sending the smoke into the air in graceful circles that were lost in the darkness overhead.

Mr. Parker told the boys how he once killed a bear, while out on a surveying-trip, armed only with a hatchet; and Russ gave them several laughable anecdotes about a loon that he captured one spring, and tamed, and kept for several years after. The boys related their exploits in capturing Nap and Lightfoot and the eagles, and the woodsmen were much amused at Claude's story of their fight with the monarchs of the air.

At ten o'clock everybody retired to rest, and slept soundly. Mr. Parker and Russ were the first up the next morning, and the boys, hearing them stirring, turned out and prepared breakfast. At eight o'clock the woodsmen left the camp, with the hearty thanks and best wishes of its occupants. Claude offered to recompense them for the time they had lost; but neither of them would take a cent, and Mr. Parker laughingly remarked, "that he guessed what they had done for the boys would not more than pay for their board and lodging."

CHAPTER XII.

Claude and Phil Visit Flint's. — The Saucy Loons. — Returning to Camp. — A Large Flock of Ducks. — Successful Shooting. — St. Clair, Le Roy, and Wingate Start for Arnold's Bog. — A Quiet Sunday. — Writing to Old Chums. — A Circus in Camp. — Maynard Takes a Bath. — The First Snow. — Worrying About the Absent Ones. — Camp-fire Flickerings. — A Wakeful Night. — An Unsuccessful Moose Chase. — Return of the Wanderers.

As fuel had run quite low after the departure of their guests, the boys, with the exception of Adams and Maynard, spent the rest of the forenoon in cutting and bringing in wood, obtaining enough, according to Claude's opinion, to last a week.

The afternoon was passed in reading and writing, mending clothing, and other odd jobs that suggested themselves.

As they sat around the camp-fire in the evening, Adams informed his friends that there were only potatoes enough for breakfast, and that the flour was getting low.

"We shall have to go for some more, then," said Claude. "We can't get along without spuds."

"It's quite a trip from here down to Flint's," suggested Maynard.

"I know it is; but you would find that we should miss potatoes and flour more than any other articles of food. It is not necessary for all of us to go. Two will be enough, and I will go for one. We can go down one day, and back the next, easy enough. Who will go with me?"

"I," said Phil.

"And I, and I," shouted St. Clair and Wingate.

"Phil spoke first, so I'll take him, and we must get away decently early. Have breakfast, say, at six o'clock, and start at seven."

"I will see that you have your breakfast on time," observed Adams.

"We shall want a lunch also," added Phil. "But we can get our supper at Flint's."

"I will see to that in the morning," responded Maynard.

"I hope we shall not all sleep until seven or eight o'clock," said Claude, as they went to bed.

"I'll be up in season," declared Adams; "I'll keep it on my mind."

True to his promise, Adams turned out early, and had breakfast ready at six, and Maynard had their lunch all put up, and at seven, amid a chorus of good wishes from their friends, Claude and Phil started down river.

The stream still felt the effect of the recent heavy rain, and the boys found more water in the river, and a stronger current than they had seen any time before, while the navigation was a great deal easier. Claude had his gun, and Phil his rifle, but they saw nothing worth shooting during the forenoon, and at half-past eleven they reached Little Boy's Falls. They carried their boat around the falls, and then sat down on the bank of the river, and eat their lunch.

As they were about to start, Phil felt an uncomfortable crawling and itching on his legs, and investigation showed that his feet had been resting on an ant-hill, and about a hundred of the little insects, more or less, had found their way under his clothing.

Jumping to his feet he danced and slapped, but all to no purpose, and finally was compelled to take Claude's advice, and strip. A careful examination of his lower clothing allowed him to free himself from his unwelcome visitors, and, as soon as he had dressed, the boys pushed off the boat, and resumed their course.

"I wouldn't advise you to sit on an ant-hill again," laughed Claude.

"I don't mean to. How the little wretches did bite!"

At two o'clock they had entered the lake, and, rowing between the islands, made their way along the eastern shore.

Just below Moose Brook they discovered two loons, who mocked them with their peculiar cries, until Phil, declaring it was more than flesh and blood could stand, dropped the oars, and sent a bullet whizzing toward them.

The two loons were about three feet apart, and the bullet struck the water between them.

"Why don't you give them a shot, Claude?"

"Can't reach them with my gun."

"Try my rifle," and Phil slipped a cartridge in.

Claude took careful aim, but just as he pulled the trigger the loons disappeared beneath the water.

"There is not much satisfaction in shooting at those fellows, they are under water more than half the time. Take your rifle, and I'll take the oars, now."

The boys exchanged seats, and once more the boat sped onward. As they neared the foot of the lake a blue heron came from the direction of the outlet, and passed them lazily, flapping his wings about a long rifle-shot distant.

"I'll give him one for luck," said Phil, and, dropping his paddle, he blazed away.

The only effect of the shot was to cause the heron to change his course a little, and give utterance to a cry, whether of fright or derision, the boys could not tell.

"Head for the carry, now, Phil."

"All right."

A few moments later the boys reached the shore, and after taking care of their boat, took the bags, and their weapons, and started over the carry.

It was six o'clock when they reached Spoff's camp, and found supper was just ready. Telling Flint they had come for some flour and potatoes, they washed up and went into the dining-room. They found ten sportsmen at the table, and they were soon on good terms with them, and took part in the conversation, which was entirely upon fishing and hunting.

They passed a very pleasant evening with the guests, and occupied a bed together upstairs. The gentlemen all reported the fishing good, and, according to Spoff's tell, deer were so thick that you had to dodge when in the woods around the camp to keep from being run over by them.

After breakfast the next morning Mr. Flint and one of his men backed over a bag of potatoes, each, to the lake, and the boys took twenty-five pounds of flour, each, and telling Spoff they should be coming down that way in a week or so, launched their boat, loaded their potatoes, and pulled northward.

Although bright and pleasant there was some tingle in the air, for there had been quite a frost the night before, and the boys pulled and paddled energetically to get warmed up.

They crossed the lake without incident, but as they shot around one of the islands at the head of the lake, and neared the river, they discovered a large flock of black duck, which were in-shore, feeding.

Phil, being in the stern, paddling, discovered them first.

"Great guns! Claude!" he exclaimed, "look at the ducks; the water is black with them."

"Where?" whispered Claude.

"A little over the port bow. I should think there was a hundred of them."

Turning half around, Claude ceased rowing a few moments, and took a look in the direction indicated by Phil.

"Ye gods and little fishes! what a sight! I never saw so many ducks before in my life. Where is my gun?"

"Here," and Phil passed it along.

Claude slipped a couple of cartridges into his gun, and laid two more on the seat beside him, then, taking the oars again, rowed carefully toward the flock.

"Is your rifle loaded, Phil?"

"Yes."

"We will get as near to them as we can, and give it to them when they rise. Gracious! I wish you had a gun instead of a rifle."

"So do I."

Claude pulled as noiselessly as possible, and by good luck succeeded in getting within fair gunshot just as two or three of the flock nearest them became alarmed at the strange object approaching. With a startled " Quack! quack!" and a whirring of wings, they were up and away, heading toward Indian Cove.

As the flock left the water, the boys pulled trigger, and the moment they had fired they loaded again, and banged away at them the second time. Then Claude laid aside his gun, and, grasping the oars, sent the light craft dashing up to the dead and wounded ducks. They picked up eleven dead ones, and saw three that were wounded swimming in the direction the flock had taken. These Phil brought to bag with his rifle, shooting one at a time.

When Phil had shot the last of the wounded ones, Claude turned the boat toward the lower part of the cove, where the ducks had gone.

"Let me know, Phil, as soon as you sight them again. I don't believe we can get up to them the second time with the boat, but we will row as near to them as we can, and then land and go through the woods, and get a shot at them from the shore. What do you think of it?"

"A good idea, if we don't frighten them away."

After ten minutes' rowing, Phil caught sight of the flock at the extreme lower end of the cove, and informed Claude as to their whereabouts.

Rowing more carefully, Claude brought the boat to within a-half-mile of the ducks, and then, pulling in to the shore, the boys landed and secured their boat.

Taking their weapons and plenty of cartridges, they stole carefully through the woods, just far enough back from the lake to keep the water in sight.

Ten minutes' stealthy creeping brought them opposite the flock, which were feeding on some wild-rice, about fifty yards away.

Getting into position they took aim and fired, knocking over several of the wild fowl, and throwing the flock into confusion.

Instead of flying as before, the ducks swam around in circles, and thus the boys were enabled to get a second shot at them.

This, however, put them to flight; and, rising into the air, they swept across the narrow point at the south side of the cove, and headed down the lake.

"This is the last chance we shall have at them," said Claude; "but we have made them feel sick. There's a dozen floating around out there, sure. Let's hurry back to the boat and pick them up."

A few moments sufficed to set them once more afloat, and Phil rowed rapidly to the dead ducks. They secured fifteen of the birds, but did not see any wounded ones, and the boys concluded they had either killed all they had shot, or that the wounded ones had hid nearer the shore where the weeds were thicker.

However, they felt perfectly satisfied with their success, and, after picking up the last duck they could find, headed the boat for the inlet.

"A pretty good haul," chuckled Phil, as he gazed at the dead birds before him.

"Yes, twenty-nine duck is not a bad morning's work."

When they reached the inlet the boys changed places, as Claude had been rowing all the time since their start.

They reached Little Boy's Falls just before one o'clock, and, after carrying the boat and their rods around, sat down to eat the lunch they had brought with them from Flint's.

"I'd like to know what the rest of the fellows are up to," remarked Phil, as he chewed away on a sandwich.

"I don't know; but they will find something to amuse themselves about, you can bet. All I hope is that none of them will go off and get into such a scrape as we found ourselves in at the cave."

"I hope not."

"The berries must be all gone," said Claude; "suppose we pick a few for supper while we are here. These raspberries are splendid, and I am very fond of them."

"So am I. We can make some birch-bark baskets to carry them in."

"Correct, old man."

"I heard Maynard say that there were plenty of blueberries on the Camel's Rump."

"We'll go up there some day, Phil, and get some. But I don't want anything more of Skeleton Cave."

"Nor I."

After picking a couple of quarts of berries, the boys launched their boat and continued up river. They reached the camp just before six, and found Adams and Maynard expecting them.

"Where are the rest of the fellows?" Claude asked, as the cook and his assistant came down to the boat.

"Gone on an expedition to the North Pole, I guess," replied Adams, laughing.

"What do you mean?" queried Phil.

"After you had gone, yesterday morning, they packed up a lot of grub, took their weapons, a blanket apiece, an axe, and some other things, and started up river in the 'Go Ahead.' St. Clair said they were going over to Arnold's Bog, and try and get a moose, and that they might not be back before Monday night. Said we need not be worried about them if we did not see them for a week."

"I hope they won't get lost," said Claude; "they ought not to have gone off that way."

"I'll risk them," responded Maynard. "I had half a mind to go with them, but I thought it would not be fair to go off and leave Jack alone for a couple of days."

"Nor safe, either," asserted Claude. "What have you been doing since we left?"

"Nothing. Have been right here in camp all the time. We've had some fun with Nap and Lightfoot, though. We have been riding them bareback."

"Nonsense!"

"It's a fact! Ask Jack."

"Yes, sir," declared Adams. "Frank rode Nap, and I Lightfoot. It was as good as a circus at first; but after a while we trained them so they carried us first-rate."

"I would rather see you do it than hear you tell of it," laughed Phil, incredulously.

"You can, to-morrow," retorted Maynard.

"Well, let's have supper; I'm about starved," declared

Claude. "However, we may as well take up the flour and potatoes and ducks, first.

'Ducks? Where are they?" Adams asked.

'In the stern of the boat. Don't you see them, or are you as blind as a bat?"

"Gracious! what a stack of ducks!" exclaimed Adams, as his eyes lighted on them. "Have you been shooting with a gatling gun, Claude!"

"No, sir. Phil and I knocked them over with my gun and his rifle."

"Where did you find them?" asked Maynard, eagerly.

"On the lake. It will be a good job for you to-morrow to pick them!" and Claude gave the assistant cook a good-natured punch in the ribs.

"I'll help you," said Adams.

"Here, Phil, take this bag of potatoes," and Claude passed one out. "Here's the other, Maynard. Now, Jack, help me take out the boat, and then you and I will take up the ducks and the flour."

After the boat was unloaded, Phil and Claude helped a little about supper, and it was ready at seven o'clock.

"I shouldn't wonder if we had a snow-squall before long," said Claude, when they were seated at the table. "This is the coolest evening we've had."

"I don't want to see any," declared Adams, energetically. "I hate it."

"They get it up here pretty early some years, I'm told," replied Claude.

"By Jove! I miss the other fellows," said Phil, when they were gathered an hour later around the camp-fire.

"So do I," added Claude.

"I tell you, boys, Jack and I missed you the night you were in the cave. I don't believe I slept an hour all night!" and Maynard looked sober at the recollection.

"Or I either," asserted Adams. "As soon as I fell asleep, I would get to dreaming about you, and keep waking up."

As Claude and Phil felt rather tired from their two days' expedition, the boys went to bed early, having agreed not to have breakfast the next morning until ten o'clock, as it was Sunday, and they intended to spend the day in camp.

About half-past eight Sunday morning Adams awoke, and singing out to Maynard to "get up," turned out and dressed himself.

Going out-doors he found there had been a frost and a heavy fog, the latter just beginning to rise.

The sun had not yet pierced the fog, and everything around was cold and wet. Going into the kitchen, he started a fire in the stove, muttering as he worked about the fog. Maynard soon joined him, and together they proceeded to get breakfast.

Before it was ready Claude and Phil made their appearance, joking and stretching, as if they had been sleeping a week. After performing their toilet they came around to the kitchen to watch the cooks.

"I had a rousing sleep last night," said Phil, as they stood around the stove.

"I wish Foster and Robbins were with us to-day," remarked Claude. "How they would enjoy it!"

"So do I," added Maynard; "they were two mighty good fellows!"

"And poor Smithy, too," said Adams. "I tell you I felt bad when he died; there never was a better fellow drew breath!" and the tears came into Adams' eyes as he thought of his dead friend.

"Peace to his memory!" responded Claude. "If there is such a place as heaven, I believe he went to it."

"So do I," added Maynard.

"I believe I shall write to Foster to-day," remarked Claude; "it would stir him up to get a letter from us dated in the woods."

"Not a bad thought," asserted Maynard; "and I'll write to Robbins. I suppose he is having a gay time down in Florida among the oranges and bananas."

"Breakfast is ready," said Adams.

"And I am ready for it," added Claude. "Don't those beans smell good?"

"First-rate," returned Phil. "You Boston people understand cooking beans."

"Yes, that's a New England patent," laughed Maynard.

By the time breakfast was over the sun had come out bright and warm, and while the cook, with Phil's assistance, was clearing away the table and washing the dishes, Claude and Maynard wrote their letters.

In the afternoon they all took a bath in the river, and then passed away a couple of hours in reading. Dinner was served at four o'clock, Adams declaring that two meals on Sunday were enough, and his friends agreed to the arrangement.

Around the camp-fire, in the evening, Adams gave up his berth, and told Maynard he could consider himself cook for the next week, and as there was no one else in camp but Claude, and as he had already served both as cook and assistant, it devolved upon Phil to become Maynard's assistant.

"I don't mind being an assistant," laughed Phil; "but I pity you the week I am cook, for you know I did not take lessons in the art, as the rest of you did."

"Maynard is a good cook," declared Claude; "you must watch him sharp next week, and learn to go it alone the week after."

"I'll do the best I can," responded the young man from Brooklyn, and the little party broke up and retired to rest.

Monday morning came in cloudy and cool. The boys stopped in camp during the forenoon, and Adams and Maynard proved to the satisfaction of both Claude and Phil that they could ride Nap and Lightfoot.

Maynard began the show by unfastening the chain from the tree; then, making a slip noose over Nap's nose, he straddled the bear, and rode him triumphantly around the camp. But the act ended differently from what he had intended; for after a while, when near the river, the bear suddenly dashed into the stream, and, lowering his head with a jerk, sent Maynard flying over it, and he lit with a splash in two feet of water, and went all under before he could gain a footing. He emerged, dripping from head to foot, while Nap, who really acted as if he enjoyed the joke, ambled back to his quarters, and Claude chained him up.

Although a good-natured fellow, Maynard lost his temper, and, picking up a club was about to give the bear a good beating; but his friends, nearly choking with laughter, interceded for Bruin, and Maynard, thinking better of it, went to the tent and put on some dry clothing.

"Look out you don't get served the same way!" warned Claude, as Adams went up to Lightfoot, and led him out of the pen the boys had built for him.

"No danger; Lightfoot isn't tricky. He's as gentle as a lamb," and Adams gave the buck a handful of salt, and then mounted him.

The deer trotted around the camp several times, and appeared perfectly unconcerned about the odd burden he carried on his back.

Phil pronounced the show a success, and then Adams took Lightfoot back to his pen and secured him.

"How are the eagles getting along?" Claude asked, as Maynard made his appearance in a dry suit.

"First-rate!" replied the impromptu bather. "I call them Romulus and Remus. They will eat out of your hand; but you have to look out for them, for they bite too hard sometimes."

"What did you name them after Romans for?" queried Phil. "They are American birds."

"The old Roman standard had an eagle on it," retorted Maynard.

"You ought to have named them Ben Butler and Daniel Pratt," laughed Claude.

"Yes, to have named one after the 'Great American Traveller' would have been very appropriate," declared Adams.

After dinner, as it still continued cloudy, the boys thought it would be a good time for fishing, and went down the river three miles to some rapids, where, in two hours' fishing, they took one hundred and twenty-five trout, none, however, weighing over a pound.

They expected their missing friends to supper, but they did not come, and, after they had eaten, the table was cleared away.

It grew cold rapidly after the sun went down, and the sky looked like a storm.

"I would give ten dollars if those fellows were back here," remarked Claude, breaking an uncomfortably long silence, as the boys sat warming their feet around the camp-fire.

"I shall not feel anyway worried about them before to-morrow night," added Maynard. "It must be twenty odd miles from here to Arnold's Bog."

"I guess they will turn up by to-morrow night," said Phil. "They would know we should be anxious about them if they stopped away too long."

"I am going to bed," said Adams; "I feel sleepy."

This broke up the party, and his friends retired with him to the tent.

Phil was the first one out in the morning, and was surprised to find three inches of snow on the ground.

"Get up, fellows," he cried. "It's a regular winter morning. The ground is covered with snow."

'Start a fire in the stove," said Maynard. "I'll be with you in a few minutes."

"I thought we should find snow this morning," remarked Claude. "There was a regular chill in the air last night."

"It will soon go after the sun gets up," observed Adams.

"I guess the fellows had a cold time of it last night," said Claude.

"I'll bet they wished they were here in the tent," added Maynard, as he went out to see to the breakfast.

The boys found the walking very disagreeable, and, as every bush and tree was covered with the fleecy material, they could scarcely move without some of it shaking down on them. Rain in the woods is far preferable to the first snow-storm.

"I'll soon have one dry place around here," declared Claude, as he went into the store-tent for some dry material, and, returning, started a huge camp-fire, whose heat soon eat into the snow for a circle of twenty feet around it, sending up clouds of steam from the damp ground.

By the time they had eaten breakfast the sun began to make itself felt, and it gave promise of a warm day; it turned out to be one of the hottest they had experienced for some time, and before night the snow had disappeared, wherever it was fully exposed to the sun.

With the exception of a short row on the river, the boys had remained in camp, as there was no pleasure in the woods, the melting snow being worse than rain, and, as the ducks and trout they had captured the day before amply supplied the larder, there was no call for them to take a disagreeable tramp.

Expecting their absent friends, as they did that night without fail, Maynard prepared a nice supper, and had it all ready at six o'clock.

But half-past six came, and still there were no signs of the wanderers.

The boys waited until seven o'clock, and then reluctantly sat down to the evening meal, not without many gloomy forebodings as to where their companions could be.

"I don't like it,—I tell you, I don't like it!" repeated Claude, as he stopped eating to give expression to this opinion.

"The fellows' not turning up, I suppose you mean?" suggested Maynard.

"Yes."

"If they get back all right, I think we had all better keep together, after this," said Phil.

"So do I," responded Adams.

"You see they have been gone five days, now," and Claude stared into vacancy, as if he saw them all before him.

"I would like to know if they reached the bog that night," Phil said.

"I don't believe they would go over there in a day, if it is twenty miles," asserted Maynard. "That is a pretty hard day's tramp in the woods, and they did not know the way, either."

"How much provision did they take?" questioned Claude.

"Oh, they took enough to last them a week!" replied Adams. "That is, if they could get any fish or game to go with it. I told St. Clair, when he was putting it up, that he was taking twice as much as he needed. And he laughed, and said that they did not mean to go hungry. I'll risk them on the grub."

"If they don't come to-night, I think we had better go after them to-morrow," ventured Maynard, "and try and look them up."

"Where are we going to look?" demanded Claude, sharply. "How do we know, in the first place, whether they went to Arnold's Bog or not?"

"Well, they said they were going,—that's all I know about it."

"They might have changed their minds after they left here," continued Claude; "and if they did go, we don't know which route they took, or which way they would come back. I wish they had been contented to cruise around here."

Supper over, and the work done up, the boys gathered around the camp-fire as usual, and the conversation again turned on the absentees.

"Didn't you tell me, Adams," said Claude, "that the boys started up the river?"

"Yes, they certainly went that way."

"They took a queer route to Arnold's Bog, then, for the trail starts from Otter Creek, below us."

"By Jove! you are right, Claude," exclaimed Maynard. "I never thought of that."

Adams gave a long whistle. It had not occurred to him either.

"Then they have not gone there," declared Phil.

"That don't necessarily follow," replied Claude; "because they could leave the river anywhere above, and by travelling east, or a little north of east, reach the bog. But, if I had been going there, I should have gone down to Otter Creek, and followed the spotted line from there. That would be the most direct way to go."

Until ten o'clock the boys sat by the blazing fire, arguing all the points of the case; but when they went to bed they were no nearer a solution of the mystery of their companions' absence than they had been before.

They had scarcely dropped asleep when a crash resounded through the forest, that awoke and startled them, and for some moments they could not think what was up.

They listened awhile, and not hearing anything more, Claude remarked that he guessed it must have been some old tree gone down; and with that explanation they were silenced, if not convinced.

A little after midnight they were awakened again by a series of discordant cries that brought them to their feet, while a feeling of alarm crept over them. The noise was soon repeated, and Claude declared it was a screech-owl, in a tree near them, and, pulling on his pants and slippers, he caught up his gun, and going out, discovered the tree that contained the owl, and fired both barrels at random into the foliage. The shots were followed by the flapping of wings, and they heard no more from the owl.

About two hours after they were again awakened by Nap, who was growling and rattling his chain, and, rushing out, beheld a large moose stamping around the bear. The moon shone fair upon him, and, forgetting caution in their excitement, they sprang for their guns with a shout, and the moose, alarmed by their cries, gave a startled snort, and went crashing away through the underbrush.

"I would like to know if the gentleman with the cloven foot has taken a contract to keep us awake all night?" asked Claude, angrily, after the moose had disappeared.

"Can't say," laughed Maynard; "but I wish I could have drawn a bead on that moose. Wasn't he a rouser?"

"As large as a small elephant," declared Adams.

"He and Nap would have had a fight in about five minutes more," remarked Phil.

"We'll warm him up to-morrow, if we can get within sight of him," observed Claude, as they sought their blankets for the fourth time.

Nothing further occurred to trouble them during the night; but having been broken of their rest so much made them oversleep, and it was eight o'clock when Maynard, who was the first to awaken, turned out. The others soon joined him, and breakfast was prepared and eaten in a hurry. Then, taking their guns and rifles, with a supply of ammunition, they started on the trail of the moose, which, as Phil laughingly remarked, "was as plain as the nose on a man's face."

"I don't believe he will go far," said Claude, as they hurried along in pursuit.

But the young gentleman was mistaken, for they followed the trail for two miles down the river on that side, and then came to a place where the animal had crossed.

The water was shallow, and, without waiting to pull off boots or stockings, they waded across, and, after some little delay, picked up the trail on the other side.

They started on now with renewed ardor, cheered by the thought that, perhaps, they had not much farther to go; but, after travelling until noon without coming in sight of the game, they came to the conclusion that they did not want the moose, and, tired and hungry, returned to camp. It had been a veritable case of "sour grapes" for them.

They had hoped to find their friends awaiting them on their return, but the camp was deserted except by their pets, and, with many misgivings for the safety of their friends, they proceeded to get supper, which was ready at six o'clock.

They were just sitting down to the table when they heard voices, and, looking eagerly at each other, they rushed to the bank of the river, and beheld the "Go Ahead" coming in to the landing.

They gave a regular yell when they beheld their friends all right, which was answered by the party in the boat, and a moment later they were all shaking hands.

"How are you, fellows?" said St. Clair, as he jumped on shore; "it seems as if I had been gone a month."

"Have you been to supper?" asked Wingate.

"No," replied Adams; "we were just sitting down."

"Glory hallelujah! I am hungry enough to eat a shark."

"Where under the sun have you been?" queried Claude.

"Wait until after supper, and we will tell you," answered St. Clair.

"We were very anxious about you," said Maynard.

"I suppose so," responded Le Roy; "but we couldn't get here any sooner. We have had an awful tramp; if you don't believe it, ask the other fellows."

CHAPTER XIII.

Around the Camp-Fire. — St. Clair's Story. — A Night at Black Pond. — Deer by Moonlight. — Arnold's Bog. — The Camp at the Forks. — Moose-Hunting at Night. — A Sleepy Hunter. — The Battle between the Moose. — Locked Horns. — Large Game. — A Visit from Indians. — Building a Raft. — Lake Megantic. — A Night at a Hotel. — Return up the Lake. — A Hard Tramp. — Lost. — Climbing a Mountain. — The Forks Again. — Back to Camp.

" Now give an account of yourselves," said Claude, as the boys, contented and happy, gathered around the huge camp-fire, which had been piled high with wood, for the night was again chilly.

" It's a long story," returned St. Clair, " and it will take some time to tell it."

" No matter," added Maynard; " we have the night before us. Blaze away!"

" Perhaps you wondered at our starting up river to go to Arnold's Bog," began St. Clair.

" We didn't think anything about it at the time," answered Maynard; " but Claude spoke of it after he and Phil came back from Flint's."

" Exactly. Well, I know how to go to Arnold's Bog as well as any of you, but although we started for that place we were in no particular hurry to get to it. We had a roving commission, and I intended to explore the country a little.

" We started up river, as you know, but we took it

easy, and did not reach the Forks until noon. Then we had dinner. Afterward we took our boat out of the water, carried her into the bushes, and covered her over with limbs, completely concealing her, while the oars and paddle we hid in another place."

"A wise precaution," observed Phil.

"Then we started up the East Branch, keeping on the south side of the stream. We shot two partridges before we had gone half a mile, and saw three others, but missed them.

"Reaching the trail that led to Black Pond, we turned into it, but although the spotted line was plain enough, the path was somewhat overgrown, and was plentifully interspersed with windfalls, making it hard travelling for us, as we each carried quite a load."

"Sin is always heavy," laughed Adams.

"About four o'clock we hove in sight of the pond, and, as an Irishman would say, the first thing we shot was a deer that we missed."

"A deer?" queried Maynard.

"Yes. A noble fellow he was, too. He stood at the edge of the pond, tail toward us. But the noise of our approach frightened him, and, turning, he galloped into the wooks. We all fired at him, and we all missed."

"If he had taken to the water we should have had him sure," added Wingate.

"I guess we should; but his head was level. He took to the woods, and that was the last we saw of him. We followed the shore of the pond around to the outlet, crossed the stream, and, as it was then five o'clock, prepared to camp.

"While Le Roy and I built a brush-camp, Wingate strung up his rod and went to fishing.

"He had splendid luck, and, in half an hour, took thirty trout, running from half a pound to a pound each."

"I tell you, boys, it was good sport." And Wingate's eyes sparkled at the remembrance.

"By the time Wingate had dressed the trout, we had a good fire under way, and, cutting up a few slices of pork, soon had the trout in the frying-pan.

"After supper we spread one of our blankets over the boughs we had gathered, reserving the other two to cover us. Then we built up a rousing fire outside the hut, and laid around it, and took our ease.

"Before turning in for the night we heard several noises in the pond near us, as if animals of some kind were in the water, and an old loon, some distance away, serenaded us with his melancholy music.

"Although cool, the evening was very pleasant. The moon lighted up the whole pond, except where the trees around the shores overshadowed the water, and a gentle breeze, that just rippled the surface, gave the most enchanting effect to the moonlight.

"Leaving our fire to burn itself out we rose to go to bed. As we started toward the camp I descried a dark speck in the middle of the pond, some distance away from us, moving rapidly toward the opposite shore. It was a deer.

"Wingate and Le Roy rushed for their rifles, and opened fire upon the animal; but they did not hit it, and we watched until it disappeared in the shadow of the trees. Then we crawled between our blankets.

"We had a good night's rest, — slept like troopers, — and did not awake until seven the next morning.

"We were a little chagrined at having slept so long, as we had intended to make an early start, and all took hold and helped to get breakfast.

"At half-past eight we scattered our fire, and, shouldering our packs, struck out in a north-easterly direction.

"Crossing a valley we skirted a lofty mountain for some distance. Then crossed some more flat land, through the centre of which ran a small brook, that I judge is one of the tributaries of the Magalloway; then began to climb a high mountain, which, from certain indications we saw upon reaching the summit, was a part of the chain of mountains that form the boundary."

"How was the travelling?" Claude asked.

"Hard. The underbrush was troublesome, and when we were among large trees we found a great many windfalls. Any way, when we reached the top of the mountain we were tired enough to stop, and we did.

"Looking at my watch I found it was noon, and we took a cold dinner, as we did not wish to stop to build a fire."

"Could you see anything from the top of the mountain?" inquired Maynard.

"Yes; mountains in every direction, thickly wooded, a few being bare on top. We counted a dozen or more silvery specks that denoted water; but we could not tell what they were. I tell you I never saw such a wilderness in my life. One huge forest as far as the eye could reach, on every hand.

"At one o'clock we descended the mountain on the

east side, and after two hours' travelling, lost the clean timbered forest, and came upon stunted and dead trees, and wet land, which we concluded must be Arnold's Bog.

"We tried to cross it where we were, and reach the high land, on the opposite side; but finding the water so deep that we should be compelled to wade, we gave up the idea, and, turning north, travelled until we cleared the bog-land, and reached the forks of Arnold's River, where we concluded to camp, on the side we then stood.

"It was mighty hard travelling around the edge of the bog, and it was five o'clock when we arrived at the Forks, about used up. I never felt more tired in my life."

"Do you good," returned Adams, smiling.

"The quick water in front of our camping-site was suggestive of trout, and while Wingate and Le Roy built a camp I went to fishing, and I found the trout plenty enough to keep me busy.

"After taking enough for our supper and breakfast, I started a fire, and prepared supper, Andrew and Tom furnishing the firewood.

"We rested awhile after eating, and about dark we lighted our lantern, for the sky was overcast, and we could not see to walk very plainly, and, guided by its rays, started for the bog.

"We followed around the edge until we found signs of moose, and then, roosting on the limbs of some old stubs, that were just high enough to keep our feet from the water, we waited the coming of the moose.

"But they 'didn't come for a cent', that is, not in our immediate vicinity, and although we heard them crashing and splashing some distance from us, nary a moose did we see."

"Why didn't you go where they were?" asked Claude, excitedly.

"Why didn't we? The best reason I can give you is because we had not quite lost our common-sense. If you would like to go perambulating around Arnold's Bog in the night, you can, but none of it for me. Why, the water is two feet deep in some places, and it is full of pot-holes, old stumps, and everything else. If we had carried a boat with us, it would have been different.

"We stuck to our perch until we were sleepy and half-frozen, and finally Le Roy dropped the lantern, and it went out, but by good luck the chimney was not broken."

"Went to sleep, I suppose," observed Phil, with a laugh.

"You would go to sleep if you had been roosting on a stump for three hours, after tramping all day," retorted Le Roy.

"I thought then," continued St. Clair, "that we had better get back to camp. Fishing up the lantern we lighted it, and started, too tired and sleepy to care whether we saw any moose or not. But although we heard several on the way back, and knew there was game in the vicinity, we did not see any, and when we reached camp we did not waste much time in getting between our blankets, I assure you."

"You were a healthy set of hunters!" and Adams poked St. Clair in the ribs, and winked at Claude, who laughed heartily.

"You fellows are running ahead of your ticket," re-

A Moose Fight.

torted St. Clair; "for we shot a moose all the same, if we didn't see one the first night."

"You want a little glue to make that yarn hold together," declared Maynard.

"Are you telling this story, or am I" demanded St. Clair, with some asperity. "If you are going to tell it I will take a back seat."

"Oh, stop your bickering, fellows!" cried Claude. "Go ahead with your story, Andrew; you are doing well."

"As you may well imagine, we did not hurry any about getting up Sunday morning, and it was eleven o'clock before we turned out. Then we cooked our dinner and ate it, wishing all the time that the rest of you were with us.

"After the meal was over we fell into conversation, and, knowing that Arnold's River flowed into Megantic Lake, we concluded, after some talk, to try and build a raft, the next day, and sail down to the lake, the rapids ending a little way below us.

"We took a walk down to the dead-water during the afternoon, and, searching about, found some good-sized cedars that would answer admirably for the construction of our raft.

"We saw in the vicinity of our camp numerous signs of deer, caribou, and moose, and there is no doubt but what large game is very plentiful in that vicinity.

"We ate our supper and started a large fire afterwards to sit by, and, while we were speaking of the best way to build our raft, we heard an awful racket toward the bog, and, taking our fire-arms, rushed in the direction of the noise.

"It sounded like a succession of heavy shocks, accompanied by loud bellowings and snortings.

"It was not dark yet, and following the direction of the noise, we soon came to a sight that, I think, must be rarely witnessed."

"What was that?" interrupted Claude.

"A regular prize-fight between two bull moose."

"Great Scott!" ejaculated Adams.

"They were at it hot and heavy — give and take — and no quarter asked. They would back off a rod or two, and then, making a dive at each other, bring their heads together with a crash that I thought would split them open. And the snorting and bellowing beat all that I ever heard.

"Whispering together that we would not spoil the fun, we crept up as near as we dared, and then watched the battle.

"It was hard telling how it would go, but suddenly something occurred that neither of the moose had reckoned on."

"What was that?" broke in Maynard.

"Rushing together with more courage than sense, their heads struck with a crash, and their horns became locked in such a manner that they could not tear them apart."

"They were in a bad fix," said Phil.

"You're right, they were. In vain they pulled, and backed, and swerved from one side to the other, like two accomplished wrestlers, both intent on victory. But the locked horns would not yield, and as it began to grow dark, we concluded that the moose must call it a draw game, and that we would step in and finish it for them."

"I should like to have been there," cried Claude, excitedly.

"So should I," added Maynard.

"We accordingly opened fire on them. I had my gun, and Tom and Charlie their rifles. The first round we fired was a surprise party to them, as up to that time they were unaware of our presence. But after they received our shots the way they tore around was a caution to snakes.

"Fearing that in their tremendous struggles they might break their horns, and thus free themselves, we loaded and fired as fast as possible, until they laid stretched out before us as dead as door-nails.

"Then we cut out their tongues, and made our way back to camp, and went to bed early, and had another good night's sleep.

"The next morning while we were eating breakfast we were surprised to see an Indian on the opposite side of the river. In front of our camp were shallow rapids, and the red man waded across and came up to where we were sitting.

"He asked us what we were doing, where we had come from, and so on; and we told him who we were, what we had come there for, and then questioned him.

"He informed us he belonged to the St. Francis tribe of Indians, and said he had come down here for a hunt. He told us his family were with him, and that they were camped a short distance below us on the opposite side of the river.

"I told him about our shooting the moose, and that we were going to build a raft and go down to Lake Megantic. I asked him if he would take off the heads and skin the moose for us, telling him that if he would we would give him the meat.

"He said he would go back and get his son, a young man, to come and help him. In half an hour they returned. They had two long hunting-knives, and taking our axe, we went over to where the moose lay, and the Indians went to work.

"They cleaned the horns and cut off the heads, took off the hides, and then cut up the meat, and we carried about twenty pounds, from one of the hind-quarters, to camp.

"The Indians then offered to help us build the raft, and we all went to work, and by noon it was completed."

"How large was it?" asked Adams.

"About six feet wide and fifteen feet long. The Indians made us three rough paddles, and we also procured three long poles, to help navigate our craft.

"When everything was ready, we took a cold lunch, and at one o'clock started for the raft. The Indian told us that he was going to come and camp in the place we had left, so they would be nearer the meat.

"We carried our things down to the raft, and, placing them in the centre of the craft, pushed off, and started down-river. The Indian had told us it was good water clear to the lake, so we had no fear of rapids.

"The raft was made of two tiers of logs, one over the other, and stood several inches out of the water, and bore us along nicely.

"We paddled until we reached the lake, and then, finding the wind was fair, — it blew from the south, — we rigged one of our blankets on two of the poles for a sail, and went booming down the lake in fine style."

"That must have been fun!" remarked Maynard.

"It was better than paddling, I tell you. At six o'clock we reached the outlet, and, landing, went up to a new hotel, kept by a man named Bruce. We stopped there overnight, and after breakfast Tuesday morning concluded it was about time for us to be getting back to camp, more especially as we found two inches of snow on the ground."

"We had three here," observed Claude.

"The wind was not fair for us to sail up the lake, and we hired two men and a bateau, for two dollars, to bring us back to the head of the lake.

"In talking with the landlord Tuesday evening, I found that we could send our moose heads and skins out to Sherbrooke from there; and I wrote Norton a letter, telling him I had expressed two moose heads and skins to him, and to fix them up, and send them to me at Boston, by express, the first of October.

"We had a very pleasant sail up the lake; but, instead of entering Arnold's River again, the men landed us on the lake shore, and put us on a trail that they told us led to the head-waters of Parmachenee.

"We followed it until noon, when we ate a cold luncheon, resting half an hour, then pushed on.

"The walking during the forenoon was horrible. The bushes and trees, loaded with snow, wet us about through, and after dinner, before we had been an hour on the road, we lost the trail."

"That was a nice pickle to be in!" suggested Phil.

"Yes, very pleasant. We blundered around for a couple of hours, without having any idea where we were, except that we knew we were on this side of the boundary. For it was in crossing the height of land that we lost the trail.

"Finally, Wingate proposed we should climb a mountain near us, and see if we could observe anything we recognized from the summit.

"I thought this good advice, and up the mountain we went. It was a hard climb. When we reached the summit we studied the landscape, and discovered a small sheet of water that we concluded was Parmachenee Lake.

"Taking the bearing of this by compass, we descended the mountain, and after an hour's walk, reached a stream that flowed toward the lake.

"After some argument we concluded it must be the Ledge Ridge branch of the Magalloway, and to-day we found we were right in our supposition.

"As it was five o'clock when we reached the stream, we thought the best thing we could do was to camp for the night, as we were both hungry and tired.

"Wingate and I started a fire and built a camp, Le Roy caught two dozen small trout in a pool on the stream, a short distance below us, and we had our supper and went to bed.

"This morning we turned out at six o'clock determined to reach you, if possible, to-night; as we knew you would begin to feel anxious about us.

"The river furnished us with some more trout, and it took the last scrap of pork we had to fry them with.

"Believing now that the stream we were on was one of the branches of the Magalloway, we concluded the best thing we could do was to stick to it, and follow it until we came out to some spot we were familiar with.

"Shouldering our packs once more, we took up our line of march. It was very rough country to travel through. Rocky, and, in some places, huge ledges walled in the river, and we went around them, rather than climb over them. Close to the stream we often encountered alder-bushes, so thick that we were forced to give them a wide berth; but we never lost sight of the water, except for a few moments at a time.

"About noon we reached a dam, and this gave us courage, for we were certain now that we were on the right track.

"At half-past twelve we reached the Forks, and gave a cheer as we recognized the place.

"Throwing down our 'collateral,' as the river drivers call their baggage, we went to where our boat was hid, and found it all right, also the oars and paddle.

"We carried the boat to the river, and placed it in the water, and then started a fire, and ate what we had left, for our dinner. And you can guess it was a pretty thin meal.

"About half-past one we embarked, and without anything to trouble us, came down the river all right, and here we are."

"And glad enough we were to see you!" returned Claude.

"How did you like Lake Megantic?" Phil asked.

"Not very well. It is two or three times as large as Parmachenee, but not near as pretty."

"Is there a steamboat on it?" inquired Maynard.

"No. But the hotel man told me they were going to build one this winter."

"Is there any fishing in the lake?" queried Adams.

"The landlord said it contained trout and bass. But we did not fish it any."

"Do you know what time it is, fellows?" asked Phil, hauling out his watch.

"Bedtime, I guess," replied Wingate.

"I should say so," responded Phil, "it's twelve o'clock."

The boys had been so interested in St. Clair's story that no note of time had been kept, but at Phil's announcement they promptly adjourned to their tent.

CHAPTER XIV.

Moving Down-river. — Rafting the Menagerie. — Camping at the Foot of the Lake. — The Pursued and Pursuers. — Fighting the Hounds. — Lightfoot's Death. — Removal to Forks of the Magalloway. — A Fifty-Dollar Bear. — Down River again. — Upper Metalluc Pond. — Camping Over-night. — Early Risers. — Good Duck Shooting.

GOING to bed at midnight does not tend to early-rising, and it was nine o'clock Thursday morning, before the party had finished breakfast.

"I think," said Claude as they arose from the table, "that we had better be getting down-river. We ought to reach home by the second or third of October, at the farthest; and as we do not care to hurry any, and will want to stop along on the way, that we had better leave here to-morrow. As we shall have to lead Nap and Lightfoot through the woods, we can't go a great way in a day."

"Suppose we leave here to-morrow morning, and go down as far as Little Boy's Falls, and camp there to-morrow night. Everything will have to be carried around there, and if we stop there to-morrow night, it will save one loading and unloading of the boats," remarked Wingate.

"I like that plan," observed Maynard.

While they were talking, Mr. Parker and Russ suddenly made their appcarance from the woods back of the camp, and told the boys that they were on their way down to the settlements, and if they had any mail to send out they would take it.

The boys tried to coax them to stop and have some dinner, but Mr. Parker said they were in a hurry, and must get along. Claude and Maynard gave them their letters, and the woodsmen, bidding them take care of themselves, headed down-river.

"How are you going to cross the lake?" Adams called after them.

"We've a canoe hid in the bushes near Little Boy's Falls, that we shall launch, as soon as we get to it," returned Russ; and a moment later the two men had disappeared in the woods.

The rest of the forenoon was spent in picking up and packing as far as possible.

After dinner all but Maynard and Phil went over to Rump Pond fishing, and returned about five o'clock with fifty small trout and the boat.

In the evening around the camp-fire Wingate suggested that they should build a raft somewhere below the falls, and take the animals across the lake on it, instead of making the tiresome tramp through the woods.

This proposition was hailed with enthusiasm by the others, and it was unhesitatingly decided to do it.

"A chromo to the first one who wakes in the morning," laughed Claude, as the party rose from the camp-fire.

The night passed quietly, and Phil, much to his own surprise, was the first one to wake. He looked at his watch, and found it was only five o'clock, but knowing it would take a couple of hours to pack up and load the boats after breakfast, he turned out and dressed; then, calling Maynard and the others, went out and started a fire in the stove.

All of the fellows rose promptly, and while Maynard and Phil were preparing breakfast, their friends struck both of the tents, and packed them up.

At half-past six breakfast was ready, and at seven the boys had all eaten, and were busy loading the boats. By stowing things snug, everything was loaded into the three boats, and at nine the little flotilla started down-river, Claude, St. Clair, and Wingate in the boats, and the other members of the party, escorting Nap and Lightfoot, by land. The box containing Ben Butler and Daniel Pratt had been packed in the "Fairy," and the eagles did not have to work their passage.

"We shall reach the falls first, Maynard," cried Claude, as the boats left the landing, "and will get dinner."

"All right; you ought to get there an hour or two before we do, even if the animals don't give us any trouble. If they do, no knowing when you will see us."

The boats, in charge of their three owners, made the run down-river without any difficulty, except from an occasional piece of shallow water. But such slight obstacles as these were easily surmounted, and at eleven o'clock the boys were at the falls.

They unloaded the boats, and set up the tents a couple of rods below, then started a fire, and made preparations for dinner."

"The venison is all gone," said Claude; "we shall

have to cook some trout, and have some canned-beef for dinner.

"I wish we had about fifty pounds of that moose-meat here that we gave the Indians," added St. Clair, who was assisting him.

"Perhaps we can scare up some partridges around here somewhere after dinner," remarked Wingate.

"I hope we can," returned Claude; "for there is nothing suits my taste better than a nice plump partridge."

Maynard and his party arrived at half-past twelve, not having had any difficulty with the animals, except in getting through the thick growth occasionally. They were tied up at a safe distance from each other, and then dinner was served.

"If there had been a path along by the river," said Maynard, "I would have mounted Nap, and rode him down here."

"Perhaps then you would have taken another bath," laughed Phil.

In the afternoon Maynard and Phil stopped in camp, but the rest of the party went out for the purpose of making additions to the larder. Claude, St. Clair, and Adams started off on some of the logging-roads, to look for partridges, and Wingate and Le Roy tried their luck on the river with their rods.

During the afternoon Phil went into the store-tent for some sugar, and caught a hedge-hog stealing their pork; he ran for his rifle, and shot the porcupine through the head, killing him instantly. Picking him carefully up by the tail, to avoid getting the quills in his hands, he carried him out, and showed him to Maynard, saying, "How would this fellow do for a roast?"

"I don't know whether they are good to eat or not; but it would be quite a job to skin him. Pick out a few of his quills and throw him into the river."

"What do you want of the quills?"

"I want to take a few home to keep in a cabinet of curiosities I am picking up."

"Do you suppose, Maynard, that these porcupines can shoot their quills at any one when they are alive?"

"Do I? Not much. Cuvier and other French naturalists used to say so; but that was about as unreliable as many other of their statements. The fact that the quills come out so easy is what probably gave foundation for the shooting story."

"Did you ever catch a woodchuck, Maynard?"

"No; but I have no doubt they are good to eat. They live on vegetables and grasses, and become as fat as pigs."

"Everything is ready for supper but cooking what game or fish the boys bring in," said Maynard, "and now let's chop some wood for the camp-fire this evening."

Getting their axes the boys went off two or three rods from where the tents were pitched, and began cutting some sticks into four-foot lengths. While engaged at this a small white animal, not larger than a rat, attracted their attention. Phil saw it first, running out of the end of a hollow log.

"Look at that little rascal, Maynard!" he cried, pointing to the animal. "What is it? A white rabbit?"

"No; it's a weasel. Isn't he pretty?"

"Yes; they are the fellows that suck eggs, aint they?"

"Yes; and kill chickens, too. But there are none for them to meddle with up here."

"See how spry that little chap is! No wonder they say, 'You can't catch a weasel asleep.'"

When the boys had cut up and carried a good pile of wood to camp it was time to get supper.

Phil started to call the fishermen, but met them before he had taken a dozen steps.

"Have you had any luck?" inquired Phil. "We want some trout for supper."

"We have forty-one, all dressed," said Le Roy.

"Good boys! I suppose they will bear rinsing a little?"

"Did you ever see a fish that wouldn't?" queried Wingate. "It's almost impossible to get all the slime off them."

While the fish were being cooked, the gunners returned with four partridges, and Maynard told them he would cook them for breakfast.

"I should like to take a trip up into the Moosehead Lake region, some time," said Claude, as the boys reclined around the camp-fire after supper.

"Suppose we go up there another year," proposed Maynard. "We shall have done this country pretty well by the time we get home."

"We will talk it over this winter," suggested Wingate.

"I should like to climb Mt. Katahdin," remarked Le Roy. "It is the second highest mountain in New

England, and, according to 'Farrar's Guide to Northern Maine,' it is much harder to climb than Mount Washington."

"We'll give it a try," asserted Claude, "if we go up that way next summer."

"We must try and find some good cedar, to-morrow, for the raft," said Wingate. "That is what we built ours with over on Arnold's River."

"I noticed some a little way this side of the outlet, when we went down to Flint's for the potatoes the other day," observed Phil.

"Then we can camp in the vicinity of it," replied Claude.

"We ought to put in two or three days at Lincoln Pond on our way down-river," suggested St. Clair.

"We will if we have time," replied Claude.

The next morning the party left the falls at nine o'clock, the same arrangements being made as on the day before.

At eleven o'clock the boats reached the proposed camping-spot, near the cedar growth that Phil had spoken of, and the boys landed and unloaded the things.

By the time the tents were up and the fires under way, the "travelling menagerie," as Phil jocosely termed it, had arrived.

Dinner over, the boys commenced an attack upon the cedars, and by five o'clock had a sufficient number cut down, trimmed up, and rolled to the bank of the river, for the construction of the raft.

The work was then abandoned until the following day, and while Maynard and Phil proceeded to get supper, their companions cut up and brought in a large pile of fuel, as they expected to stop where they were until Monday morning.

"How are we going to fasten those logs together?" queried Phil, when the party were discussing their future movements in the evening.

"If we only had an auger," said Adams, "it would be easy enough."

"But we have none," replied Claude. "I have been thinking that matter over. We shall have to make a double-decker. The first layer of logs we will place side by side, then place two poles across them long enough to reach from one side to the other. Then with that long line we have we can fasten them together. It will not be very strong, but I guess it will hold. Then we can roll the upper tier of logs on the cross-sticks, and fasten them in place with some alder withes. This can be done by cutting small alder limbs about six feet long, and looping them about the lower and upper logs, bringing the upper ends together, and twisting them, and then sticking the ends in just as you have seen them on a bale of hay. I don't know as we can build a very secure raft, that way, but I guess it will answer our purpose. If any of you can show me a better way, I am open to conviction, as the darkey said when he stole the chickens."

"How did the Indians build your raft, St. Clair?" inquired Phil.

"They had an auger, and made it similar to the head-works the lumbermen use."

"I don't see but what Claude's plan is safe enough," declared Maynard.

A Rainy Sunday.

"It is thickening up," remarked Le Roy, while the boys went to bed. "I should not wonder if it stormed to-morrow."

It was eight o'clock when the tired sleepers awoke Sunday morning, and the first sound they heard was the rain pouring down on the tent.

"It's raining," cried Phil, with a sour expression on his face, as he listened to the storm.

"Let it come," remarked Claude. "We can't do anything to that raft now, and I am glad of it. On principle I don't believe in working Sundays, but I looked upon that job as a matter of necessity. But the Lord evidently thinks different, and we shall have to lie still."

"It will be nice getting breakfast," growled Phil, as he pulled on his rubber-coat, after dressing.

"It will do you good," laughed Adams.

"I suppose you take us for ducks," observed Maynard, as he began dressing.

"No; you are a couple of old drakes," spoke up Le Roy.

Leaving their companions to arise at their leisure, Maynard and Phil went out-doors, and, in a pouring rain, began preparations for breakfast. Their wood was soaking wet, and Phil had to go to some white birches near them and collect a quantity of bark, before they could start a fire, and even then it was with some difficulty that they coaxed the fires to burn.

By the time the breakfast was well under way their companions were up; and Maynard, dripping like a mermaid, went in to set the table.

"Rain any where you come from?" laughed Claude.

"You will say so when you get out-doors; and it's an awful cold storm."

"We can't expect fair weather all the time," sagely remarked Wingate. "I think we have had more than our share of it on this trip so far."

"Right you are," replied St. Clair. "We have no reason to growl at the weather."

The party stuck to their tent the most of the day, and in the evening, although the rain had stopped and the indications were that the storm was over, it was so cold, wet, and cheerless out-doors that the camp-fire was dispensed with, and they went to bed early, after appointing Phil as cook and Wingate as his assistant.

Monday morning dawned bright and pleasant, and as soon as breakfast was over the building of the raft began. The boys prosecuted the work with energy, and when, at half-past twelve, Phil called them to dinner, their rude craft was completed. As soon as the mid-day meal was over, the things were packed up, the tents were taken down, and the heavier articles loaded upon the raft. Then the boats were loaded; and after this, Nap, by a piece of bread and molasses, and Lightfoot, by means of a handful of salt, were enticed upon the raft and securely tied, while the tents and some other things were piled up between them. Maynard had found an old board, about twelve feet long, by the side of the river, — a stray waif probably from some lumberman's camp, — and out of this, by the aid of an axe, he had fashioned a rough steering-oar. As he had more control over Nap than either of his friends he had agreed, at the request of Claude, to look after the animals and steer the raft, his friend promising to keep an eye on the craft and promptly render him any assistance needed.

At last all was ready, and Maynard, stepping on the raft, pushed it away from the bank of the river. Claude and Phil, in the "Fairy," then hitched on to the forward end; the "Water-Witch," with Wingate and Adams, then fastened to the "Fairy;" and the "Go-Ahead," with St. Clair and Le Roy, took the lead, after being secured to the "Water-Witch." Thus arranged the boats started down-river, towing the raft behind them, with Maynard at the helm.

They soon reached the lake, the current in the river helping them considerably at the start.

They had concluded to go to Bose Buck Cove, at the south-western extremity of the lake, and camp a day or two, and make the ascent of Bose Buck mountain.

The raft towed much easier than they had expected; and, without any accident or trouble of any kind, they reached the place where they intended to camp at five o'clock, and, taking the raft close to the shore, landed the animals and secured them. Afterwards the boats were unloaded, the tents set up, and, while Phil and Wingate began overhauling the stores for supper, Claude started the fires, and the other members took a look around for fuel, and, using the axes and hatchet, by supper-time had a goodly pile gathered.

The next morning all of the party, with the exception of Phil and Wingate, who had concluded to stay in camp, left the tent at eight o'clock, taking a lunch with them, to climb Bose Buck.

They followed a path that led from near their encampment, running as far as the Little Magalloway, and crossing this, took a straight course through the woods for the top of the mountain. After leaving the path at the river, the route was rough and hard, and they found the climb quite difficult. Reaching the summit they rested an hour, and ate their lunch, and then started homeward, being rather disappointed in not having obtained better views from the mountain.

Between the river and the camp they came across a flock of seven partridges, and secured five. Just after they had shot the partridges, they heard the baying of hounds, and Claude said that somebody must be out hunting deer with dogs.

During the forenoon Wingate and Phil went over to the outlet in the "Water-Witch," and spent several hours in fishing, returning to camp at one o'clock with a good string of trout. After eating their dinner, they busied themselves about the camp cutting wood, reading, and fooling with Nap, until four o'clock came, and they began to think of supper. While Wingate was building a fire in the stove they heard the noise of hounds in the woods west of them.

"That sounds like dogs yelping," said Wingate.

"Yes; I guess there are some fellows out with hounds after deer," returned Phil.

Soon they heard the hounds again, and this time more distinct. "I'll bet the deer is heading for the lake," said Wingate.

"I hope he is," replied Phil. "If he reaches it before the dogs do, he will be all right, for if the hounds follow him into the water, I will go out in one of the boats and drive them back. I don't believe in hunting deer that way."

"Nor I either. It don't give them any kind of a chance. I'll go in the boat with you, Phil, if the deer and the dogs take to the water."

A few moments later they were startled by hearing a noise close at hand, and the next moment a splendid buck, accompanied by a doe, passed through the camp on the gallop and dashed into the water near them, heading for the opposite side of the lake. "Great Scott! there were two of them!" shouted Wingate as the boys stood looking at the deer.

"And they have run them nearly to death, I suppose," remarked Phil.

"They would not be fit to eat if they were shot now," added Wingate.

The boys took a few steps nearer the water, and watched the hunted animals as they swam gallantly for their lives.

Their interest in them, however, ceased very suddenly when they heard the hounds giving voice close behind them, and they turned around just in time to behold two dogs emerge from the woods, and, springing into the camp, make an attack on Lightfoot and Nap.

"Thunder and guns, Phil! those hounds are after our pets! I suppose they think they are the deer they have been chasing;" and rushing into camp followed by Phil, they shouted to the dogs, to frighten them from their attack.

"Let's get that hound away from Lightfoot first if we can," cried Wingate; "Nap will take care of himself."

As the boys reached Lightfoot they found the hound was hanging to his throat, and a stream of blood was pouring down his breast.

Wingate was about to lay hold of the dog, but Phil interfered. "Don't touch him now, Charlie, he may bite you; and as we are strangers to him, I don't believe we can make him loose his grip. Our rifles are what we want."

The two boys darted into the tent, and in a moment were out with their rifles loaded. Phil rushed up to the hound, who now had the deer down, and putting the muzzle of his rifle to one of the hound's ears, sent a bullet through his head, killing him almost instantly.

Quick as the boys had been, however, they were not able to save their pet, for the hound had torn his throat all open, and there was no chance whatever for him to recover from his wounds, and Wingate reluctantly shot him, to put him out of his pain.

The boys felt bad at losing the deer, for all of the party were much attached to it, it having become so tame as to eat out of their hands, and to come up to them and court a caress when they were near enough.

Turning around to help Nap, they found that he did not require any help, as the hound lay dead with his bowels ripped open, while the blood was running from a dozen wounds in various parts of his body.

The boys had heard the barking and growling, but had not witnessed the combat, as they had stood back to the dog and the bear, while trying to save Lightfoot.

Nap stood over the dead hound smelling of him and nosing him over, and occasionally lapping some of the blood that streamed from the dog's wounds. The boys could not see that Nap was injured any, but they did not like the idea of his lapping the hound's blood, thinking it might make him ugly to them, and Wingate caught hold of the hound's tail, and dragged him out of the bear's sight.

Phil took the other hound and pulled him along to his mate, and then the cooks proceeded with their work, which had been interrupted.

Ten minutes afterwards two rough-looking men, who evidently owned the hounds, came rapidly out of the woods, and, entering the camp, stood still when they saw Lightfoot lying on the ground. They were armed with double-barrel shot-guns, and had knives in sheaths belted around them.

"Here's one of our deer," cried the oldest of the two men, "and the other must have tooken to the lake."

"You have made quite a mistake, gentlemen," declared Wingate, as the two boys confronted them; "that deer belongs to us. It was one we had caught alive and tamed, but your hound killed it, and I had rather given twenty-five dollars than had him do it."

"That's too thin!" asserted the younger of the two men. "I don't believe you could catch a deer alive anyway. That deer belongs to us, and we're goin' to have him. Whar'd the other one go to? The hounds were after two of 'em."

"This is not your deer," replied Phil, indignantly; "don't you see the rope on his neck, and that he is still fastened to the tree, as he was while alive? The two deer your hounds were chasing swam across the lake."

At this announcement the two men turned to look out on the lake, and espied Nap chained to a tree.

"Thunder, Bill! There's a bear!" and the men looked at their guns.

"He will not hurt you, if you keep away from him," said Wingate; "we are taming him."

"Are you fellows in the menagerie business?" sneeringly asked the man who had spoken of the bear.

"No, we are not," answered Phil, sharply.

"Whar' did the hounds go?" asked the man called Bill.

"They are about here somewhere," answered Wingate, cautiously, with a warning glance at Phil.

Just then, much to the relief of Wingate and Phil, their friends returned from the mountain.

The boys were astounded when they saw the deer lying dead.

"Who killed Lightfoot?" shouted Adams, savagely, as he bent over the deer.

Wingate began to narrate the facts in the case, but before he had spoken a dozen words the hunters, who had found their hounds, rushed up to the boys, but moderated their pace somewhat when they found what an addition had been made to the party.

"Who killed them ar dogs?" inquired the older, angrily.

"The bear killed one, and I shot the other," returned Phil, coolly, who, knowing that his party were more than a match for the two men, thought it as well to be explicit.

"Yer did? Wall, you'll have ter pay for them hounds, if there's any law in the State," growled the younger of the men. "What did yer shoot him fur?"

"Because he killed our tame deer."

"If I were you," said Claude, "I would not say much about law. I suppose you know it is against the law to hunt deer with dogs, and you have already laid yourself liable to arrest, and here are plenty of witnesses to convict you both. But we have no intention of doing it; the whole thing is an accident, in one sense of the word, and we feel as bad about our deer as you do your dogs. We intended to take him home with us to Boston."

"Wall, I don't see as we can make anything out of this crowd," remarked the older of the men to his companion. "Let's put for camp," and the strangers, with a parting scowl at the boys, started off.

"Why don't you bury the hounds before you go?" cried Maynard.

"Bury them yourself, if you want ter; if you don't, you can eat them. They'll make good sassingers," replied the younger of the fellows, with a coarse laugh, as the men moved rapidly away.

After their disagreeable visitors were out of sight, the boys had their supper, and afterwards went down to the shore of the lake, scooped a deep hole in the sand, and tumbled the bodies of the two dogs into it and covered them up.

Then they took the head and skin off of Lightfoot, and dressed him, for the buck was fat and in fine order.

Wednesday morning, after breakfast, they packed up again, and getting Nap aboard the raft, towed it over to the outlet, and pitched their tents, intending to stop here until the next day.

In the afternoon, Claude and Maynard went over to Flint's, and finding him at home, asked him if he thought they could run their boats down from the lake to the Forks of the Magalloway.

He told them that there would be no danger if they were careful, as the river was higher than usual at that season of the year, and advised them to start from below the dam.

Claude told him about the death of the hounds, and Flint seemed highly amused at the way Nap had disposed of the one that had attacked him. He said the men were probably from Colebrook, and he advised the boys not to leave their camp alone until they left the lake, as the men might visit it in their absence and play some mean trick upon them.

The boys thought this good advice to follow, as they considered the two men capable of committing any rascally act that came into their heads.

"This is our last night at Parmachenee," remarked Claude, as the boys gathered around their camp-fire in the evening.

"For this season," echoed Maynard.

"But I hope we shall come up here again some summer," declared Phil. "We have had a splendid time."

"That is so," added Wingate, "and it's a charming little lake. In fact, the whole country is pretty."

As the boys are on the point of leaving Parmachence Lake, we would say that, while this sheet of water is not as large as several others in the Androscoggin system, it is the gem of them all, so far as beauty is concerned, lying, as it does, in a dense wilderness, surrounded by lofty mountains, and offers unequalled facilities to campers-out, the fishing and hunting in the vicinity being equal to that in any part of the State of Maine, which, up to the present time, is more than half an unbroken forest. Parties who think of visiting this section of Maine will find in "Farrar's Androscoggin Lakes Illustrated," all the information necessary to enable them to make a pleasant and successful trip.

After breakfast, Thursday morning, the boys prepared for their removal to the Forks, and when all was ready, the party, with the exception of Maynard and Wingate, started with the boats, while the other two boys led Nap across the carry, the road ending at the Forks.

The bear was in good-humor, and, after feeding him, Maynard mounted upon his back and rode, Wingate leading the animal along by the chain. The carry was four miles long, and when Maynard had ridden half the distance he dismounted and Wingate took his place.

When they reached Flint's Camp several gentlemen who were stopping there came out to look at the bear, accompanied by Spoff, and they all laughed heartily at the queer steed Wingate rode.

"Is he a trotter or a pacer?" asked one of the gentlemen, smiling.

"I don't care about his doing any trotting when I'm on his back," replied Wingate.

"How long have you had him?" asked another of the party.

"About a month," replied Maynard.

"Will he do any tricks?" inquired Spoff.

"Get me a piece of bread and molasses, and I'll show you," returned Maynard. "Be sure and put plenty of molasses on it."

Spoff obtained the bread, and Wingate, dismounting,

Maynard made Nap set up, and placed the bread on his nose.

"Now," said the bear's instructor, "ready, aim, fire!" and at the word "fire" Nap tossed the bread into the air and caught it handsomely in his mouth as it came down.

"He's quite a cuss!" said Spoff, and the audience laughed at the deft manner in which the bear had caught the sweet morsel.

"What are you going to do with him?" asked one of the party as Wingate mounted the bear again.

"Carry him home with us," replied Maynard.

Bidding the gentlemen good-morning, the boys went along, and reached the river just as the boats arrived.

"Have any trouble on the river, Claude?"

"Not a bit, Wingate. The water was rather rough in two or three places, but we came along nicely, and did not hurt the boats a particle."

"Have any trouble with Nap?' inquired Phil.

"No, none at all," laughed Maynard, "and we made him perform to an admiring audience at Flint's Camp."

"Perform?"

"Yes; he did the great bread-tossing act!" and again Maynard laughed.

As the party only intended to stop one night at the Forks, they camped on the west side of the river. In the afternoon they all went to look at a beaver dam, about two miles distant, that Mr. Flint had told them of, with the exception of Claude and Phil, who had visited one over to Second Lake. They not feeling like fishing, walked over to Flint's, and spent the afternoon at his camp.

The boys all appeared at the supper table, and Claude asked them if they found the beaver dam.

Wingate told him that they had, and that they all thought it was worth going to see.

"Did you see any beavers?" inquired Phil.

"Nary a beaver," answered Le Roy.

"In talking with Flint this afternoon," said Claude, "he told me that there were two trails to Lincoln Pond: one starts from just below the Big Rips on the river, and strikes the pond at the upper end, and the other leaves the pond on the west side, and runs to the upper Metalluc Pond, near the east side of the river. The last trail is a good deal the shortest, and I thought we could visit the pond by one trail and come back to the river by the other."

"But we shall lose eight or ten miles of the river that way; and, as the scenery is very fine, I don't like to do it," replied Maynard.

After a debate on the matter, the boys decided to go down the river in their boats to the upper Metalluc Pond, and cross to Lincoln Pond from there.

While they were eating breakfast the next morning they were surprised by a visit from one of the gentlemen who were stopping at Flint's Camp.

Claude asked him if he had been to breakfast, and, upon learning that he had not, invited him to take a seat with them, and the gentleman accepted.

During the course of the meal the visitor informed the boys that he had taken a fancy to the bear, which he had seen when Maynard and Wingate brought him across the carry, and wanted to buy him. He told them that he was stopping up in the woods for his health, and intended to remain until the first of November, and, as the time hung heavily some days, he thought he could amuse himself by having the bear about the camp.

At first the boys utterly refused to entertain the proposition, but the gentleman was persistent, and showed them how much trouble Nap would be to them, more especially if they were going to Lincoln Pond, which he had learned was their next camping-place; said he would use the bear kindly, and finally offered them twenty-five dollars for the animal.

The opinion of the party now became divided, and, seeing this, the gentleman increased his offer until he rose to fifty dollars.

The last bid set the boys to arguing the case lively, and finally the gentleman proposed that they should take a vote on it, and this they did, Claude, Maynard, and Wingate voting to keep the bear, and their four friends to sell it.

As the gentleman was afraid he would have trouble in conducting his new purchase home alone, Maynard unchained the bear and led him over to Flint's.

He returned with the fifty dollars, and asked his friends what he should do with it.

"Keep it until we get home," said Claude, "and then we can decide."

"I feel as if it was blood-money," remarked Maynard, looking at it discontentedly.

"Nonsense!" declared Adams.

"Put it in your pocket-book," continued St. Clair. "None of us cared particularly for the money, but the gentleman was sick, and wanted Nap so much that I did not have a heart to refuse him."

Umbagog Lake, from Steamboat Landing, Cambridge, N.H.

"And besides," added Le Roy, "it is getting to be too much like work carting him around the country. I think we are well rid of him, leaving the money entirely out of the question."

Maynard did not agree with them; but, as the bear was gone, he made the best of it. Neither Wingate nor Claude had been very particular about keeping the animal, but had voted against selling him more out of regard for Maynard than for any especial love they had entertained for Nap.

The things were now packed up, and the boats loaded, and a little after nine the flotilla swung out into the river. They soon reached the Big Rips, and went down this inclined plane like a shot, then over the rapids below, reaching "good water" without any accident.

The current along that part of the river they were now sailing was very swift, and they did not have to exert themselves much with the oars. The banks of the river were thickly wooded, and the foliage, which had begun to assume its brilliant fall colors, attracted their attention from its beauty.

Several times, as they rounded some of the curves in the river, they came across flocks of ducks feeding; but the boats were loaded so deeply they thought it prudent to make no attempts at shooting.

Just before entering the meadows they were excited by seeing some large animal, which they took to be a caribou, wading across the river.

Phil, whose rifle was loaded, gave him a shot, but the caribou disappeared in the forest on the east side of the river, apparently unhurt.

At one o'clock they reached the entrance to the upper Metalluc Pond, and poling their boats through the narrow outlet, entered the pond, and landed at the northern end near the trail.

Disembarking, and unloading the boats, the cooks proceeded to get dinner, while the other members of the party pitchèd the tents, and took care of the stores, and the other articles.

In the afternoon Claude and Maynard walked over to Lincoln Pond to look at a logging-camp that was situated at the upper end, and see if it would do for them to live in while they were there, as, if so, it would save carrying over the tents. They carried the " Fairy " with them, and left her there. They found the camp in good condition, — a stove, and some cooking utensils in it, — and congratulated themselves on being able to leave quite a number of their heaviest things at Metalluc Pond.

On their return the boys questioned them about the place, and Claude gave them all the information he had acquired.

During the night they heard ducks quacking in the pond, and Claude and Phil turning out early the next morning, took one of the boats, and succeeded in shooting fifteen, and getting back to camp with them before either of their friends were up.

CHAPTER XV.

Early Birds. — Fine Duck-Shooting. — Moving. — The Camp at Lincoln Pond. — A Prolonged Storm. — Housed-up. — Fair Weather. — Early Fishing. — Splendid Luck. — Three and Four Pounders. — A Windy Day. — A Poor Hunt. — Bears as Thieves. — A Logger's Story of an Inquisitive Bear.

It was half-past six when Claude and Phil returned, and, going into the tent, Claude called out, —

"Wake up here, you sluggards! and see what Phil and I have brought you for dinner."

The boys roused up at his voice, and gazed at the ducks with astonishment.

"'The early bird gets the worm,'" remarked Claude, laughing, as his companions turned out and dressed.

"You did well — for you," said Maynard, as he examined the birds.

Wingate hurried out to assist Phil about the breakfast, and the ducks were taken care of by Phil, who did not intend to cook any of them until dinner-time.

During the forenoon the entire party, each loaded with all he could carry, made a trip over to Lincoln Pond and back, and then had dinner. After the meal was over they took down the tents, and carrying them and the stove, also some other articles, which they would not need until their return, hid them in the woods, a little way from the river, completely covering them with brush. After disposing of these things, they took what was left, and started for the pond once more.

"I wish we had let these eagles go with the bear," declared Maynard, as, with the box containing the birds on his shoulder, he tramped along, sweating under his load.

"I will change with you when you get tired," said Claude, who was bending under a load of supplies.

"I can stand it, I guess," replied Maynard; "and this is the only place we shall have to carry them."

The party were loaded quite heavily, and could not make very rapid progress, and it was five o'clock when they reached the logging-camp.

While Phil and Wingate prepared supper the other members of the party put the camp to rights, and cut up a supply of fuel, and brought it in-doors.

During the night a storm began, which the boys concluded must be the line-storm, as it lasted, with but little intermission, until Tuesday night. It rained hard most of the time, and the wind blew a gale from the south.

It was so rough on the pond that the boys could not fish with any comfort; and for three days, while the storm lasted, they spent the most of the time in camp, finding it more comfortable in a cold storm than their tent would have been.

Phil's week of cooking ended Sunday night, and Wingate was promoted to the office of chief cook, with Le Roy for an assistant.

"I hope this storm will clear up to-night," remarked Maynard, as they sat around the stove Tuesday evening; "I don't like being housed up so much day-times."

"Nor I either," added Claude; "and I don't like sitting around this stove evenings. It is much pleasanter having a large fire out-doors."

"Correct," returned Maynard.

"There ought to be good fishing after this rough weather," said Adams.

"And I'll bet there will be," replied Phil.

Wednesday morning Adams awoke about half-past four, and, running to the door, looked out and found the rain had stopped, and that the clouds, which were already running from the north-west, betokened a fair day.

He awoke Phil, and hurriedly dressing, they took their fishing-tackle, and embarking in the "Fairy," pulled across to a point on the eastern shore, and, anchoring, began to cast their flies.

They had not long to wait for a rise, for the water seemed alive with trout, and in less than ten minutes after they had made their first cast each one had landed a trout, weighing about two pounds apiece.

From where they were fishing they could command a view of nearly the whole pond, it being only two miles long by about a mile wide, and, when they had been enjoying the sport half an hour, they saw some of the boys take the other two boats and row down near the outlet and begin fishing there.

Besides a number of medium-sized trout they took two that were larger than anything they had seen on their present trip; but, not having scales with them, could not weigh them until they returned to camp.

At half-past seven Phil noticed a white speck fluttering from a stick near the shore in front of the camp, and concluding that it was a sign that breakfast was ready, they reluctantly pulled up their anchor and rowed for camp.

The fishing was as good as when they began, and Phil wanted to stop longer, but Adams, who was hungry, thought too much of his breakfast, and persuaded Phil that they had caught all the trout they needed at once; and as they had thirty, I think he was right.

The first thing they did on reaching camp was to weigh their two largest trout, and Phil's hauled down four pounds, while the one belonging to Adams stopped at three and one-half.

"By Jove! those are pretty fish," said Wingate, as he and Le Roy watched the weighing.

"They are beauties," added Le Roy, " and their size would not disgrace the Richardson Lakes. I had no idea there were such large trout in this pond."

"'They are few and far between, I guess," observed Phil.

While they were talking about their fish the other two boats came in, but the occupants of these had not done so well. Claude, who had been in the "Water Witch" alone, had only taken six fish, the largest of which weighed two pounds.

Maynard and St. Clair, who were together, had captured fifteen trout, the largest weighing a pound and three-quarters.

As it was, however, the five boys had brought in over seventy pounds of trout, being, with their other provisions, all they would need for several days.

The rest of the forenoon the party stopped around the camp, and cut up a lot of large logs for an out-door fire.

The wind blew a gale all day, although the sun shone bright and pleasant, but the air was decidedly cool.

During the afternoon the boys, with the exception of the cooks, who had quite a job before them to dress the morning's supply of fish, went out on some of the logging roads in the vicinity to see what they could shoot. They discovered plenty of deer sign, but the only game they succeeded in bagging was two partridges.

By evening the wind had gone down, and a large fire was built out-doors at a safe distance from the camp.

"We must climb Speckled Mountain before we go home," declared Wingate, as they reclined around the camp-fire, enjoying its warmth and glow.

"That is on the road to Bethel, I believe," asserted Phil.

"Yes,"' said Claude. "It forms one side of Grafton Notch, and is just opposite of Bald Pate, that we made the ascent of from Andover two years ago.

"Suppose it will be as hard to climb as Bald Pate was?" queried Adams.

"Harder, I think," answered Claude. "It is a higher mountain, and I believe there is no path to the summit. We shall have to pick our way through the woods until we get clear of the forest."

"How do you suppose Nap is getting along, Maynard?" asked Le Roy.

"All right, I guess. I think that gentleman will be kind to him. I shouldn't be surprised, however, if he gave him to Flint when he went home."

"You are wrong," remarked Claude. "The gentleman told me he owned a large place in New York, just out of the city, — Yonkers, I think, is where he lives, — and that he should take Nap home with him."

"He better not," said Adams, as the shadow of a smile played across his face, " Nap will be *Bruin* mischief around the house if he does."

"One dollar fine and three months at the Island for that," laughed Claude.

"I have heard bears are great thieves where they have a chance," observed St. Clair.

"Can't say as to that," replied Maynard.

St. Clair was right in his statement, as all woodsmen familiar with the habits of bears will testify, and they frequently annoy the inmates of logging camps very much by their thievish proclivities.

Springer, in his "Forest Life and Forest Trees," gives a good illustration of a bear's curiosity, and also tells of the fate that befell the marauder. He says: "We have sometimes been diverted as well as annoyed by their thievish tricks. In one instance we were followed several days by one of them on our passage up river, who seemed equally bent on mischief and plunder. The first of our acquaintance with him occurred while encamped at the mouth of a small stream, whose channel we were improving by the removal of large rocks which obstructed log-driving. Our camp was merely temporary, so that all our goods were exposed. While we were asleep during the night he came upon the premises and selected from the baggage a bundle containing all the winter clothing of one of the men, boots, shaving-tools, etc.

"His curiosity was too great to allow of a far removal

of the pack without an examination of its contents, and never did deputy inspector or constable perform a more thorough search. Duties on the package were inadmissible; the goods were esteemed contraband, and were accordingly confiscated. The wearing apparel was torn into shreds. There were a pair of stout cowhide boots, of which he tried the flavor; they were chewed up and spoiled. The razor did not escape his inquisitiveness. Whether he attempted to shave we say not, but he tested its palatableness by chewing up the handle.

"From this position we removed a few miles farther up stream, where we were to construct a dam, the object of which was to flow the lake, to obtain a good head of water for spring driving. This job being somewhat lengthy we erected a more permanent camp for our convenience. A few evenings after our settlement at this point, while all hands were in camp, we heard some one moving about on the roof, where a ten-gallon keg of molasses was deposited. At first it was supposed to be a trick by some one of the crew; but, on looking round, there was no one missing.

"Suspecting with more certainty the character of our visitor, we seized a firebrand or two, and sallied forth like a disturbed garrison of ants, when we discovered that we were minus a keg of molasses. Following in the direction of the retreating thief, we found the keg but a few rods distant, setting on one end with the other torn out. He evidently had intended a feast, but, intimidated by the firebrands and the hallooing, he had retreated precipitately into his native haunts; but only, as it would seem, to plan another theft. About two hours afterward, when all was still, a noise was again heard in the door-yard similar to that of a hog rooting among the chips, where the cook had thrown his potato-pearings. Peering through the crack of the camp-door, sure enough, there was Bruin again, apparently as much at home as a house-dog.

"We had a gun, but improvidently had left our ammunition at another place of deposit, about a hundred yards distant. Resolved upon chastising him for his insolence, in the event of another visit, the lantern was lighted, and the ammunition soon brought to camp.

"The gun was now charged with powder and two bullets. We waited some time for his return, first removing a strip from the camp-door for a port-hole. Hearing nothing of him, all hands turned in again. About twelve o'clock at night he made us his third visit in the door-yard, as before, and directly in front of the camp, offering a most inviting shot. Creeping softly to the door, and passing the muzzle of the gun through the prepared aperture, our eye glanced along the barrel, thence to a dark object not thirty feet distant. A gentle but nervous pressure upon the trigger, a flash, a sheet of fire, and the very woods shook with the reverberating report, which sent Bruin away upon a plunging gallop. The copious effusion of warm blood which spirted on the chips was evidence that the leaden messenger had faithfully done its duty. A portion of his lights were shot away, and dropped to the ground, which convinced us that he was mortally wounded, and that it would not be possible for him to run far. Seizing as many firebrands as could be procured, with axes, and the gun reloaded, all hands dashed into the forest after him, half naked, just as they had risen from the bed, leaping, yelling, and swinging firebrands, like so many wild spirits from the region of fire.

"Guided in the pursuit by the cracking of rotten limbs and the rustling of leaves as he heavily plunged on, we pursued him through a dense swamp. From the increased distinctness with which we heard his step, it was evident we were gaining upon him. Soon we heard his labored breathing. Just before we overtook him he emerged from the swamp, and with much exertion, ascended a slight elevation, covered with a fine growth of canoe birch, where, from exhaustion and loss of blood, he lay down, and suffered us to surround him. The inflammable bark of the birch was instantly ignited all round us, presenting a brilliant and wild illumination, which lent its influence to a most unbounded enthusiasm, while our war-dance was performed around the captured and slain marauder. Taken altogether, the scene presented one of the most lively collections of material for the pencil that we have ever contemplated. There were uncommon brilliancy, life, and animation in the group. After despatching, we strung him up and dressed him on the spot, taking only one quarter of his carcass, with the hide, back to camp.

"A portion of this was served up next morning for breakfast, but while the sinewy, human-like appearance of the foreleg might have whetted the appetite of a cannibal, a contrary influence was exerted on ours.

CHAPTER XVI.

A Deer-Hunt. — A Ludicrous Fright. — A Sociable Bear. — Trailing a Caribou. — Peculiar Pedestrianism. — Successful Shots. — The Caribou Killed. — Aid from Camp. — Boat-racing on Lincoln Pond. — Formation of the Lake and Forest Club. — Peppering a Loon. — Last Night in Camp.

"WHAT are you going to do to-day, Claude?" inquired Maynard, as they all sat around the breakfast table Thursday morning.

"I don't know. What do you say to going out somewhere, and try and get a shot at a deer? Wingate says there is only meat enough for dinner."

"I would like to go, for one."

"So would I," spoke up St. Clair.

"Any more?" inquired Claude, glancing around the table.

"I don't care to go," remarked Adams. "I noticed some blueberries near here yesterday, and the cooks and myself are going after some as soon as they do up their work."

"I guess I'll stay at home, also," said Phil, "and cruise around the camp a little; then I can be at home to dinner."

As soon as they had eaten breakfast Claude and his two companions, taking their guns and rifle, with plenty of ammunition and a lunch, — for they had very little expectation of being back to camp by dinner-time, started into the woods, taking a circle round the head of the pond, and then bearing away from it in an easterly direction.

About two hours after they had left camp they came upon the trail of some large animal; but the ground where they then were was soft and swampy, and they could not tell what it was; but they were of the opinion that it was either a moose, caribou, or bear.

They followed it until they came out upon dry and firm land, and then concluded that it was a caribou, as a careful examination of the footprints showed them to be very much like oxen, and they knew it was highly improbable, although not impossible, that an ox should be roaming at large through the forest.

Having made up their minds that the animal they were chasing was a caribou, they determined to hunt it down if possible, as the entire party had highly relished the meat that was sent them by Tom Chester, and ever since they had reached the woods they had been trying to get a shot at one.

"We will have that caribou, fellows," cried Claude, with enthusiasm, as they once more started on the trail, "if we follow him clear to the Cupsuptic River."

"My gracious, Claude! that is seven or eight miles," declared Maynard.

"What of that? — we are good for it," said St. Clair.

"But it is just as far back," suggested Maynard.

"Well, it won't kill us," answered Claude.

"I can stand it if you can," and Maynard made no further objections, for at the pace they were travelling talking became very tiresome.

About half-past eleven they reached a slight hill, the trail leading over it. At the top their direct progress was barred, by a cluster of windfalls, blown over and piled in every direction, the work of the late storm, the boys judged from the fresh breaks on the trees, and the rough appearance of the ground, where some had been uprooted.

"Great Scott!" exclaimed Maynard, "he can't have gone over this pile of stuff!" and he looked wonderingly at his companions, for the trail had led straight toward the centre of the snarl of broken and uprooted trees.

At this point the boys lost the trail, and, making a long circle of the tangled mass before them, reached the other side, and, after a half-hour's search, discovered the animal's tracks once more.

"Look here, fellows, it's past twelve o'clock," said Maynard, consulting his watch. "Suppose we dispose of our luncheon before we go any farther?"

"We may as well eat it now as any time," replied Claude, and sitting down on an old fallen pine, covered with moss, that had lain there perhaps for more years than the united ages of the boys, proceeded to dispose of what Wingate had put up for them.

Judging from the fresher appearance of the trail that led from near where they were sitting they concluded that their game was not very far in advance of them, and they eagerly discussed, while eating, their chances of soon sighting the caribou.

They were talking so earnestly that they did not hear the light step made by a bear, which had come from the windfalls, among which he had been lying; and the first they knew of his presence, Maynard, who was between his two friends, felt something cold and soft against his cheek, and, turning, rubbed noses with the bear.

If the earth had opened before them and Mephistopheles, surrounded by fire and blue smoke, had appeared, the boys would not have been any more surprised.

Never did electric shock start a person any quicker, than Maynard started as he caught a glimpse of that black head.

With his eyes almost bursting from his head and his hair standing on end he gave vent to a shriek that echoed through the forest, and rushed away from the log upon which he had been sitting.

His companions turning as he arose, also beheld Bruin, and the suddenness of his appearance, added to Maynard's wild screech, was too much even for Claude, who prided himself on his bravery, and he and St. Clair also yelled and jumped, frightening the bear as badly as the boys themselves had been frightened, and the animal took to his heels and disappeared in the woods before the hunters had found out that they were more frightened than hurt.

The whole scene was ludicrous beyond expression, and if "Puck" could have been there to have done justice to it the paper containing the sketch would have run through forty editions.

"Well," remarked Maynard, after a few moments, drawing a long breath, and smoothing his hair down, "if I didn't think that old Cloven-foot had come for me then, may I never eat another meal."

By this time the comical sense of the situation had dawned upon Claude, and he began to laugh. He was soon joined by his two friends, and they laughed until the tears fairly ran down their cheeks.

Every time they attempted to speak a spasm of laughter would seize one or the other, and they would break out again in a united howl that made the woods ring.

"Anyhow," remarked St. Clair, after half an hour's vent had somewhat relieved their mirth, "we are even with the bear. He was as badly frightened as we were, and I'll bet he is running yet."

"I have no doubt of that," returned Claude, "and now we must push on after the caribou if we intend to come up with him to-day."

"I am ready," observed St. Clair, as he picked up his gun, which, with the others, leaned against the log they had been sitting on, the boys in their scare not having touched them.

Claude and Maynard took their weapons, and once more the three boys pushed forward on the trail.

After following it for a mile, they discovered that the sun, which had been at their back after first leaving the place where they had been so badly frightened, was now in their faces, and the boys stopped for a moment, while Maynard consulted his pocket-compass. The dial showed they were travelling west, and convinced them beyond question that the game had made a turn, and was now travelling toward the pond.

"So much the better," declared Claude, when this point had been decided, "for now every mile we travel brings us nearer to camp."

"I don't see how those animals can get through some of the places they do," remarked Maynard, as they travelled onward.

"They just lay their horns back on their shoulders, as moose do, I expect, and push through by main strength."

The trail ran nearly due west, and after following it in this direction for about two hours, the party reached a tract of land, covered with loose stones and immense boulders, with a scant growth of soft wood.

Many of the large rocks were covered with caribou moss, and they soon found signs that the animal had been lately feeding.

The boys now began to grow excited, for they knew that the tract of land on which they were travelling extended to the borders of the pond, and they expected to see the caribou at any moment.

Up to this time they had been walking with their pieces unloaded to avoid accident, but now they slipped in the cartridges, and putting the hammers at half-cock, moved carefully forward.

Peering keenly at each stunted tree, and watching sharply each moss-covered boulder, they stole silently along, earnest and expectant.

Just as they came to a spot from which through the thin growth they could discern the sparkling waters of the pond, Claude, who was slightly in advance, stopped suddenly, and raised his hand with a warning motion.

"What is it?" whispered his friends, eagerly.

"The caribou! Don't you see him feeding on the moss on that leaning spruce?"

"He's too far away for a sure shot," said Maynard.

"Yes, we must get nearer to him."

Dropping on their hands and knees, the boys crawled toward the unconscious animal as stealthily as possible.

They had reached a point where they thought they might risk a shot successfully, when the caribou started along toward the outlet of the pond, and in a few seconds had increased the distance between himself and his pursuers by several rods.

"Confound him!" whispered Claude; "I was just going to fire. We shall have to crawl nearer."

The peculiar locomotion that the boys were now driven to was anything but pleasant. It is bad enough to crawl on your hands and knees where the ground is smooth and level and free from obstructions, but when, as was the case with our hunting party, the ground was full of treacherous holes, many of them being covered with bog moss, that sank a foot or more the moment the boys' hands or knees touched it, and rocks of all sizes, while occasional windfalls, clumps of bushes, and limbs, added to the difficulty of rapid progress, it is decidedly worse.

"He has stopped again!" softly said Maynard.

"I hope he will wait long enough this time for us to tickle his ribs," remarked St. Clair; "this kind of travelling may suit an Indian, but it never was intended for a white man."

Crawling and wiggling along, stopping occasionally to watch the animal, and keeping as still as mice, when their game left off browsing, they once more succeeded in getting within shooting distance.

"Aim behind his fore-shoulder, Frank, and I"— said Claude; but Frank didn't aim, because just then the caribou, who seemed to be picking out dainties in the eating line, shambled off again.

"By the Pied Piper of Hamlin!" exclaimed Frank,

impatiently, "are we to chase that fellow all over the country on our hands and knees?"

"Have patience," urged Claude.

"I have," whispered Frank, "and presently I shall have two holes in the knees of my breeches. I have a great mind to send a rifle-bullet after him."

"Don't do it!" entreated St. Clair.

"If you did not kill him or wound him mortally he would escape us, for our guns will not throw that distance with any effect. I wish we had all taken rifles."

"So do I," added Claude, earnestly. Crawling a short distance further they reached a large pine stump, and stopping for a moment, Claude rose up behind it, and peered around, one side toward the caribou.

"He has just reached the outlet," whispered the leader, as he dropped down again, "and will probably drink there. I hope we can get a shot at him before he crosses the brook."

"If we don't," returned St. Clair, "we shall lose him, for I'll be hanged if I am going to cross that brook on my hands and knees."

"You can't do it," declared Maynard, as they crawled forward again; "the water is too deep."

Fortune favored them this time as the caribou seemed in no hurry to cross the stream, and, worming themselves along, they at last reached a place from which they could fire with some degree of certainty.

As the animal stooped to drink, his right side was exposed to them, and they gave him a volley. He jumped, staggered, and fell into the water, and was dead when the boys reached him.

Upon examination it was found that several buck shot

had gone into his neck, and others into his hind flank, while Frank's bullet had struck him at the upper part of the foreleg, and, breaking the bone, had made a ragged wound, in itself sufficient to have killed him.

The animal was in good condition, and must have weighed six or seven hundred. He had a noble set of antlers, and the boys determined to save them.

It took their united strength to get the caribou out of the water, and then it was a question what to do with him.

Finally Frank offered to walk to camp, about two miles distant, and come back with some help in two of the boats, while Claude and St. Clair skinned the animal as he lay. It was then five o'clock, and Frank promised to make the best time possible.

As soon as he had disappeared the boys went to work, and with their knives succeeded in cutting off the head, which they laid carefully to one side.

Skinning the animal they found to be a slow job on account of his weight, but they finally managed it, and then waited for the axe Frank was to bring before cutting the carcass up.

Soon after six they descried two boats leaving the camp, and at half-past they were at the outlet, bringing Phil, Maynard, Le Roy, and Adams.

"Give us your axe, Maynard," cried Claude, as the boats reached the shore, "and I'll soon have this fellow in quarters, and we can handle the meat a little easier."

After finishing their work, the meat, head, and hide, were loaded into the boats, and the boys rowed to camp. It was about dark when they arrived, and after eight before they sat down to supper.

Friday was cloudy and cold, with an appearance of snow. The boys remained in camp during the forenoon, the hunting party, especially, being tired from their tramp of the day before.

About ten o'clock the boys noticed a large volume of smoke floating over the pond that came from toward the river, and concluded that there must be a fire in the woods in that direction. The smoke continued all day, but towards evening was not so heavy.

As the party sat around the camp-fire after supper, Claude made a proposition that they should form a club, and call it the "Lake and Forest Club," and after they returned home should hire a suitable room and hold one meeting per week.

The boys eagerly listened while he went on to give them his ideas. The membership fee was to be five dollars, with a further payment of fifty cents per week from each member, the number of the club limited to twenty-five persons. He thought that with such a membership as that a suitable number could be induced each summer to make a trip to the woods, one of his objects being to keep up their excursions and go somewhere every year.

Their club-room was to be plainly but comfortably furnished, and from the funds of the club a complete library of books on hunting and fishing was to be procured, and such additions of new volumes made as the members might vote for. When he had finished speaking Maynard moved that Claude be made president, and the motion was promptly carried. Afterward, Maynard was elected vice-president, Wingate, recording and corresponding secretary, and Adams, treasurer. Claude and Le Roy were chosen a committee to hire a suitable room, and were given power to fit it up on their arrival home. Maynard and Adams were chosen a committee to canvass for members, and St. Clair and Wingate a committee to prepare a constitution and by-laws for the regulation of the club, which was to be presented and voted upon at the first meeting held in Boston, such meeting to be called when and where the president saw fit.

Phil laughingly told them that he would join the club, although he would not be able to be present at many of the meetings.

"Well, Mr. President," said Adams, addressing Claude with mock gravity, "I move that we adjourn, for I am going to bed."

While eating breakfast Saturday morning it suddenly occurred to Claude that the things they had left over at Metalluc Pond might have been burnt by the fire of the day before, and he spoke of it.

His friends as well as himself were rather troubled by this view of the case, and the idea, having entered their minds, gave them no peace. Soon after breakfast they determined to satisfy themselves in regard to their fears, and the whole party, excepting the cooks, took the trail, and went over to the river.

Before they reached the pond their worst suspicions were confirmed, for they suddenly emerged from green woods into brown and blackened trees, and the ground beneath their feet was covered with ashes which still sent forth smoke and heat.

The fire had changed the appearance of the locality, and it was some time before they found where they had cached their things. When they did they found everything ruined. The tents, table, stools, and whatever else would burn had disappeared in smoke, and the stove and cooking utensils were cracked, broken, or spoiled.

"Guess we are about a hundred and twenty-five dollars out," remarked Claude, with rather a wry face, as he gazed at the ruins the fire had left.

"There is no discount on that," added Maynard.

"By Jove! it's an expensive fire for us."

"How do you suppose it started?" queried Adams.

"Some of those careless countrymen from down river have camped here, and probably left their fire when they went away," asserted Claude. "Half of them are so shiftless that they would think nothing of doing it. A man in the woods always wants to be careful how he leaves a fire, for he never can tell what damage it will do."

"This will upset our plans a little," said Phil; "we cannot stay here to-morrow night without a tent or cooking utensils."

"You are right," remarked Claude; "we shall have to spend Sunday where we are, and turn out early Monday morning and get our things over here in time to get down to Fred Flint's to spend the night. We can go down to his camp, at the head of Aziscohos Falls, in five hours."

"We can bring everything over in three trips," said Maynard.

"I think we can in two," added Le Roy.

"It's after eleven o'clock," remarked Adams; "and it will not do us any good to stand here and cry over spilled milk. Come on fellows, it will be dinner-time before we get back to camp."

The cooks were astonished and vexed at the news their friends brought; but there being no remedy for it, the whole party made up their minds that they would not worry over the accident, as they called it, although every one of them knew that they had lost their property through the carelessness of some shiftless natives.

In the afternoon they had two boat-races on the pond, it being the last week-day they would spend there. The first one was from the landing in front of the camp, diagonally across the pond to a point and back, the whole distance being about a mile and a half, as near as the boys could estimate it.

Each fellow was to row over the course alone, having the choice of either of the three boats, and those on shore were to time the rowers.

Claude, Wingate, and St. Clair started first, each rowing his own boat, and their friends, sitting on a log outside the camp, timed them, watches in hand.

They turned the point on the opposite shore in the following order: Wingate ahead, St. Clair second, and Claude last. But things were changed on the return, and Claude came in ahead; time, twenty minutes; St. Clair, second; time, twenty-two minutes; Wingate, last; time, twenty-four minutes.

Le Roy, Adams, and Phil then rowed over the course, each selecting the boat he liked best, and came to the landing in the following order: Le Roy ahead; time, twenty-two minutes and a half; Adams, second; time, twenty-one minutes; Phil, last, time, twenty-five minutes.

It was now Maynard's turn, and he selected the "Go-Ahead" to row in. He was one of the best oarsmen in the party, and the boys felt sure that he would make as good, or even a better record than Claude.

He leaped into the boat lightly, and, taking the oars, began rowing a long, regular stroke, that apparently required little exertion, but that sent the boat spinning handsomely through the water.

"I tell you, boys," laughed Adams, "Frank is going to be the dark horse. He will beat us all."

"I don't believe he will beat Claude's time a great deal," declared Phil.

"He will not be far behind me, I can assure you," said Claude. "Frank can handle the sculls about as well as any amateur oarsman I ever met."

"He has turned the point," cried Wingate, "and has been just eleven minutes and a half."

"But he is doing his level best, now," remarked Le Roy. "See how quickly his oars flash!"

Frank knew that every one of the party was watching him, and was determined to beat Claude's time if it lay in the boat and himself to do it. He took it moderately going over, but on his return he warmed up to the work, and every stroke he pulled was pulled to win. When half-way back to the landing his exertions became tremendous, and he rapidly shortened the remaining gap, reaching the landing in eighteen minutes and ten seconds, and was received with cheers by his friends.

The second race was to be from the landing to the outlet and back, a distance of nearly four miles.

Maynard, having made the best time in the single race, was unanimously chosen referee and time-keeper, and declared out of the double one.

The crews for the three boats were selected in the following manner: The three fellows with the best records outside of Maynard's had choice of boats and men. This gave Claude the first chance, and he chose his own boat to row in and Le Roy to row with him. Adams, who had the next choice, took Wingate and the "Water-Witch"; while St. Clair had his own boat, with Phil for a companion.

The boys took their places in the boats, and at a signal from Maynard they dashed away together. There being only one pair of oars to each boat, one of the crew rowed and the other paddled, and when they reached the turning-point, the outlet, the oarsman and steersman in each boat changed seats.

Claude and Le Roy reached the outlet first, but, in changing seats, clumsily capsized their boat, and both of them went into the water, which was about four feet deep. They did not mind their bad luck, but righted their boat, and, floating her to shore, emptied the water out of her, and took their places just as the other boats swung around and headed up the pond, their occupants laughing at the "Fairy's" mishap.

"Confound them! they have the lead now, Claude, and are laughing at us, besides."

"Let them laugh, we shall gain the race all the same. Take the oars — ready — now off we go!" and Claude, with a stroke of the paddle, headed the boat toward the landing.

"I'll sicken them," said Le Roy, as he bent to the oars, and drove the boat ahead at a pace that soon enabled them to slowly crawl up to the other boats, and, when about half-way to camp, pass them.

Duck Shooting at South Arm, Lake Welokennebacook.

"They can laugh now, if they want to," said Claude.

"They are not feeling so funny as they were," puffed Le Roy, as he strained his muscles to widen the gap between the "Fairy" and her pursuers.

Each boat's crew were now spurting; but, although the "Go-Ahead" and "Water-Witch" sometimes changed places, the "Fairy" continued to lead, and came in ahead, Maynard declaring her the winner; time, fifty minutes. The "Go-Ahead" came in second; time, fifty-five minutes, twenty seconds, and the "Water-Witch" wound up with a record of fifty-seven minutes.

In the evening, after supper, in talking over the preparations for removal down river, it was decided to carry the boats across to the river Sunday afternoon, as that would enable the party to get the balance of their things across the carry in two trips.

The boys arose late Sunday forenoon, and it was nearly twelve o'clock when dinner was over.

About one o'clock they were on the point of starting for the river, when the cry of a loon was heard from the pond, and the boys descried him out on the water, halfway to the outlet.

"I want that loon to set up, and I am going to have it!" cried Claude. "Lend me your rifle, will you, Wingate, and I'll see if I can't get him?"

"You will only fool away an hour for nothing," remarked St. Clair.

"Suppose three or four of us help you, Claude?" proposed Maynard, as he went into camp and brought out his rifle.

"All right; all I want is the loon. I don't care who

shoots it. Come out in the boat with me, will you Wingate?"

"Certainly."

Claude and Wingate started in the "Fairy," followed by Maynard and Adams in the "Water-Witch," and Phil and St. Clair in the "Go-Ahead." Claude, Maynard, and Phil were to do the shooting, and the other three boys the rowing.

"I guess I'll watch the battle from the window of the camp," said Le Roy, as the boys started. "I don't care to get a stray bullet in my skin."

"You had better keep under cover, if Claude is going to fire many times," asserted Wingate, mischievously, as he dipped his oars in the water and sent the "Fairy" speeding towards the loon.

When the boats were within rifle-shot the oarsmen took in their oars, and, going to the stern of the boats, plied the paddles, the riflemen sitting in the bow.

As the boys were about to fire, the loon, glancing in their direction, went down, probably thinking he had too much company.

"No knowing where he will come up," cried Claude. "Suppose we scatter some. I will stay here, and you paddle to the right, Phil, and Adams go to the left."

The commander's orders were obeyed, and in about two minutes the loon rose some way to the left of Adams. The boys were on the lookout for him, and three rifle bullets sped towards him; but neither did any damage. The loon hallooed derisively, and the boys loaded and fired again. This time two bullets struck within a couple of inches of his head, while the third went into the water just behind him. Not liking the singing of the bullets he dove again, and the boats were paddled a little nearer the spot where he was last seen.

With rifles cocked the boys sat expectantly awaiting his reappearance. In a short time he came up within ten feet of them; as his head bobbed above water, and he caught a glimpse of the boats, he gave a startled cry, and dove as quick as a flash of lightning.

He had come up so near them as to astonish them, and he was out of sight again before a shot was fired.

"By Jove!" exclaimed Maynard, laughing, "he was frightened that time. Did you notice what a funny noise he made?"

"I noticed he did not stop long," remarked Claude.

"Didn't his old head go under water quick?" and Adams laughed as he gave a turn or two to his paddle.

It was nearly three minutes this time before the frightened bird appeared, and then his head bobbed up a long distance off between them and the camp.

"If a fellow was only at camp, now," observed Phil, "he could get a good shot at him."

The boats were turned in that direction, but, before they had gone fifty feet, Le Roy, stepped from the camp with his rifle, and walked to the edge of the pond.

"Tom is going to fire at him," said Maynard.

"I hope he won't shoot any of us," declared Phil.

The boys saw Le Roy drop on one knee, and take aim. A second later a report echoed across the pond, and the loon turned over on his back.

"Good for Tom!" shouted St. Clair; "he has fixed him."

The boats were now rowed to the dead bird, and Claude, upon inspection, found that Le Roy's bullet had gone through the neck of the loon, killing him instantly.

As the boys approached the shore Le Roy hailed them.

"If there are any more loons out there you want shot drive them in here, and I will kill them for you!" and a self-satisfied smile played across the assistant cook's face as he stood leaning upon his rifle.

"That was a good shot, Tom, we are all willing to acknowledge," said Claude as the boats grounded on the shore.

"Let Le Roy take the loon to camp, Claude, and we will shoulder these boats, and get them across the carry. It will be five o'clock before we can get back, and we shall want something to eat by that time;" and Maynard, picking up one end of the "Water-Witch," motioned to Adams to lift the other.

Shouldering the boats the boys struck into the carry path, and after a two hours' hard tramp, deposited their burdens among a thick growth of alder-bushes beside the river.

The fire was about extinguished now, and they considered it safe to leave the boats where they had placed them, as it was some distance away from the burned place.

"Next Sunday we shall be at home," remarked St. Clair, as the party sat at the dinner-table.

"Yes. It will seem odd to go to church again," observed Adams; "all days are alike up here in the woods."

"More so than they should be," said Claude.

"This is our last camp-fire for this year," asserted

View on Androscoggin River between Bethel and Newry Corner.

Maynard, as the boys gathered out-doors for their regular evening chat.

"I hope we shall gather around a great many more before we die," responded Wingate.

"I say Amen to that," returned Claude.

As it was the intention of the party to be up at daylight the next morning, if any could wake, they retired early, and by nine o'clock every one was asleep, and the solemn stillness of the forest encircled the lonely camp and its occupants.

CHAPTER XVII.

A Noisy Waking. — Good-by, Lincoln Pond. — Down to Flint's. — The Brown Farm. — A Surprise Party. — Old Friends. — A Charming Re-union. — The Ride on the Steamboat. — The Lakeside. — A Good Hotel. — Trading in a Country Store. — A Beautiful Drive. — Climbing Speckled Mountain. — The View from the Summit. — Moose Cave. — The Jail. — Screw Auger Falls. — Arrival at Bethel. — Homeward Bound.

WINGATE awoke Monday morning a few moments before five, and, getting up carefully, he discovered that the rest of the party were still wrapped in slumber. He dressed quietly, without awakening any one, and then, taking Claude's gun, stole softly to the door; pointing the muzzle outside, he discharged both barrels nearly at the same moment.

The noise brought the sleepers to their feet, and, with cries of alarm, they inquired what was the matter.

"Nothing. I was only calling you fellows up," declared the cook, coolly, as he proceeded to start a fire in the stove.

"You need not make so much racket about it the next time," growled Adams, who had half a mind to lie down again.

"The sooner we dress the better, boys," said Claude, cheerfully; "we can pack up some of our things before we eat."

All was now hurry and bustle, every one being busy until six o'clock, when they sat down to breakfast.

At seven all of the party, with the exception of the cooks, crossed the carry with a load, leaving the things near the boats, which they found just as they had left them the day before. After resting fifteen minutes they returned to camp, reaching it at half-past ten, and at eleven they had dinner, the last meal they would eat of their own preparing.

By one o'clock everything was ready for their final trip, and, extinguishing the fire in the stove and fastening the door of the camp, they picked up their baggage, Claude carrying the box with the eagles, which was now anything but a light load, and at half-past two reached the river.

A half hour was spent in loading the boats, and at three o'clock they pushed away from the shore, and headed for Aziscohos Falls.

Just below the Narrows they passed a bateau containing loggers, there being ten in the party, who were going up to Parmachenee Lake to make some repairs on the dam.

The boys had a good run down river, and at half-past seven, somewhat tired and very hungry, they landed at Fred Flint's Camp.

Fred heard their voices, and came down to the river to meet them.

Claude asked him if he could give them some supper, and take care of them over night, and he replied with a laugh "that he guessed he could;" and after helping them unload their boats, he led the way to camp, and requested the cook to get their supper under way as soon as possible.

While supper was progressing, the boys, assisted by

Fred, carried all their baggage and what stores they had left up to the camp. The boats were left out-doors, but everything else was carried into the house, and then the party washed up and sat down to rest. At half-past eight the cook called them to supper, and they gathered around a well-supplied table, and, as Adams said, "They proved to the landlord's satisfaction that they were hungry."

After supper Claude asked Mr. Flint if he knew when the steamer would be at Magalloway; and Fred told him it was coming up the next day.

"Then we must hit it without fail," remarked Claude. "Have you team enough to take our boats and baggage down to the landing?"

"No, I haven't. But I can go over to Clark's early in the morning, and get him to come up and help me."

"That will do," replied Claude.

The boys went to bed early, and, as Wingate observed, "it seemed odd to them to lie in a bed again." They talked, and laughed, and joked over the events they had passed through until nearly midnight, and then fell asleep, and the first any of the party knew was Fred singing out to them the next morning that breakfast was ready.

"My goodness!" exclaimed Adams, "I have not slept five minutes!" But on looking at his watch, he was surprised to find that it was seven o'clock.

Fred had sent one of his hired men over to Clark's early in the morning, and about eight o'clock his neighbor made his appearance with a two-horse team, on which the boats and part of the baggage were loaded, Fred taking the remainder.

As the carry road was quite rough, the boys concluded to walk it, the distance being only three miles. From the upper settlement the road was good, and from there to the steamboat landing the party could ride, although the boys intended when they reached the Brown Farm to stop and take dinner.

They had a very pleasant ride down to the hotel, the road running near to the river, and following the narrow valley all the way. They arrived at the house at eleven o'clock, and left the teams, Fred and the other driver promising to unload the boats carefully.

The landlord was glad to see the boys again; they having been there two years before, and, sitting down on the piazza, they indulged in a pleasant chat. At the expiration of half an hour he excused himself, and went out to the stable to harness up his team, and drive down and meet the boat.

"Suppose there will be any passengers on the steamer?" remarked Wingate, after the landlord had left them.

"It is rather late for city people now," replied Claude, "unless there might be some fellows on their way up river hunting."

"I don't believe my folks came down to the Lakes this year," observed Phil. "If they had I should have heard from them up here somewhere."

"Did they talk very strongly of coming?" asked Claude.

"Yes. When I left home they told me they should go to Mt. Desert through August, then go up to the mountains and spend two or three weeks, and be over in this vicinity the last of September."

"I wish they had come," responded St. Clair, earnestly.

"Of course you do!" laughed Claude, in an exasperating way.

About half-past twelve the teams appeared in sight, and, to the surprise of the boys, the hotel team was loaded, while Flint's carried three besides the driver. As the vehicles swung up to the house Phil and St. Clair jumped to their feet.

"By gracious!" cried Phil; "if it isn't the folks. I wonder where they have come from?"

"And there's Violet, and three other young ladies," said St. Clair, blushing as he made the remark; for his friends were looking at him with a mischievous smile on their faces.

The hotel team reached the piazza first, and Phil and St. Clair were beside it as soon as it had stopped.

"How do you do, mother? How are you, Violet?" said Phil, as he helped his mother from the wagon, while St. Clair, bowing to Mrs. De Ruyter, and shaking hands with her, then spoke to Violet and assisted her from her seat.

"Come, make yourselves useful, fellows!" cried Phil, as he helped one of the young ladies out, and Claude and Maynard took care of the other two on the opposite side of the carriage.

Fred now drove up, and Mr. De Ruyter, descending from the buckboard, shook hands with Phil and his friends. In the other gentlemen the two boys recognized Mr. Peyton and Mr. Grayson, who had been members of the mountain party two years before.

The whole company entered the house, and then Phil

introduced his friends to the two Miss Graysons, and Miss Peyton, whom they had not met before. As soon as the ladies were ready, the dinner was served, and at the table Mr. De Ruyter informed Phil that they had been stopping at the new hotel in Cambridge, at the foot of Lake Umbagog, for a week, and were intending to return home the next day. The pleasantness of the morning had tempted them to take a sail on the steamer, and, although they expected to hear from the boys, they had no idea of meeting them.

"I am glad you met us, father," cried Phil. "Won't it be jolly? We can all go home together."

They had a merry time at dinner, and Mrs. De Ruyter said she could scarcely hear herself talk there was such a noise. The boys related some of their adventures to the no small amusement of the party, especially the incident of the sociable bear, the day the boys shot the caribou at Lincoln Pond.

It is hard saying how long the party would have remained at the table had not Mr. Lowe come in and told them that the steamer was whistling for them, it being already past her hour of sailing.

This announcement hurried them up, and, getting ready, they took seats in the teams and were driven to the boat-landing. Here Claude settled with Mr. Flint, and, after he had paid him, informed him that if he wanted three quarters of as nice caribou-meat as he ever ate in his life all he had to do was to go up to the camp at Lincoln Pond and get it, as the boys had been obliged to leave it; and he promised to go the next day.

Bidding Fred good-by, Claude joined his friends on the steamer, and the boat a moment later was underway. [The scenery from here to the foot of the lake is very fine, but as it is fully described in "Eastward Ho!" the first volume of this series, we will say nothing of it here.]

The party had a very nice time on the way homeward, and they saw all that was to be seen, as the boat ran over her whole course, making the customary stops at Errol and Sunday Cove.

The young ladies and gentlemen cultivated each others' acquaintance on their way down, leaving the old people to themselves.

Phil and St. Clair told the girls that their party were going to climb Speckled Mountain on their way to Bethel; and the girls thought it would be delightful, and said they should like to go also.

Claude informed them that there was no path, as there was to Aziscohos, and that it would be too hard a tramp for them; and the young ladies reluctantly gave up the idea.

At six o'clock the steamer reached the wharf at Cambridge, and the party adjourned to the hotel. After supper they sat before a cheerful open wood-fire, in the office, and talked over arrangements for getting home.

It was finally decided that Mr. De Ruyter and his party should leave for Bethel the next day, and await the arrival of the boys, who would get along some time Thursday, and that Friday morning they would leave Bethel for home.

"Here is a letter for you, Mr. Maynard," said the landlord, approaching Maynard after supper.

The young fellow took it, and noticed that it had a

Florida post-mark. "Hurrah, fellows!" he cried; "I have a letter from Robbins."

"Read it aloud," suggested Claude.

"Do," added Violet. "I should like to hear from Mr. Robbins."

"Here goes, then":—

TAMPA, Sept. 24, 1876.

DEAR OLD FELLOW:—

Your pleasant letter from the wilds of Maine came safely to hand, and I hasten to answer it, in hopes that you may receive this before you get away from the lakes. I was very much interested in the incidents you relate of your trip, and should like nothing better than to visit the Maine woods again with another such jolly crowd as we had before. Do you remember Foster's ride on the bear? I cannot think of it even to this day without laughing. I suppose he is shooting grizzlies now in California.

I like down here very much. My uncle has a large orange-grove, over seven hundred trees, and is setting out more all the time. There is plenty of game down here, and also good fishing. About twenty miles south of where we live is a rousing place for hunting, there being plenty of deer, ducks, bears, alligators, and everything else. Uncle and I went off on a week's trip last winter, and had a splendid time, shooting and fishing.

And, by the way, a thought strikes me. Why can't you all come down here some winter? I can assure you a cordial welcome from my uncle, who, despite the fact of his being a successful orange-grower and a smart business man, appears to me more like a boy than any man of his age I ever saw. Do come, sometime, prepared to spend two months, and I will get away for a month or so, and we will go on a camping-out trip down here; and you can make up your mind that we shall have anything but a slow time. Remember me personally to each individual member of the party, and when you reach home write me again.

Hoping in the course of time to see you in Florida, I remain,

Very truly, your friend,

GEORGE ROBBINS.

P. S. Do you remember the day I was lost and caught the porcupine bare-handed?

"That is not a bad idea of Robbins'," declared Claude, as Maynard folded up his letter.

"What do you mean?" asked Phil.

"Why, our going down there sometime. That would just suit me. I was never south of New York in my life."

"You would have to make a winter trip of it, then, boys," said Mr. De Ruyter, laughing.

"We could skip our vacation in summer one year and take it during the winter in Florida," remarked St. Clair.

"We can talk it over this winter, sometime, when we meet at the club," added Maynard.

Wednesday morning dawned warm and pleasant, and the party were up early, and by half-past seven had finished breakfast. It had been arranged the night before that both parties should travel together to the point where the boys were to ascend the mountain.

The teams were driven to the door, each a three-seated Concord wagon, capable of carrying nine people, and half of each party went in both wagons, so that the young fellows could have a chance to converse with the girls on the way. Just as they were starting Mr. De Ruyter paid the landlord a high compliment, informing him that he had the best beds and set the best table of any house they had stopped at that summer, and told him that the whole party had been very much pleased with their accommodations there, and that none of them would forget the Lakeside in a hurry. The young people cordially indorsed Mr. De Ruyter's statement, and bade the landlord "good-by" as the teams drove away.

Before leaving Claude had made a bargain with the landlord to send their three boats and all their baggage to Bethel that day by an extra team, as there was no room on the ones they were to ride in, and paid him for the service, and the boys left without their traps to look after.

When the teams reached the top of the hill they stopped a moment, and the two parties took a last look at the beautiful Lake Umbagog, bathed in the morning sunlight and surrounded by its lofty forest-clad mountains, now decked in all the gorgeousness of autumnal coloring.

"Stop for me at the store," cried Claude, jumping from the first team, and running ahead. St. Clair, who was in the second, followed him, suspecting his errand.

"Wait a moment, Claude," called Andrew, as he hurried forward. "What are you going to do, — buy out the store?"

"Not exactly," laughed his friend, as they went along together; "I thought I would invest in some candy and peanuts, and treat the crowd."

"I had an idea what you were up to. Get what you want for those in your team, and I will take care of the people in mine."

"All right."

The boys entered the store, and found a tall, slab-sided, good-natured, native leaning over the counter, talking "loggin'" with two or three countrymen who lived in the neighborhood.

Their conversation stopped short as they saw the boys, and they looked at them as if they would stare them out of countenance. They moved a little as the boys approached the counter, but stood with ears and mouths wide open, eager to catch the first word the strangers should utter, while their eyes scanned them from head to foot.

"Have you any candy?" asked Claude.

"And peanuts?" added St. Clair.

"Yaas," responded the store-keeper; "how many do you want?"

"I will have three pounds of candy, mixed, and three quarts of peanuts," answered Claude.

"And I the same," said St. Clair.

The magnitude of the order astonished the merchant, and he had to think it over a moment before he began to fill it, while the two by-standers looked at the boys as if they thought they were young Goulds or Vanderbilts.

"Ben up ter the lakes?" asked the merchant, sociably, as he weighed out the candy.

"We have come from Parmachenee," returned Claude.

"Have a pretty good time up there?"

"Yes, sir."

The teams now stopped in front of the store. This was too much for the two countrymen, and they immediately deserted the boys for the larger game outside, and, taking their places on the platform before the door, they did two hours' worth of common staring in five minutes. The two teams with their occupants were a harvest for them, and they made the most of their time, until the boys appeared, and the horses were once more put in motion.

Claude and St. Clair divided their purchases among their friends, and the girls thanked them for the treat. The candy was not very nice, but they had just as good a time eating it as they would if it had been Bailey's best.

"A good hunter would be able to trail us from that store to the Notch by peanut-shells," said Claude, laughing, as he dropped a handful over the side of the wagon.

"Be sure and look at Moose Cave and the Jail," said Miss Grayson, "when you go along, to-morrow, Mr. Emerson; they are really worth seeing."

"Trust us for that, Miss Grayson," returned Claude; "we shall look at everything along the road you may depend."

"What a lovely day this is for October!" remarked Phil.

"Charming!" replied Miss Peyton. "And how warm it is! I think you will find it hot on the mountain."

"I guess we shall," observed Maynard.

At half-past ten the teams reached the northern end of the Notch, and the boys, taking their lunch, bade the young ladies and the old people farewell, saying they would be at the hotel in Bethel to dinner with them the next day. As the wagons rolled away the boys raised their caps and shouted their "good-bys," and the girls responded with a waving of handkerchiefs and a shaking of parasols.

"By Jove! it looks like quite a journey to that highest peak," remarked Adams, as the boys left the road and started for the summit of Speckled Mountain.

And a journey they found it before they reached the top. The climbing soon became difficult, and they were obliged to go out of a straight line quite often in order to avoid some perpendicular piece of ledge. They found traces of several slides whose old tracks they crossed.

When nearly half-way to the summit they reached a brook, and with some difficulty followed it until nearly clear of the forest, when, getting a glance at the highest peak, they left the stream and took an air-line for it. They were soon beyond the last tree, and only barren ledge lay before them. It was half-past two when they finally stood on top, tired and hungry, and their clothing showing marks of their hard scramble.

There was very little air stirring, and the sun shone hotly down upon them. Their dinner was brought forth as soon as they had sat down, and they paid very little attention to the views around them until they had partly appeased their hunger.

"I never was so hungry in my life," declared Adams, as, with a piece of meat in one hand and a slice of bread in the other, he gazed at his companions.

"I felt rather hollow, myself," remarked Claude. "This is a hard old mountain to climb. It beats any we have tackled yet."

"I agree with you," observed Maynard; "but what a magnificent view there is from here! It is much finer than that from Bald Pate."

"Sure!" said Wingate. "There is Bald Pate opposite of us. We can see both peaks from this side, I noticed when I was in the team, and I presume that is why the people over this way call the mountain Saddleback. From Andover, you remember, we could only see one peak."

When the party stood up, and began to gaze around them, they found they were fairly looking down upon Bald Pate, "Old Spec," being at least five hundred feet higher. The view stretched away, mile upon mile, in every direction. Northward, deeply embosomed in the midst of the vast forest bouquet, Lake Umbagog sparkled like a diamond, and beyond it for miles could be traced the Magalloway Valley, with an occasional silver thread that showed where the river once in a while escaped from the leafy folds of the forest. Still farther away the mountains about Parmachenee, and the chain of peaks that composed the boundary, lay sharply defined against the sky, the last thing visible in that direction.

North-easterly, the other lakes of the Androscoggin chain, Molechunkamunk, Welokennebacook, Mooseluemaguntic, Cupsuptic, and Oquossoc, wound in and out for sixty miles amid the forest-clad mountains that skirted their shores. Westward of these beautiful sheets of water, the Saddleback mountain in Greenvale, Mount Blue, Mount Abraham, the twin Bigelow Peaks, and many others whose names the boys had not the slightest idea of, towered grandly skywards.

North-west the peaks around Dixville Notch, and others along the valley of the Connecticut, lay piled so thickly that from where the party stood it actually looked to them as if a person could step from one mountain-top to another, even without the traditional three-mile boots.

From different points of observation glimpses of the Androscoggin River and valley were obtained, and to the south-west the higher peaks of the White Mountains barred all vision beyond their gigantic walls. The air was unusually clear, and, without the aid of the glass, a white speck on the summit of Mount Washington, denoting the hotel, could plainly and easily be distinguished.

South-west, a large number of mountains of all shapes, but not so high as the northern peaks, lay scattered about like pebbles on a sandy beach, and beyond these a silvery gleam, stretching away into infinite space, convinced them that they gazed upon old ocean, about fifty miles distant as the crow flies.

With eating and sight-seeing an hour glided rapidly away, and Claude, telling the boys it was high time for them to be moving, if they wished to gain the road before dark, took a bee-line down the mountain.

Claude had ordered their team to be at the path leading to Moose Cave at four o'clock, not doubting but what the party would be there to meet it. But it had taken them so much longer to climb the mountain than they expected that it was half-past three when they began the descent, and six when they reached the road.

On their way down they slipped about and stumbled considerably, and had several narrow escapes from a bad accident. In many places the way before them was so steep that they did not dare attempt the descent in a straight line, and were obliged to zigzag either to the right or left for some distance. It grew dark rapidly after they entered the forest, and they were all very glad upon emerging from the woods and large boulders among which they had been stumbling for the last half hour.

"Glory hallelujah, fellows! I am glad we are out of that!" exclaimed Phil, as they started briskly down the road, having come out on it a little farther north than they had intended.

"That is no fool of a mountain to get up and down," observed Le Roy.

"I believe it is the toughest climb I ever had," remarked Wingate.

We remember one summer being on the steamer "Welokennebacook," on her afternoon trip from South Arm to Upper Dam Landing, and making a stop at the Middle Dam.

Among the passengers who came aboard the steamer at the place was a fine-appearing, gentlemanly-looking foreigner, who proved to be a German professor in some college, the name of which has slipped our memory. His only baggage consisted of a small valise. His clothing was very nice with the exception that it had been darned and patched in many places, and his hat had also been torn, and bore several marks of pitch.

As he talked English fluently, I fell into conversation with him, and after a short time he alluded to his clothes. He told me that his suit had been whole, in fact, a new one, when he left New York, but that on his way from Bethel to Lake Umbagog he had walked the entire distance, and when he saw the immense peak of Speckled Mountain it so interested him that he could not resist the inclination to make the ascent, and he went up without any guide.

It was late when he reached the summit, and stopping too long on top, entranced by the view, he became lost in the woods on his way down, and hungry and tired, passed a very disagreeable night in the forest. His clothing had been so badly used up that he was compelled to stop at the first farm-house he reached and have the rents in his suit mended; and he wound up his story, which both interested and amused me, by begging me to tell him what the first place was he would reach where he could procure another suit.

"I guess you fellows found it harder work climbing Old Spec than you thought it would be, didn't ye?" inquired the driver, who had been waiting a couple of hours.

"We did," returned Claude. "We found it to be a great deal like work. But I am sorry that we have kept you waiting so long."

"Don't say nuthing 'bout it, — it's all right. But ye can't see the cave or falls now. It's too dark."

"We can drive back here in the morning before we go to Bethel," suggested Maynard. "It can't be a great distance from the hotel where we stop to-night."

"'Bout five miles from here ter the Popple Tavum," answered the driver.

"You have just spelled it, Frank!" declared Claude. "We can see the sights in the morning."

It was a little after seven when the team stopped at Poplar Tavern, and the boys gladly entered its open portals, and suggested to the landlord, if he did not want them to breed a famine in that neighborhood, to have their supper on the table in the shortest possible time.

During the evening the young fellows arranged with the driver to leave the house at six o'clock the next morning and visit the three places they had missed, and then stop at the hotel again on their way to Bethel, and take breakfast; and this programme was carried out.

The driver called them Thursday morning in ample time, and they were ready as soon as the team drew up at the door. The air was sharp and frosty, not nearly as warm as the day before.

An hour's drive brought them to the path leading to Moose Cave, and five minutes' walk enabled them to reach the bank of Bear River, whose waters had worn out a large hole in the rock at this point. The cave is said to have received its name from the fact that a wounded moose once took shelter in it to avoid his pursuers.

Retracing their way to the team, which the driver had turned during their absence, they drove along, and stopped next at the Jail, another huge chasm, close beside the road. This place, like the other, owed its existence to the unwearied rush of waters which for ages had helped to develop its size and depth. The hole into which they were now carefully peering was nearly circular in shape, with perpendicular walls, whose height can be readily imagined when we state that large trees growing from the bottom of the Jail, barely reached the level of the road.

"The Jail is a good name for that place," remarked Phil, as they gazed at the stream so far below them. "I should hate to fall in there!"

"It would not be the fall that would hurt you," laughed Adams; "it would be the 'bringing up,' as the Irishman said."

The next stop was at Screw Auger Falls, and here the boys were astonished at the wonderful display of the action of water on stone. For a long distance in this vicinity the waters of Bear River have forced their way through the solid granite, and, working deeper each year, have worn a spiral channel for many yards, being in some places nearly seventy feet deep. While at some points a good leaper could vault across the channel, at other spots it widens to a distance of thirty or forty feet. A mill once stood over the large circular chasm, but several years ago was destroyed by fire. Part of the dam a short distance above is all that remains to tell the story.

Once more the boys entered the team, and away they sped to the hotel, and to breakfast.

"I should like to follow that river up the whole distance through the Notch," remarked Claude as they rattled along; "there must be a lot of places on it worth seeing that are not generally known."

"I have no doubt of it," added Phil.

At nine o'clock they reached the hotel and stopped an hour to breakfast, and the driver fed his horses. After settling their hotel bill, the team was harnessed, and they took their seats as before.

The driver sent his horses along at a good pace, and at twelve o'clock they crossed the covered bridge over the

Androscoggin, and a half hour later were deposited in front of the Elms, and found their friends awaiting them on the piazza.

Then came pleasant greetings and many hand-shakings, and, filing into the parlor of the hotel, the boys related their experiences in climbing Speckled Mountain.

The afternoon and evening at Bethel were passed very pleasantly, and slipped away almost before the boys knew it.

Friday morning the young fellows made their appearance in city dress once more, and as soon as breakfast was over Claude and Maynard went down to the depot to see to their boats and other things.

The landlord sent the rest of the party to the depot in carriages, and for five minutes the young fellows and the gentlemen were busy getting checks for their baggage. For a wonder the train came along on time, and the two parties secured seats in the Pullman car. Claude had found a chance for their boats in the express car, and at a quarter of ten the train moved away from the station.

The party reached Boston in safety, and Phil and his folks left for New York the same evening by the Shore Line.

If my readers, who have followed the boys through "Eastward Ho!" and this present volume, care to continue their acquaintance, they can renew it in the third volume of this series, entitled, "Down the West Branch; or, Camps and Tramps around Katahdin."

www.ingramcontent.com/pod-product-compliance
Lightning Source LLC
Chambersburg PA
CBHW051244300426
44114CB00011B/888